MINERS
OF THE
RED MOUNTAIN

Indian Labor in Potosí,
1545–1650

Peter Bakewell

UNIVERSITY OF NEW MEXICO PRESS
Albuquerque

Library of Congress Cataloging in Publication Data

Bakewell, P. J. (Peter John), 1943–
    Miners of the Red Mountain.

    Bibliography: p.
    Includes index.
    1. Silver miners—Bolivia—Potosí (Dept.)—History.
2. Silver mines and mining—Bolivia—Potosí (Dept.)—
History. 3. Indians of South America—Bolivia—Potosí
(Dept.)—Employment—History. I. Title.
HD8039.M732B53   1984   331.7'6223423'098414   84-7582

Manufactured in the United States of America.
Library of Congress Catalog Card Number 84-7582.
International Standard Book Number 0-8263-0769-8.
First edition

I. M. B. and W. B.
in memoriam

Contents

Illustrations

Preface

It is perhaps a drawback to have a great deal of time in which to undertake a piece of historical research. The combined generosity of Trinity College, Cambridge, and the Social Science Research Council of London enabled me to spend much of the period from 1970 to 1974 peering into the early history of Potosí in various archives in Europe and South America. The archives proved bountiful. Piles of notes and reels of microfilm multiplied. When the time to assemble came, I began to suspect the existence of a law of historical writing that my seniors, perhaps for kindness's sake, had not previously revealed to me: that the difficulty of synthesis increases as the square (or perhaps some higher power) of the quantity of material to be synthesized. What now finally appears is indeed less than I originally set out to write. The present small book began life as a chapter on mining labor in what was to be a general study of silver production in Potosí in the town's first century. As the pages accumulated, however, I realized that the labor question was as much as my mental apparatus could accommodate and organize at one time. And, on reflection, it did not seem an unreasonable idea to devote a brief work to the origins and development of the labor systems of Potosí, especially since the *mita* that served the town's silver producing industry had long been so prominent a feature in historians' general view of colonial Spanish labor arrangements. Now, therefore, I have laid out what seems to me important about *mitayos*, and also about *mingas*; and the way is that much clearer than before to tackle other aspects of the history of early Potosí.

Many have helped me bring my research on Potosí this far. I should first mention the late Professor David Joslin, of Cambridge

University, who suggested that, after Zacatecas, Potosí was a challenge that might be met. My research began in the Archivo General de Indias, whose staff I should thank for their attentions on that and other occasions. Life in Seville would have been much the poorer, and research less rewarding, without the presence of many friends there, some of them historians, and others not. I recall with especial gratitude the companionship of José Guillermo García Valdecasas, María Isabel Paredes Vera, Cristina García Bernal, María Angeles Eugenio Martínez, José Luis Mora Mérida, Julián Ruiz Rivera, and Manuel Fernández Escalante.

In South America I should thank the staffs of the Biblioteca Nacional of Peru, and the Archivo General de la Nación of Argentina, for their helpful service. And in Bolivia itself I have many obligations to acknowledge. The late Don Armando Alba, Director of the Museum of the Casa Nacional de la Moneda in Potosí, made fully accessible the archive housed there—remarkable for both its good condition and its range—and offered aid in research in diverse ways. His assistant, Don Mario Chacón Torres, now Director of the archive himself, was equally helpful. Living in Potosí—always interesting, and not so forbiddingly cold as repute would have it—was made more enjoyable by the friendship and hospitality of Don Jack Aitken Soux. His knowledge of Quechua and of things *potosino* was always generously shared.

In Sucre, Dr. Gunnar Mendoza L., Director of the Archivo Nacional de Bolivia, proved a powerful ally. His lifelong work of cataloguing that splendid collection has made its riches easily accessible to the researcher; and his knowledge of the contents of his archive makes his guidance indispensable to the newcomer. Beyond this, for the historian of Potosí, one of Dr. Mendoza's greatest services has been to edit and annotate, in conjunction with Professor Lewis Hanke, the vast *Historia de la Villa Imperial de Potosí* of Bartolomé Arzáns de Orsúa y Vela. And I should also express my appreciation to Dr. Hanke for his editing and publication of Luis Capoche's *Relación general de la Villa Imperial de Potosí*. In so far as any single work can be indispensable to a historian, Capoche's *Relación* is so to the historian of mining in Potosí in the first century.

Finally, I should like to record my debt to Judith Hope Reynolds, companion of countless hours of work in the archives of five countries. Much information gathered by her appears in this book. Its presence is acknowledged here, and specifically in footnotes marked with her initials.

PETER BAKEWELL

Albuquerque
November 1983

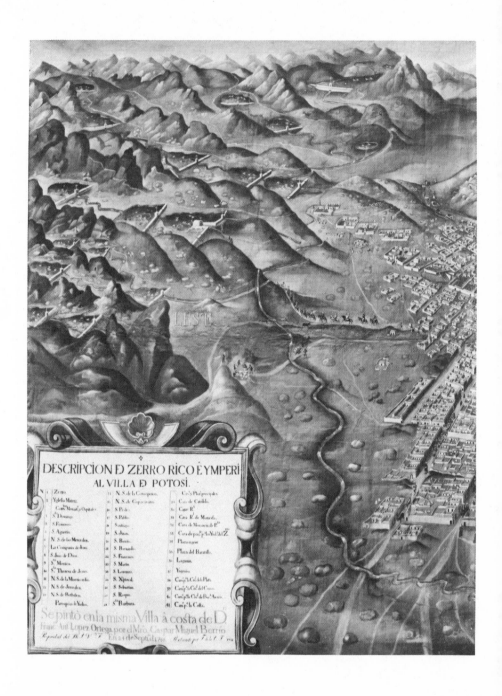

Gaspar Miguel Berrío, *Descripcion de zerro rico e ymperial villa de Potosi* (1758). Note the numerous dams in the Kari-Kari massif to the east of the town.

Abbreviations
and Conventions Used

AAGN	Archivo General de la Nación, Argentina (Buenos Aires)
AGI	Archivo General de Indias (Seville)
BAN	Archivo Nacional de Bolivia (Sucre)
BL	British Library
CIM	Proceedings, VI Congreso Internacional de Minería, *La minería hispana e iberoamericana. Contribución a su investigación histórica.* León 1970.
HAHR	*Hispanic American Historical Review*
PBN	Biblioteca Nacional, Peru (Lima)
PCM	Casa Nacional de la Moneda, Bolivia (Potosí)
SAU	Archivo de la Universidad (Seville)
SBN	Biblioteca Nacional, Spain (Madrid)

Sums of money are usually expressed in *pesos de plata corriente* of 272 maravedís.

References to the *Recopilación de leyes de los reinos de las Indias* of 1681 are given in the order: book, title, law—for example, 1. 11. 21.

The spelling of Spanish has generally been modernized; but Quechua words are spelled as they appear in colonial manuscripts.

*Miners
of the
Red Mountain*

1

Introduction

Silver Mining in Potosí and its district

Potosí es un cerro muy hermoso; al derredor de él no hay otro ninguno.

(Juan de Matienzo, *Gobierno del Perú* [1567], *ch. XL.**)

Potosí is an acquired taste. Even one of its early citizens who had good reason to think well of the town, since he prospered there, wrote severely of the conditions it offered for human existence.

The cerro and Imperial Town of Potosí are situated in cold terrain, which receives much snow, is sterile and unproductive, and almost uninhabitable because of its unpleasant and nasty climate. Before the cerro was discovered, nobody lived here, on account of the displeasing nature of the place. It is dry and cold and exceedingly windy, especially in May, June, July and August, when some strong winds called tomahavis come up (so called because they blow from [the direction of] a town of that name).[1] They are violent and very cold and bring so much dust and sand that they darken the air and

---

*What is interesting about the second part of Matienzo's remark is that it is wrong. Another substantial hill, Huacacchi, rises 2 kilometers to the south-west of the cerro. Perhaps Matienzo wished to let the cerro stand in splendorous isolation. Or perhaps his own perception of topography had been distorted by the aura of wonder and wealth that already hung about the cerro. Huacacchi, in contrast, held no silver. Being therefore out of mind, it perhaps went out of sight. Huacacchi is a hispanized spelling of the Quechua verb *Waqachiy:* to make cry. The hill's barrenness was a matter for tears.

1.   Tomave, to use the modern spelling, is 100 kilometers west–south–west of Potosí.

3

cause much unpleasantness, although they do not carry sickness. It rains little in this town. The rains begin at the end of November, and are heaviest in January and February. They stop in early March. Nothing in the way of food can be raised in Potosí or its surroundings, except some potatoes (which grow like truffles) and green barley, which does not form grain, because the cold is continuous and outdoes that of Old Castile and Flanders, for there is no time in which the elements are in peace and harmony, enabling the land to yield its fruit to him who possesses it. The land is much folded and naked, without trees or greenery. It lies 21-2/3 degrees south of the equator, and, for somewhere within the tropics, is cold, where it should be temperate and warm, as are [other] lands at this remove from the pole. But that is prevented by the height and elevation of this land and by the intemperate winds that sweep over it."

In this happy vein, Luis Capoche, a silver miner and refiner of Potosí, began his *Relación general de la Villa Imperial de Potosí*, composed in 1585.[2] A hundred and twenty or so years later, another remarkable colonial chronicler of Potosí, Bartolomé Arzáns de Orsúa y Vela, took a different line.

The very celebrated, always illustrious, august, magnanimous, noble and rich Town of Potosí; a world in miniature; honor and glory of America; center of Peru; empress of the cities and towns of this new world; queen of her opulent province; princess of native places; mistress of treasures and fortunes; benign and merciful mother of foreign sons. . . .

And so on for two ample paragraphs.[3]

The truth, in its usual disobliging way, lies between the two descriptions. Capoche wrote to emphasize success in adversity—the wresting of great wealth for Spain from a resistant land. He could not know it, but the peak of that wealth, in quantity of silver produced, was to be reached within seven years of his completing the *Relación*. In no other year of Potosí's history was as much silver produced as in 1592. Arzáns wrote of glories past,

2.   Lewis Hanke (ed.), in Biblioteca de Autores Españoles, tomo CXXII (Madrid 1959), p. 75. Modern measurement places Potosí at 19° 48' S. by 65° 42' W.

3.   *Historia de la Villa Imperial de Potosí*, Lewis Hanke and Gunnar Mendoza (eds.), (3 tomos, Providence, Rhode Island, 1965), tomo 1, p. 3.

weaving from the history and still young legends of Potosí a baroque tapestry of words that is the verbal equivalent of the altarpieces wrought from the local silver. The town in his day was far poorer and less populous than in Capoche's, and was always so to remain.

Capoche's view has prevailed. The world thinks of Potosí—or that part of the world that is aware of it—as high and harsh and inhospitable. Inhospitable it may be, but far from uninhabitable. The town is indeed high—perhaps higher than Capoche could know—at roughly 4,000 meters (13,100 feet). But its climate is much moderated by its lying, as Capoche noted, within the tropics.[4] Only in May, June, July, and August does the temperature fall below freezing on more than half the nights of the month. In the coldest month, July, the average minimum temperature is -3° C (26.6° F), and the average extreme minimum from year to year is -7.5° C (or 18.5° F). No frosts occur in December, January, or February, and on average only one or two in March, April, and November. Temperatures, to be sure, never rise above the cool. The average high reaches its peak in October, at 16.5° C (61.7° F), and falls to its low point in June, at 13.5° C (56.3° F). Despite the altitude, therefore, not only is the minimum temperature less severe than usually supposed, but the range between maximum and minimum is rather narrow, in the characteristic way of tropical climates.

The town receives, however, rather less precipitation than might be expected in tropical latitudes. It lies on the edge of the highland Atacama desert area of southern Bolivia and northern Argentina and Chile. Like the rest of that area, it receives no appreciable moisture from the Pacific. It is close enough, however, to the inland side of the eastern Andean ranges of Bolivia to receive substantial precipitation in the summer months from the Amazon basin. Total annual precipitation at Potosí is some 600 mm (25 inches), with over 100 mm in both January and February, and over 80 mm in April and December. Hardly any moisture falls in the period from May to August. Summer precipitation often comes as snow or hail,

4. The town's altitude is variously estimated, and is difficult to specify since the site is on a slope. Four thousand meters is a useful approximation. The cerro reaches 4,790 meters (15,700 feet). Salomón Rivas and Raúl Carrasco, *Geología y yacimientos minerales de la región de Potosí* (2 tomos, Servicio geológico de Bolivia "Geobol," Ministerio de Minas, Boletín 11, La Paz, 1968), tomo 1, pp. 13, 68.

especially on the cerro itself, and brings with it an unpleasantly
dank chill. This, along with the dryness of the winter months, and
an unawareness of the reversal of seasons in the Southern Hemi-
sphere, led early Spanish inhabitants to confuse summer with
winter. Capoche, for instance, at one point refers to winter rains,
where, strictly speaking, summer rains would be the correct description.[5] It is not hard to sympathize with the mistake. A wet
summer evening in Potosí has a wintry feel to it.

If Potosí's temperatures are nevertheless more bearable than
Capoche would have his readers believe, so are the town's site
and surroundings a little less forbidding than he suggests. It is true
that Potosí is set in a well churned landscape. Geomorphologically
speaking, the site lies on the eastern slopes of the Cordillera de
los Frailes, one of the ranges of the Andes that border the Bolivian
altiplano on its eastern edge. The distance from that edge to Potosí
is about 100 kilometers. The area around the town is, in general,
one of folded parallel ranges, trending north-south; but the regu-
larity of the folds has been disturbed by igneous intrusions and
even more by the erosion of water and ice. After the *cerro rico* itself,
the most striking feature of Potosí's local terrain is the Kari-Kari
massif. This is a large igneous mass, with peaks rising to 5,200
meters (c. 17,000 feet), and about 32 by 12 kilometers in area. It
looms darkly over the town to the east and south-east. But however forbidding, it has played a central role in the history of silver
at Potosí, since in colonial times it was the source and store of
power for refining. Its height drew relief rainfall; and its glaciated
valleys provided sites where dams could be built and rainwater
stored in reservoirs that, through canals and modified natural
channels, supplied energy to the waterwheels of the refining mills
in the town below. Without the Kari-Kari range, the colonial silver industry of Potosí could have existed only on a modest scale.[6]

So in this respect, at least, the ruggedness itself of the terrain
around Potosí brought a crucial advantage. Nor is the soil of that
landscape so barren as Capoche described it. The modern visitor

5. *Relación*, p. 117. Data on climate are from Rivas and Carrasco, *Geología*,
tomo 1, fig. 4, facing p. 26. They refer to the period from 1959 to 1963.

6. Animal power would have been expensive, because of the lack of nearby
pasture. For the history of the reservoirs of Potosí, see William E. Rudolph, "The
lakes of Potosí," *The Geographical Review*, vol. XXVI (New York 1936), pp. 529–54.

to Potosí is surprised to find poppies flowering in the main plaza during the summer, and hummingbirds feeding from them. The higher slopes of the mountains are, it is true, bare except for a partial covering of *ichu (stipa pungens)*—a tough grass, apparently always brown. Even this, however, has and had its uses. It serves well as thatch. And it is the standard fodder for llamas and alpacas—animals still, as ever, fundamental to Indian economic life as sources of wool, and, in the case of the llama, carrying power. The colonial mining industry would have been hard pressed without the llama as a carrier of ore, mercury, fuel, and all sorts of general supplies.

Lower on the slopes grow two native plants that served colonial mining well: the *kehuiña* and the *yareta*. The *kehuiña (polilepsis incana)* is a small, stunted tree that can survive at heights of up to 5,000 meters (c. 16,400 feet). It is too small to yield useful construction timbers, but served in colonial times as a source of fuel (wood and charcoal). The *yareta (azorella glabra)* is an oddity. On the surface it resembles a cushion of bright yellow-green moss, sometimes several feet across. Its value lies in its long, woody, and resinous root system, which, again, can be used as fuel, and was so used in colonial days.

The most productive land around Potosí lies in the valleys among the mountains. Many of these have narrow alluvial floors, at about 3,500 meters (c. 11,500 feet), on which crops can be grown. These are not limited to the potatoes and green barley that Capoche mentions. Beans and maize flourish here, along with hardier vegetables and fruit. Examples of such areas are the Cayara valley some 12 kilometers to the west of Potosí, and the Tarapaya valley about 15 kilometers to the north. These sites, and other similar places nearby, are certainly too small to have supplied more than a fraction of Potosí's food needs in colonial times. But their existence just as surely should not be passed over in silence.[7]

At the center of the landscape of Potosí stands the cerro rico, as much the navel of early colonial Spanish South America as Cuzco had been of the Incaic domains. Its peak lies 4 kilometers south of the main plaza of the town, and some 800 meters (2,600 feet) above it. After almost 450 years of continuous working, the cerro has

---

7. Information on vegetation is from observation by the author, and from Federico E. Ahlfeld, *Geografía física de Bolivia* (Cochabamba 1969), pp. 52–60.

become a massive slag heap on its surface—but a noble slag heap, still dominating the town and its life as it always has. Oxidation of discarded ores has given it an attractive reddish-brown tinge—a certain warmth, from least from a distance.

The heart of the cerro, and the root of the wealth it has yielded, is an igneous volcanic stock, formed during the Tertiary. This stock, at its greatest horizontal extent, is an oval mass of about 1,500 by 1,100 meters. Vertically it is an inverted cone, with the wide end forming much of the upper part of the cerro, and the narrow end tapering down to a volcanic dyke that, 900 meters below the top of the hill, is only 50 meters thick. It was up this dyke that the volcanic material forming the stock originally welled, carrying with it the metallic minerals that were eventually to form the great veins of silver that made Potosí rich. The upper, and therefore volcanic, section of the cerro contains thirty-five veins and major branches. These converge downwards to form six main groups. Enrichment of the ores by oxidation has taken place to a depth of 500 meters. The combination of densely packed veins and enrichment provided early Spanish miners with a mass of high-grade silver ore without equal in colonial Ibero-America, either then or later. The accessibility and concentration of ores in the upper cerro allowed, once fitting technology had been introduced, an immensely rapid growth of silver production in the sixteenth century. On the other hand, those same qualities of accessibility and concentration led to rapid depletion of the good ores. Once that had happened—and the process was under way before 1600—the path of production from the cerro could only be downward. The hill yielded its best in the space of some fifty years.[8]

The silver ores of the cerro became known to the Spanish in 1545. Several picturesque stories of the discovery exist, in which an Indian pursuing an errant llama stumbles across an outcropping of ore, which he eventually reveals to his Spanish master.[9] As Gunnar Mendoza has pointed out, however, it is unlikely that the

8.   Geological information on the cerro is from Rivas and Carrasco, *Geología*, tomo 2, pp. 49–60.
9.   See Manuel Ballesteros Gaibrois, *Descubrimiento y fundación del Potosí* (Zaragoza 1950).

Potosí deposits were unknown to the native people before 1545. One account of the conquest and early history of Peru, that of Pedro Pizarro, indeed alludes to actual working of the ores by Indians before the Spanish came on the scene. And it is of course beyond doubt that the nearby silver mines of Porco, 36 kilometers to the south-west of Potosí, were being extensively worked under Inca direction at the time of the conquest. Mendoza suggests that the Potosí deposits were certainly known to local people, but that, as happened elsewhere in early Spanish America, there was reluctance to reveal them to the conquerors. Eventually, however, the secret was bound to escape.[10]

No native settlement existed on the site where Potosí was to develop—an alluvial terrace to the north of the cerro. Three kilometers below that site to the west, however, lay the native community of Cantumarca. The existence of this place within an hour's walk of the cerro makes it even less plausible to suppose that the silver ores of Potosí were not known to Indians before 1545, although there is nothing to suggest that the people of Cantumarca worked them. By Arzáns's account, Cantumarca ceased to exist in 1545, as a result of the Spaniards' forcing the villagers to do building work, and the villagers' subsequent violent opposition to this. After some fighting they fled to the Mataca valley, to the east of Potosí.[11]

The closest preexisting Spanish settlements to the Potosí site were Porco and La Plata (or, as it was called in those very early days, la Villa de Plata). Porco had been occupied by Spaniards since 1538, when Gonzalo Pizarro undertook the conquest of the eastern highlands of what is now Bolivia, laying the foundation of the province to which the Spanish gave the name Charcas (after one of the native groups of the region). Gonzalo and Hernando Pizarro

10. Arzáns, *Historia*, tomo 1, pp. 37–38, n. 2. Pedro Pizarro's work, quoted by Mendoza in that note, is the *Relación del descubrimiento y conquista de los reinos del Perú*, of Arequipa, 1571.

11. *Historia*, tomo 1, pp. 38–39. There exists a modern village named Cantumarca, apparently on the same site as that described by Arzáns. The place does not seem to have been occupied in the period treated in this book, although silver refineries stood there.

immediately began to work the silver ores of Porco.[12] Also as a
result of Gonzalo Pizarro's conquest of Charcas came the foundation of La Plata in mid 1539, on a site 120 kilometers northeast of
Porco (and so 80 kilometers north-east of the cerro of Potosí).[13]
Although rather far from Porco, and separated from it by extremely
rough country, La Plata was well placed as a base for further explor-
ations to the east and south. And apart from that, the site was
lower, at 2,900 meters (c. 9,500 feet), and hence more hospitable,
than other possible locations closer to the silver deposits. La Plata
grew rapidly into the administrative center of Charcas, and became
the seat of an *audiencia* in 1561.[14] Potosí and almost all the mining
district that developed around it lay within the jurisdiction of the
Audiencia of La Plata, or Charcas, as it was often called. The audiencia was the principal agent of royal authority in America for
the Potosí mining industry, outranked only by the viceroy of Peru
in Lima, who, however, because more distant, had less to do than
the audiencia with the normal business of Potosí.

A detailed study from primary sources of the urban growth of
Potosí has still to be done. It is clear enough, however, that one
major natural feature around which the town was arranged—and
possibly the predominant feature—was the stream or small river,
originating in the Kari-Kari massif, that ran westward 3 kilometers north of the peak of the cerro. One of the earliest surviving
records of a property transaction at Potosí, from July of 1549, is a
bill of sale for houses "on the other side of the river."[15] It cannot
be said for sure which side, north or south, was "the other side,"
though it would be at least arguable to suppose that it was the
north side, since buildings would have been most likely to appear
first close to the cerro, to the south of the stream.

Clearly enough, in the early years, Potosí was an unplanned and
rough settlement, like other incipient mining towns of sixteenth-
century Spanish America. One early inhabitant recalled many years

12.   Josep M. Barnadas, *Charcas, 1535–1565. Orígenes históricos de una sociedad
colonial* (La Paz 1973), pp. 34–36.
13.   Eduardo Arze Quiroga, *Historia de Bolivia. Fases del proceso hispanoamericano:
orígenes de la sociedad boliviana en el siglo XVI* (Cochabamba 1969), ch. 7.
14.   Arze Quiroga, *Historia*, ch. 13.
15.   BAN EP Soto 1549, f. 151–51v., Potosí, July 31, 1549, Gonzalo Hernández
Colmenero to Hernando de Medina, "casas . . . de la otra parte del río. . .," for
600 pesos de plata corriente.

later that in 1545 there were only "huts as [the town was] a mining camp that was then beginning to be settled."[16] By the late 1550s something much more permanent, if not orderly, was in place. Property transactions of 1559 refer to dwelling houses *(casas de morada)*, the street leading to the church of Santo Domingo, the merchants' street *(calle de los mercaderes)*, the royal (or main) street *(calle real)*, the square *(plazuela)* of Captain Juan Ortiz de Zárate, and the coca sellers' street *(calle de la coca)*.[17] Clearly enough, an urban pattern was growing. This impression is borne out by the illustration of Potosí and the cerro provided by Pedro de Cieza de León in his *Crónica del Perú*, published in Seville in 1553 (f. 260). The picture, a rudimentary line drawing, shows considerable building along both banks of a copious stream, with at least two churches on the cerro side, and some substantial structures on the north side. Cieza had visited Potosí, so his illustration would seem to be a firsthand view.[18]

Despite its apparently unplanned beginnings, Potosí possessed, by the end of the sixteenth century, a remarkably orderly street plan, at least in its center. A map *(Planta general)* of the town, dating from the late sixteenth or early seventeenth century, shows a central area of such notably regular gridiron design that the authors of the Royal Ordinances of 1573 for the laying out of new towns, if

16. ". . . bohíos, como asiento de minas que entonces se comenzaba a poblar." Testimony of Capitán Francisco Fernández Valderrama, in "Información de servicios que la Villa Imperial de Potosí ha hecho a su magestad. . .," Potosí, January 22, 1610, f. 34–34v. (BAN Minas tomo 3, item 17—Minas catalog No. 559a). Fernández said he had first entered Potosí on April 17, 1545, and was among its first settlers. A manuscript of 1548 reveals that dwellings were being built in Potosí in 1545 with the large stones that were found lying on the site, and with local agave branches *(madera de maguey)* for roof beams. The roofing material itself would most likely have been ichu. This document, dated at Potosí, April 26, 1548, reports that Potosí had been founded some three years before (" . . . puede haber tres años poco más o menos, tiempo cuando se fundó este asiento . . .")—a statement that, taken in conjunction with the *Información* cited above, firmly fixes, the beginnings of Potosí in early 1545. See PBN ms A547, "Proceso hecho a pedimento de la Hacienda Real, contra Francisco Zúñiga sobre las casas."

17. Various house sales of April and May 1559, in BAN EP Aguila 1559, ff. 301v.–02v., 374v.–75, 376–77; and in BAN EP Reinoso 1559, ff. 79v.–80.

18. See frontispiece.

magically deposited at the peak of the cerro and gazing down on the settlement, would surely have found their hearts warmed by it despite the chill of the air.[19] The central gridiron measured some 500 meters from north to south and 700 meters from east to west. The blocks in it correspond very clearly to those of central Potosí today. The maximum dimensions of the built-up area of Potosí, as shown in this plan, were 1,000 meters from north to south by about 1,500 meters from east to west; but there were many open spaces within these broad measurements, so that the town was by no means a complete rectangle.

Don Francisco de Toledo, the viceroy of Peru who visited Potosí in the early 1570s, is sometimes given credit for imposing physical order on the town.[20] The center had already been long in place by the time he arrived, however, so that he can have had little influence on its form. The viceroy certainly did try to reorganize and regularize the part of the town between the stream and the cerro, which, by the time of his visit, was largely a suburb inhabited by native mine workers and their families. (See chapter 3). To judge from the *Planta general*, his efforts were not a resounding success, at least in the matter of the layout of streets. Not only the southern Indian suburb, but also others to the west and north of the center, seem to have grown as jumbled muddles of streets and houses.[21]

As Potosí expanded, the stream remained a feature around which the town was organized. Indeed, its influence grew, because it became the boundary between the Spanish center and the largest

19.   Regulations for new towns are in clauses 110–37 of the *Ordenanzas para descubrimientos, nuevas poblaciones y pacificaciones*, given at San Lorenzo on July 3, 1573. See *HAHR* 4:4 (1921), pp. 754–94. The plan is the *Planta general de la Villa Ymperial de Potosí* in the *Atlas of Sea Charts (K3)* held by the Hispanic Society of America, New York. It is reproduced in Capoche, *Relación*, np, sixth illustration at end. The *Planta* is undated; but since it shows the Compañía, or Jesuit church, of Potosí, it cannot date from before 1581, when the permanent building was begun. (José de Mesa and Teresa Gisbert, *Bolivia: monumentos históricos y arqueológicos*, Instituto Panamericano de Geografía e Historia, Comisión de Historia, Mexico City, 1970, p. 47). The script on the *Planta* is of distinctly sixteenth-century character, so that it seems unlikely that the plan was drawn after 1620 or so.

20.   E.g., Arze Quiroga, *Historia*, p. 358.

21.   For other information on the purely urban history of early Potosí, see Arzáns, *Historia*, tomo 1, pp. cxxxi–cxxxiv; and Capoche, *Relación*, pp. 75–76.

native section of the settlement, south under the cerro. And once the silver industry began its astonishing expansion in the 1570s, as a result of the introduction of ore processing with mercury (to be recounted shortly), the stream became an even more prominent feature of Potosí—not only physically, as a dividing line, but also economically, as the source of water power for the refining mills. Indeed, it would be no exaggeration to say that the stream was the aorta of Potosí's industrial organism, especially once artifice had added to its size and importance. During the last quarter of the sixteenth century, dams and aqueducts were built in the Kari-Kari range, and the water so collected was channeled into the existing stream bed. Construction of dams began in 1573. In some cases the lakes already existed in the glaciated valleys of the massif, and the dams served merely to increase the volume of water contained. By the mid-1580s, seven dams existed, providing water for the refineries for six or seven months in wet years (whereas before they were built, the stream had supplied useful amounts of water for only three or four months).[22] Other reservoirs were added over the next forty years, so that by 1621 thirty-two of them may have been in use—possibly the maximum reached at any time during the colonial era.[23] The effect was to provide enough stored water to drive the refineries the year round in the early 1600s, given normal rainfall.

Furthermore, the original watercourse through Potosí was modified to carry this greater flow of water. According to William E. Rudolph, a section of the course 5 kilometers long was canalized, with walls of rock bound with lime mortar. The channel was 8 meters wide.[24] From it ran aqueducts to individual refineries; and the water, having passed over the waterwheel driving the ore-crushing machinery in one mill, was returned to the channel for use in the next one downstream.

The canalized stream and the refineries *(ingenios)* along it formed the *Ribera* of Potosí—a ribbon of industrial activity that transformed the ores of the cerro into refined silver.[25] The production process

---

22. Capoche, *Relación*, p. 117.
23. Rudolph, "The lakes of Potosí," p. 529.
24. Ibid., p. 536.
25. See Arzáns, *Historia*, tomo 1, pp. cxxx–cxxxi, for information on the Ribera.

begun in the mines of the cerro and carried to its conclusion in the *ingenios* below was the reason for Potosí's existence. Since it also brought to Potosí the subjects of this book—the mining and refining laborers—a few pages may usefully be devoted to it here.

In the early decades of silver production at Potosí there was a broad and important continuation of preconquest mining and refining methods. Since many of the early Indian laborers seem to have come from Porco to Potosí (see chapter 2), and Porco had been an Incaic mining center, this is hardly a surprise. Incaic techniques for extracting ore were advanced in comparison with those of other native Americans. Where possible, surface outcroppings were worked, and these might be pursued downwards with opencast pits. Tunneling was also practiced, however, with narrow galleries up to 70 meters long.[26] Firesetting seems to have been commonly used. The softened ore-bearing rock could then be more easily removed with hammers, chisels, wedges, and crowbars. Archaeologists have discovered such tools in the central Andes made from a variety of materials: stone, hard wood, horn, copper, and bronze.[27]

Naturally enough, Indian miners preferred where possible to extract pure metals. Gold, of course, almost always occurred in metallic form. And, given the immense richness in minerals of the central Andes, the miners had little difficulty in finding deposits of pure (or "native") silver in various forms: lumps, flakes, and threads in veins, or even a fine metallic dust.[28] Ores containing chemical compounds of silver were, none the less, also mined and refined. The same was true of copper: some native metal occurred, but compounds were also exploited. The final metal used in pre-Spanish times, tin, occurred only as an oxide (cassiterite).

Ores were carried from the mine to refineries in leather sacks or reed baskets. Generally speaking, the Incaic miners sited their refining plants by streams from which water could be diverted for

26. Georg Petersen G., *Minería y metalurgía en el antiguo Perú* (*Arqueológicas* 12, Museo Nacional de Antropología y Arqueología, Lima, 1970), pp. 67–68; and p. 75, drawing on Pedro Sánchez de la Hoz's account of mines near Lake Titicaca visited by a Spanish expedition in early 1534.

27. Ibid., pp. 68–70.

28. Ibid., p. 67, quoting Alvaro Alonso Barba, *Arte de los metales, en que se enseña el verdadero beneficio de los oro, y plata por azogue* (1st ed., Madrid 1630; ed. used here in subsequent references, Potosí 1967), p. 47.

washing and concentrating crushed ores. A large, rocking stone served as a crushing mill—a boulder with a curved underside and a flat top—a half-moon shaped piece of stone to whose upper surface a beam was lashed, extending outwards from each side so as to allow two men, alternately pushing down on the ends of the beam, to rock the boulder to and fro, crushing any material placed under it. The Spanish called this apparatus a *quimbalete*.[29]

Once the ore was crushed, it could be concentrated by flotation in running water. Incaic miners used stone-lined channels for this. Any particles of native metal could then be removed by hand washing in a pan or basin. Ores containing metal in compounds, on the other hand, demanded smelting. Here again, Incaic technology had made notable strides. One apparatus used was a simple hole in the ground, in which ore was placed along with fuel (wood, ichu, yareta, or llama dung).[30] A more advanced technique was that employing a wind-blown furnace, or *guayra* (from Quechua, *wayra*: air, wind). This was a furnace typically in the shape of an inverted cone, slightly wider at the top than at the base (fig. 1). Some were square in section. To judge by a late sixteenth-century illustration of Indians using guayras, the height was about 2 meters and the diameter at the top some 75 centimeters—though, of course, preconquest versions may have been different in size.[31] Guayras could be made in at least three ways. Some were of rough stones, loosely assembled so that the wind could blow through the gaps and fan the fuel. More advanced was the type built of stones set in clay. Holes were left open to allow the wind to enter. The third variety was a portable clay furnace, and apparently generally somewhat smaller than the first two: from 80 to 90 centimeters high and 40 centimeters maximum across the top. Again, holes punched in the walls allowed air to enter. Evidence exists that the third, portable type was a post-Conquest innovation.[32] All guayras were typically built or placed on exposed ridges where the wind blew strongly.[33]

29. Or *bimbalete* or *bambalete*. Petersen (*Minería*, p. 69) maintains that the term *maray*, often applied by modern writers to this sort of trituration mill, is incorrect.

30. Petersen, *Minería*, p. 83.

31. "Estos indios están guayrando," in *Atlas of Sea Charts (K3)*, Hispanic Society of America, New York.

32. Capoche (*Relación*, p. 110), attributes the design of the clay guayra to a settler in Potosí, Juan de Marroquí.

33. Petersen, *Minería*, pp. 84–85.

Most of the ores smelted by Incaic silver workers yielded a mixture of lead and silver. To separate out the lead, this mixture was placed in a muffle (a perforated crucible) and heated in a separate small furnace—round, and some 80 centimeters in diameter. To provide draught for these, the refiners used not the wind, but copper or cane blowpipes.[34]

No direct evidence exists that preconquest extractive techniques were used at Potosí; but considering that mining there in the first twenty-five years or so was very largely in the hands of Indians (see chapter 2), it is surely safe to assume that they were. Of the use of guayras and of the small refining furnaces no doubt at all exists. Pedro de Cieza de León, when he visited Potosí in 1549, was mightily struck by the success of guayras, particularly because standard Spanish smelting apparatus would not perform satisfactorily there.

It seems . . . that the silver ore cannot fuse *(correr)* with [furnaces blown by] bellows. . . . In Porco and other parts of this kingdom where they extract ore, they make large ingots of silver, and purify and separate the ore from the dross . . . with fire, having large bellows [blowing Castilian stone furnaces] for that purpose. In this Potosí, although it has been tried by many people, they have never had success with this [method of smelting]. The resistance *(reciura)* of the ore seems to be the cause of this, or some other mystery, because great masters have tried to extract [silver] with bellows, and their efforts have yielded nothing. And in the end, as men can find a remedy for everything in this life, one was not lacking to extract this silver, with as strange an invention as any in this world. And this is that, in times past, the Incas were very inventive in some places where silver was mined that would not fuse in [furnaces with] bellows (just like the silver of Potosí), and so, to profit from the ore, they made clay vessels, of the shape and manner of a basil pot in Spain, which had openings or breathing holes in many places. In these vessels they put charcoal, and ore on top of it; and they placed them on the hills or slopes where the wind was strongest, and extracted silver, which they refined and purified afterwards with small

---

34.   Ibid., p. 86. Petersen also refers here to the occasional use by pre-Conquest refiners of fixed furnaces, much larger than guayras.

bellows, or tubes through which they blew.[35] In this way was extracted the great flood of silver that has come from the cerro, the Indians taking the ore to high places all around it to produce silver. These vessels are called guayras, and at night there are so many of them all over the countryside and hillsides that they look like decorative lights *(luminarias).* And when the wind blows hard, much silver is extracted. When the wind falls, they can extract none. And so, just as the wind is useful for sailing on the sea, so it is here, for obtaining silver.[36]

Exactly why the Castilian style of furnace, with bellows, that succeeded at Porco would not function at Potosí is still a mystery. Capoche noted the same difficulty thirty-four years later, attributing it to the "dry" *(seco)* nature of ores at Potosí.[37] Some guayras were still in use there at the time he wrote his *Relación;* but by then the standard method of processing ores had become amalgamation. Capoche, at some indeterminate date before 1585, had counted exactly 6,497 guayras in use at Potosí; but by the 1580s almost all of them were dilapidated and abandoned.[38] None the less, they were still sometimes to be found in operation fifty years later, according to Father Alvaro Alonso Barba.[39]

It was in the 1570s that guayras, indeed smelting in any apparatus, ceased to be the main method of extracting silver from ores at Potosí. In that decade amalgamation—the blending of pulverized ore with mercury—became the dominant technology of refining, and so remained for the rest of the colonial era—and indeed beyond. The change of technology brought many other con-

35. Despite Cieza's implication that in some places the Incas did use bellows, no evidence exists for that. Similarly, not even small bellows were used in Incaic refining furnaces; though Cieza perhaps refers here to furnaces with bellows operated at Potosí by Indian workers after 1545.

36. Pedro de Cieza de León, *La crónica del Perú, nuevamente escrita por . . . , vecino de Sevilla* (Biblioteca de Autores Españoles, tomo XXVI, *Historiadores primitivos de Indias,* II, Madrid, 1947), p. 449, ch. cix.

37. *Relación,* p. 78. This description usually signified that an ore was lacking in natural flux. But since Capoche elsewhere (p. 110) notes the use of *soroche* (Quechua: *sorojchi,* argentiferous galena), a silver ore rich in lead, as a flux in smelting by guayra, it is not clear why the problem of "dryness" in smelting with bellows could not be solved in the same way.

38. Ibid., p. 111.

39. *Arte de los metales,* p. 133.

sequent changes: great expansion in the scale of mining itself, an increase of the regimentation and specialization of native workers in all phases of silver production, rapid growth of the native labor force, and progressive exclusion of that labor force from the profits of production, despite a great surge in output. These themes are the subject matter of succeeding chapters. For the moment, the production process itself remains the object of attention.

One of the more puzzling questions in Spanish-American mining history is the reason for the delay of some fifteen years between the development of a large-scale amalgamation process in New Spain in the mid-1550s, and the introduction of that process to the Andean silver producing regions in the early 1570s.[40] News of the Mexican process reached Peru quickly: in 1558 the colonial administration there sent a miner to Mexico to learn it. He, a Portuguese named Enrique Garcés, produced silver with the method in Peru in 1559. But amalgamation failed to catch on, despite further attempts in Potosí in the mid-sixties.[41] The reason—at least in the case of Potosí—may well have been, as Modesto Bargalló suggests,[42] that the easy profits available to Spanish mine owners from leaving mining and refining (in guayras) to Indian workers made them unwilling to learn and invest in the new techniques from Mexico, which required both new skills and substantial expenditure on plant. It is also possible that the very richness of the early ores at Potosí made amalgamation too costly, since losses of mer-

40.   A considerable bibliography now exists on the various amalgamation processes developed in colonial Spanish America. A basic account is still the *Tercera parte* (pp. 107–200) of Modesto Bargalló, *La minería y la metalurgía en la América española durante la época colonial* (Mexico City 1955). More detail is available in the primary accounts assembled by Bargalló in *La amalgamación de los minerales de plata en Hispanoamérica colonial* (Mexico City 1969). For the initial development of amalgamation on an industrial scale in Mexico—arguably the most remarkable feat of technology ever achieved in Ibero-America—see Alan Probert, "Bartolomé de Medina: the patio process and the sixteenth century silver crisis," *Journal of the West*, 8:1 (1969), pp. 90–124. The principal Andean work on amalgamation of the period discussed in this book is Alonso Barba's *Arte de los metales*, especially the *libro segundo*.

41.   Guillermo Lohmann Villena, "Enrique Garcés, descubridor del mercurio en el Perú, poeta y arbitrista," *Studia* (Lisbon), Nos. 27–28 (1969), pp. 7–62. Also Peter Bakewell, "Technological change in Potosí: the silver boom of the 1570s," *Jahrbuch für Geschichte von Staat, Wirtschaft und Gesellschaft Lateinamerikas*, Band 14 (1977), pp. 60–77; and Bargalló, *La amalgamación*, pp. 162–63.

42.   *La amalgamación*, p. 172.

cury, an expensive substance, tended to be great when the amalgamation processes of the day were applied to ores of very high silver content.

Circumstantial evidence for these suppositions comes also from the fact that amalgamation began to take hold in Potosí precisely at a time when the quality of the ore being mined had fallen severely, resulting in a movement out of the town of Indian silver producers, and a decline in production. (See p. 26 below). The first unequivocal evidence found so far of the arrival of the new technique in Potosí is from January of 1572, in the form of contracts for building refineries.[43] In February of that year, Viceroy Toledo ordered from Cuzco that Pedro Hernández de Velasco, the man traditionally given credit for adapting the Mexican amalgamation technique to Andean conditions, should receive a salary of 400 *pesos ensayados* (744 *pesos corrientes*) a year as "chief master of mercury" (*maestro mayor de azogues*) in Potosí. Hernández was clearly not the only one who had experimented with amalgamation in the town, but his part in bringing in the technique was, equally clearly, substantial.

The chief advantage of amalgamation over smelting was that it allowed profitable processing of large amounts of ore that was, for smelting purposes, of medium to low grade. Even if the ores of Potosí had been amenable to smelting in larger furnaces than guayras, the cost of extracting silver from the vast amounts of moderate ore in the cerro would have been prohibitive because of the lack of fuel in the vicinity. Indeed, the crucial superiority of amalgamation is seen in the fact that it was precisely the tailings from the previous twenty-five years of mining, discarded as too poor for smelting, that served as raw material for the early amalgamation mills.

The necessity of building what were, for the time and place, complex refining plants was the main drawback of amalgamation. To maximize the efficiency of the refining process, through optimum contact of the mercury with particles of ore, fine trituration of the ore was required. To achieve this, mechanically driven stamp mills proved essential. To begin with, refiners in Potosí made mills turned by human power. They quickly progressed to bigger machines driven by mules or horses; and finally, though still rapidly, to others powered by vertical waterwheels. These drew water from

43. Bakewell, "Technological change," p. 62.

the stream, as already outlined. By 1576, only four years after the first refineries were built, 108 mills were running in Potosí: 22 human powered, 22 animal powered, 15 water powered, and 49 with unidentified power source. Thirty-nine more were being built: 5 human powered, 15 animal powered, 18 water powered, and one unidentified. It was, apparently, the profit made from refining tailings—in essence, free ores, since the extraction cost had been paid in the guayra phase of processing—that provided capital for investment in ever larger mills. Water-driven mills were far more costly to build than the two earlier types, but made much more efficient use of both capital and labor.[44]

The typical water-driven refining mill *(ingenio de agua)* of Potosí was a large structure (fig. 2). A rectangular wall, perhaps 50 meters on a side, enclosed open-air working areas, storage sheds, stone tanks for amalgamation, the trituration mill itself, and a water-wheel. A small chapel was often included. The machinery was massive: for example, the standard waterwheel had a diameter of some 8 meters (26 feet), and by the start of the seventeenth century, the iron stamp shoes in the mill itself each weighed over 45 kilos (100 pounds), the standard weight of the shoes having roughly doubled since the mid-1570s.[45] Frequently, two milling assemblies *(cabezas de ingenio)* were built on a common shaft, one on each side of the wheel. Each cabeza usually had six to eight stamps. This was not a design original to Potosí; nor indeed was that of any of the ore-triturating machinery built there in the sixteenth century. A clear illustration of a "double-headed" mill is given by Agricola in Book VIII of *De Re Metallica*, along with drawings of other sorts of apparatus used by the refiners of Potosí.[46]

The number of refining mills in and around Potosí remained large during the period treated by this book. In 1603, for example, a time of high silver output, though not quite so high as in the 1590s, there were 48 ingenios along the Ribera of Potosí, and 17

44. For a more detailed discussion of the beginnings of amalgamation in Potosí, see ibid.

45. Dimensions of wheel are from PCM EN 8, cuadernos 11–16, 18 passim (JHR); weights of stamps from PCM EN 8, cuaderno 19, nf, Potosí, October 11, 1577 (JHR), and from PCM EN 44, f. 1096v., Potosí, June 11, 1612.

46. Georgius Agricola, *De Re Metallica*, translated from the first Latin edition of 1556 . . . by Herbert Clark Hoover and Lou Henry Hoover (New York 1950), p. 286, and Book VIII passim.

more in the valleys of Tarapaya nearby to the north and west.[47] Seven years later, when the number of ingenios could not have changed substantially, 140 cabezas were in service in Potosí and Tarapaya.[48] Some ingenios, therefore, had more than two cabezas, which suggests that some had more than two wheels, since only two cabezas could run on one shaft. In 1624, approximately 124 cabezas remained in service in Potosí and Tarapaya, with 944 stamps among them—an average of about 7.5 each. The cabezas were distributed among 85 owners.[49] By 1654 the number of operating cabezas on the Ribera was down to 64, and in Tarapaya, 4.[50]

The ore fed into the stamp mills had already been concentrated to a degree at the mouth of the mine—obviously useless material being broken off with hammers. After trituration, the pulverized ore *(harina)* was sifted, normally by being tossed against an inclined sieve, and then shoveled into refining tanks *(cajones)*, each of which held 50 *quintales* of harina (5,000 pounds). In the cajón various substances were added to the ore: enough water to give it a stirring consistency, salt (5 quintales per cajón), and a sprinkling of mercury (from 6 to 10 pounds per quintal of ore, according to its silver content—with poorer ores needing less than the richer).[51] In addition to these basic "ingredients" of the amalgamation "soup" were often added after the late 1580s, copper sulphate *(magistral)* and powdered iron, both of which were found, by empirical testing, to improve the speed and efficiency of the mercury process.[52]

Until roughly the end of the sixteenth century, amalgamation was carried out over heat. The cajones were built above vaults in which a fire could be set. In this way, according to Capoche, the

---

47. Don Pedro de Lodeña, corregidor of Potosí, to crown, Potosí, April 3, 1603, in AGI Charcas 46 (JHR).

48. Potosí, 1610. "Información de servicios que la Villa Imperial de Potosí ha hecho a su magestad, recibida por el Licenciado Alonso Maldonado de Torres . . . ," testimony of Juan Vélez, Potosí, January 15, 1610. See BAN Minas tomo 3, item 17 (Minas catalog No. 559a).

49. PCM CR 201, ff. 269–79v.—Repartimiento general of mitayos by Don Diego de Portugal, president of the Audiencia of La Plata, Potosí, November 15, 1624.

50. "Resumen de visita de minas e ingenios hecha por el corregidor don Francisco Sarmiento [de Mendoza]," Potosí, July 4, 1654, in AGI Charcas 266, item 19d.

51. Capoche, *Relación*, p. 123. These quantities should not necessarily be regarded as valid for times other than Capoche's.

52. Bargalló, *La amalgamación*, pp. 229, 247ff.

mercury drew the silver from its ore in five or six days: whereas
without heat, absorption of the silver took twenty-five days.[53] In
the seventeenth century, use of heat seems to have ceased, perhaps because of the cost of fuel.

Once the mercury had fully combined with the silver present in
the ore, in the judgment of the foreman of the ingenio, the contents of the cajón were removed and washed. Special vats equipped
with a rotating paddle served for this purpose, the paddle in some
cases being turned by Indian workers and in others by waterpower.
As water ran through the vats and the paddles turned, the heavy
amalgam of mercury and silver settled, while the rest of the triturated ore was washed away. Several vats and settling pools were
used in series, to maximize recovery of amalgam. Once collected
up, the amalgam was squeezed in a heavy cloth tube to express
free mercury, and the remaining substance *(pella)*, consisting of 80
percent mercury and 20 percent silver, was molded into conical
pieces *(piñas)* weighing 45 kilos (100 pounds), and heated for eight
to ten hours under a clay hood to distill off the mercury (which
could in part be recovered as it condensed on the inner surface of
the hood).[54] Honeycombed masses of pure silver remained once
the mercury had been removed. This, in broad and simplified form,
was the amalgamation process by which Potosí produced its silver in colonial times. No important modifications of the method,
beyond those already mentioned, took place in the first century
of mining.

Nothing introduced by the Spanish in the techniques of ore
extraction was as dramatic an innovation as amalgamation in refining. Nevertheless, a few changes were made in native practices
of mining that certainly contributed to Potosí's growth as a silver
producer. One was the use of steel-tipped tools for cutting ore,
replacing native implements that were at best tipped with bronze
or copper.[55] Another was the greater scale of mining operations.
Incaic mines had sometimes, if rarely, been as long as 70 meters.
By 1573, doubtless under the stimulus of increased demand for

53. *Relación,* p. 123.
54. Detail in this description is from Capoche, *Relación,* pp. 124–25.
55. In this connection the absence of underground blasting is worth noting.
Even in Europe, blasting did not begin until the early decades of the seventeenth
century. The first sign of it in the Potosí district (though not in Potosí itself)
appears in the 1670s. Peter Bakewell, *Antonio López de Quiroga (industrial minero
del Potosí colonial),* Universidad Boliviana "Tomás Frías" (Potosí 1973), p. 22.

ore from the fledgling amalgamation mills, mines in the cerro averaged some 200 meters (650 feet) in depth. To reach these great depths, there had come into use long, and by all accounts, precarious ladders made of leather ropes with wooden, and even woven-rush, rungs.[56] The growing depth and extent of the mines, however, had already led to another innovation, probably the most noteworthy of all those brought in by the Spanish to the business of ore extraction itself. This was the use of adits *(socavones):* near-horizontal galleries driven from the surface to intersect workings at their lower levels, with the purpose of allowing easier removal of ore as well as promoting drainage and some circulation of air. The location of Potosí's ores in one steeply sloping and conical hill made the use of adits attractive and simple. And near the summit, of course, where the densest concentrations of ore lay, the distance from the surface to the veins was short. So it is no surprise to find the first adit being started as early as 1556, the work of the Florentine miner Nicolás del Benino, and directed to cut the "Rich Vein" *(Veta Rica),* one of the main objects of the early miners' attention. The tunnel took far longer to complete than Benino expected. Only after twenty-nine years of labor, on and off, did it finally reach its mark, in April of 1585. Unexpected hardness of rock was the reason given by both Benino and Capoche for the lagging advance. Perhaps, also, the ambitious dimensions of the adit made for delays: 2.4 meters (8 feet) square in cross section. The final length was 210 meters (250 *varas).*[57]

By 1585, according to Capoche, seven other adits were under way or completed in the cerro, with a total length of 560 meters (670 varas).[58] The use of adits remained a standard feature of mining in Potosí and its district, although it is hard to conceive that later efforts can have yielded the returns provided by the early and

56.   Nicolás del Benino, "Relación muy particular del Cerro y minas de Potosí y de su calidad y labores, por . . . , dirigida a Don Francisco de Toledo, virrey del Perú, en 1573," in *Relaciones geográficas de Indias—Perú,* tomo 1, pp. 362–71 (Biblioteca de Autores Españoles, tomo CLXXXIII, Madrid 1965), here pp. 368–69. Benino gives the common depth of mines in the cerro as 100–120 *estados*—an estado being roughly the height of a man, reckoned here as between 5 and 6 feet.

57.   Information on adits is from ibid., pp. 369–70, and Capoche, *Relación,* p. 106.

58.   *Relación,* p. 107.

short tunnels cut into the densely packed high-grade ores near the top of the cerro.

Both mining and refining drew on distant places for their raw materials. Potosí's role as a market and economic stimulus for an enormous area of middle and southern South America is well established, and is beginning to be known in some detail.[59] It is no purpose of this book to undertake to add to that knowledge; but it is necessary, in order to give a rounded, if brief, account of silver production, to enumerate the types and sources of raw materials needed in mining and refining.

Enough has already been said about fuel. More problematic a commodity was large timber for making refining machinery. The largest piece needed was the drive shaft of the stamp mill—a beam typically 5.5 to 7 meters long (from 18 to 23 feet), and roughly 50 centimeters (20 inches) square. This, indeed, was the single most costly component of a refining plant.[60] Shafts of sufficient strength could not, apparently, be built up from separate pieces. A single timber was demanded, and one free of cracks. Trees big enough to yield such a piece of wood did not grow near Potosí. Typical sources of shafts in the late sixteenth and early seventeenth centuries were far away in temperate valleys in the eastern slopes of the Andes. The nearest source used was the Pilcomayo valley (at a minimum distance from Potosí of 30 kilometers), and the farthest, the Mizque valley (some 200 kilometers away). Shafts were cut on site, and dragged, by Indians or animals, to Potosí.

Hides were another essential raw material that at least in part was found in distant places. Leather had manifold uses in silver production: for bags to carry ore, for the rungs of ladders, and as a reinforcing and hinging material in machinery. It seems highly likely that the hides of llamas served these purposes in Potosí, since the llama was locally bred and was the cheapest of large domesticated animals available. Cattle, however, were also brought in in large numbers from what is now northern and central Argentina, providing both meat and leather. Another valuable import from

59. See Carlos Sempat Assadourian, *El sistema de la economía colonial. Mercado interno, regiones y espacio económico*, Instituto de Estudios Peruanos, Lima 1982.

60. In the late 1580s, for example, such a shaft cost from 800 to 1,000 pesos ensayados, whereas the large waterwheel that turned it sold for only 200 to 250 pesos ensayados.

the south was mules, which the area around Córdoba, above all other regions, raised especially for the Andean market.[61]

Of the mineral raw materials needed for silver production, iron traveled the farthest. All the iron employed in Potosí originated in Spain. Its uses were two: in machinery, as nails, straps, bearings, journals, stamp shoes and mortar blocks; and in amalgamation, in triturated form, as a reagent. Despite the length and occasional insecurity of the supply line, lack of iron never seems to have been an impediment to silver production in the part of Potosí's history studied here. Another reagent in amalgamation was copper, probably used in the sulfate form. Supply contracts of the early seventeenth century show that it had been found quite close to Potosí, and at Yura (70 kilometers to the south-west) and Chulchucani (20 kilometers to the north-east).

The essential reagent in amalgamation was, of course, mercury itself. The primary source of mercury for Potosí, as for other silver mines in the central Andes, was Huancavelica, in the mountains 220 kilometers south-east of Lima. The details of mercury supply to Potosí from Huancavelica would occupy a volume in themselves. For present purposes it is enough to say that Potosí seems never, in its first century, to have suffered any shortage of mercury long or severe enough to have hindered silver output substantially. In part this was because, in the the period roughly from 1620 to 1660, considerable amounts of mercury were exported to Peru from Almadén in Spain and from Idrija in Slovenia. These extra supplies offset a weakening trend in output at Huancavelica.[62]

The production of silver in Potosí and its district followed the pattern shown in figure 2.[63] For the purposes of this study, no elaborate explanation of changes in production is necessary; but

61.   Carlos Sempat Assadourian, "Potosí y el crecimiento económico de Córdoba en los siglos XVI y XVII," in *Homenaje al Doctor Ceferino Garzón Maceda*, Universidad Nacional de Córdoba, Córdoba 1973.

62.   See P. J. Bakewell, *Silver mining and society in colonial Mexico: Zacatecas, 1546–1700* (Cambridge [UK] 1971), pp. 161–64; Guillermo Lohmann Villena, *Las minas de Huancavelica en los siglos XVI y XVII* (Seville 1949); Gwendolyn B. Cobb, *Potosí and Huancavelica: economic bases of Perú* (Ph.D. dissertation, University of California, Berkeley 1947).

63.   For the sources of output figures, see Peter J. Bakewell, "Registered silver production in the Potosí district, 1550–1735," *Jahrbuch für Geschichte von Staat, Wirtschaft und Gesellschaft Lateinamerikas*, 12 (1975), pp. 67–103.

some commentary on the broad movements is called for. The graph of production shows three clear trends. First is the period of low and generally falling output from 1550 to the early 1570s. This corresponds with the early smelting stage of ore processing—the production of silver largely by Indians using guayras. No useful data on output in the late 1540s exist, so it is impossible to tell whether the figure for 1550 represents a peak in the early decades. Possibly it does, since several years would have been needed for production to work up from nothing in 1545. The broadly falling trend of the next twenty years or so reflects the depletion of the initial, very rich surface ores, and the growing need to begin actual mining—as indicated, for example, by the start of work in 1556 on Benino's adit. Production seems in general to have stabilized between 1555 and 1565; but after then, a severe decline set in.

Impending collapse was more than averted, and the second phase of production begun, by two large innovations of the early 1570s. Amalgamation, the first of these, has already been outlined. The second, the draft-labor system of the *mita*, is treated at length in later chapters. Amalgamation was arguably the more efficacious of the two. Without an efficient technique of bulk refining, such as amalgamation offered, the application of even vast numbers of cheap laborers to mining would have brought slight gains—if for no other reason than the scarcity, and hence potentially high cost, of fuel for smelting.

The great leap of silver output between the mid-1570s and the early eighties was the result, in addition, of the availability of the abandoned tailings already mentioned. A plentiful supply of this ore no doubt facilitated progress from the early and small human- and animal-powered mills to the more expensive, but far more efficient, water-driven refineries. The combination of cheap ore, cheap labor, and a new and efficient technology made the period from 1573 to 1582 a *decas mirabilis* for Potosí. Such an explosion of production and prosperity has never been seen there since.

That surge of ten years took a hundred and twenty to subside— in a long, downward drift that constitutes the third broad phase of production. By 1710–20 silver output was back to the levels of the early 1570s. The year of highest output was 1592, with 887,448 registered marks, or 201 metric tons, of silver. From then on, the trend was consistently down, although occasional brief resurgences interrupted it. The main depressant of production seems to have

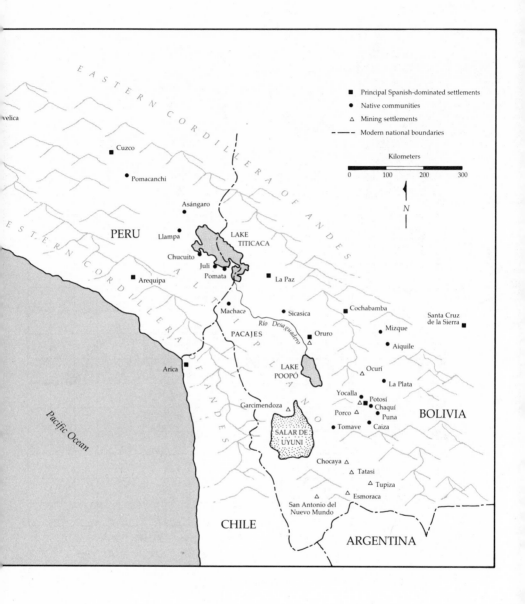

Principal Spanish-dominated settlements ■
Native communities ●
Mining settlements △
Modern national boundaries

Kilometers

0   100   200   300

N

EASTERN CORDILLERA OF ANDES

WESTERN CORDILLERA OF ANDES

ALTIPLANO

PERU

velica

Cuzco

Pomacanchi

Asángaro

Llampa

Chucuito

Juli

Pomata

Arequipa

LAKE TITICACA

La Paz

Machaca

Río Desaguadero

PACAJES

Sicasica

Oruro

Cochabamba

Santa Cruz de la Sierra

Mizque

Aiquile

LAKE POOPÓ

Arica

Ocurí

La Plata

Yocalla

Potosí

Chaquí

Porco

Puna

Garcimendoza

Pacific Ocean

SALAR DE UYUNI

Tomave

Caiza

BOLIVIA

Chocaya

Tatasi

Tupiza

Esmoraca

San Antonio del Nuevo Mundo

CHILE

ARGENTINA

Annual Registered Silver Production in the Potosí District, 1550-1710

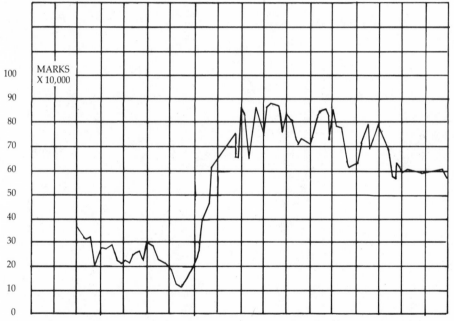

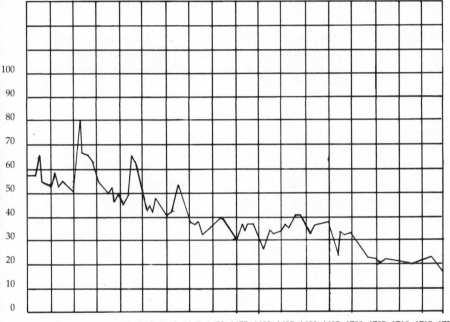

For sources see: Peter Bakewell, ''Registered Silver Production in the Potosí District, 1550-1710,'' Jahrbuch für Geschichte von Staat, Wirtschaft und Gesellschaft Lateinamerikas, 12 (1975).

Figure 1. "Estos yndios estan guayrando." This illustration, probably from the late sixteenth century, shows two native refiners tending guayras. (The Hispanic Society of America, Atlas of Sea Charts (K3).)

simply been depletion of ores in the cerro of Potosí—or, more exactly, depletion of the easily accessible ores concentrated toward the top of the cerro. Important new finds were certainly made in the lower reaches of the hill in the seventeenth century, but they were not so compact, and hence so cheap to work, as had been the group of veins beneath the summit. Richer than these discoveries in the cerro, however, were various of the strikes made in the greater district of Potosí, some of them far from the town. The first of the district mines was Porco, which, of course, predated Potosí itself. The first new ore deposit to be worked after the discovery of Potosí was Berenguela, near Cochabamba, which was being exploited by 1555.[64] Several other finds were made in the sixteenth century, mainly in the province of los Lipes, south-west of Potosí. But far more strikes came in the seventeenth century, as, no doubt, a reflection of the progressive depletion of the cerro. Some of the more durable of the deposits exploited in the first half of the century were these (the dates are of the earliest mention found in manuscript sources): Sicasica (1600), Tupiza (1602), Garcimendoza (1603), Esmoraca (1606), Tatasi (1612), Chocaya (1633), San Antonio del Nuevo Mundo (1648), and San Antonio de Padua

64.   BAN Rück collection, No. 6, Alegaciones, tomo 8, f. 28: registration of a vein in Berenguela by Juan de la Fuente, December 4, 1555.

Figure 2. An untitled view of a waterpowered ingenio for refining silver ore, with the cerro rico of Potosí in the background. Clearly visible are two large veins of ore near the summit of the cerro, many entrances to mines below the summit, and herds of llamas bringing ore down from the mines (or on their way to collect new loads). In the ingenio the arrangement of aqueduct, wheel, and stamp mill is clearly shown. Note the S-shaped cams, lifting the stamps. Piles of ore stand awaiting amalgamation. At the front left are cajones containing amalgamating material. A vat for washing processed amalgam is in the center of the courtyard. Pools of lamas (residues of washed amalgam) have collected here and there. At the foot of the cerro, and emitting smoke, are furnaces for roasting lamas, for recovery of mercury. (An anonymous and undated illustration, held by The Hispanic Society of America, in *Atlas of Sea Charts* (K3). The script on the drawing strongly suggests that it dates from the late sixteenth century.)

(1652). Oruro, where substantial mining began in 1606, was more productive than any of these: so productive, indeed, that in 1607 a separate treasury office *(caja real)* was set up there to collect royalties on silver produced. In the sense, therefore, that its silver output is not reflected in the treasury records of Potosí, Oruro did not belong to the Potosí district, though geographically it lay between Potosí and some of the places just listed. Even without Oruro, however, the district mines provided a large supplement to Potosí's output in certain periods of the seventeenth century. No separate accounting of their royalty payments (and hence of their registered production) has been found for the period before 1660. But in that year and the following one they supplied 37.1 percent and 39.1 percent respectively of the total registered output of the district; and in the whole period from 1660 to 1690, yielded an average of 25.3 percent of that production.[65] Since this silver came largely from the district deposits that had been found in the first half of the century, it would seem likely that then, too, production in the district was substantial. There was, therefore, a great deal more behind the wealth of Potosí than the cerro alone.

Research to date suggests little besides ore depletion (and the consequent extra costs of new exploration and more difficult extraction) to explain the downward drift of silver production after the early 1590s. No change took place during the seventeenth century in the royalty rate of a fifth. Other costs do not appear to have risen. Indeed, the general trend of prices, for those items whose cost can be traced, was downward from the early 1600s. (See, for example, the items in Appendix 2.) The price of mercury certainly fell; while, as already noted, the supply in the seventeenth century gives no signs of having posed difficulties for refiners. Similarly, the supply of labor seems always to have been sufficient, in the crude sense that enough workers were always at hand, either drafted or for hire, to perform the necessary tasks. A larger, or more reliable, supply of draftees would no doubt have lowered the total labor cost, and so tended to encourage silver production. But it does not seem possible to argue that Potosí suffered at any point from an absolute shortage of either skilled or unskilled men.

After this bare outline of the environment and the system of production in which they worked, it is to these workers that attention can now be turned.

65. Bakewell, "Registered silver production," table 3, pp. 99–100.

2

Indios varas, indios ventureros

En habiendo metal en alguna veta acuden tantos indios cuantos pueden cavar en la mina . . .

(Juan de Matienzo, *Gobierno del Perú [1567]*, ch. XL)

The name Potosí is commonly associated as no other in colonial Spanish American history with forced labor. The Black Legend hangs heavily around the town's history. The mita of Potosí—the mass of drafted Indian workers serving its mines and refineries— was larger than that assigned to any other single place in the empire. Working conditions in the mines of Potosí, from the time of Theodor de Bry's gloomy drawings of the late sixteenth century, have been assumed by historians and propagandists to have been as miserable as they were hazardous. Almost equally widespread is the notion that the blame for it all rests squarely on the shoulders of that irascible, impatient, bulldozing man, Don Francisco de Toledo, fifth viceroy of Peru (1569–80). While there is no denying that these persistent generalizations have their measure of truth, the reality was more varied than they allow, as the pages that follow will show. The central enquiry running through them is about coercion—but not *was there* coercion of Indian mine workers at Potosí? (for there clearly was); but rather the more elusive question of the *degree* of coercion to which those workers were subjected. This question raises many others that demand attention. How did coercion arise? To what extent was Toledo to blame for it? What, if anything, did workers receive in return for their labor? How was that labor organized? What were the conditions of work? In what measure did workers move from forced to voluntary labor, and for what reasons? These and other questions this book sets out to examine.

The labor history of Potosí in its early years can at best be dimly seen. Documentation is scarce, as would be expected. And the lack of conclusive secondary works on early colonial labor in Peru as a whole makes for further uncertainties. Difficulties arise immediately in discussing a highly important group of workers of Potosí's initial days—the *yanaconas*.

The concept of *yanaconaje* (to use the Hispanized term) is, of course, one belonging to Incaic and pre-Incaic times. An exhaustive discussion of what it meant before the conquest does not belong here. But one essential quality of being a yanacona in pre-Spanish times does need to be emphasized, because it carried over into the colonial era and is central to the condition of the Indians whom the Spanish called yanaconas. This quality was apartness from the great body of society composed principally of the common people, or *hatunrunas*. Yanaconas were a minority made up of people who did not belong to any *ayllu*—the kin group that was a basic building block of the social structure; neither did they form any ayllus of their own. To this extent, they might be said to be "free-floating" in a society whose other members had a rigidly defined place. But Incaic yanaconas were attached as personal servitors to dominant figures in society: for example, to nobles, military leaders, local *curacas*, or to the Sapa Inca himself. Many yanaconas served as agricultural workers or herdsmen; others were craftsmen; yet others, temple attendants and even responsible administrators. Recent investigation has stressed above all the variability of their social standing, which differed from region to region, and in accordance with the status of their master. One student of Incaic yanaconaje even holds it to have been an intermediate condition between the commoner status and the nobility, a condition

1. Sócrates Villar Córdoba, *La institución del yanacona en el Incanato* (Lima 1966), pp. 20–21, 37–38, 57, 62, quoted in Barnadas, *Charcas,* pp. 285–86, notes 249–52. Much has been written on the controversial topic of yanaconas. Discussion here rests heavily on Barnadas, *Charcas,* p. 284 ff., where references to other relevant works and mss may be found. See also José Matos Mar, *Yanaconaje y reforma agraria en el Perú. El caso del Valle de Chancay* (Lima 1976), pp. 21–23; and Nathan Wachtel, *La vision des vaincus. Les indiens du Pérou devant la Conquête espagnole, 1530–1570* (Paris 1971), pp. 120–21.

of high prestige to which were admitted people of unusual intelligence and ability.[1]

It was the relatively "free-floating" nature of yanaconas' status that made them peculiarly receptive to the Spanish conquerors. Of all groups in central Andean native society, it was they who ranged themselves with the Spanish most quickly and most thoroughly, readily abandoning their defeated local masters for the victors. Even before *encomiendas* of hatunrunas were granted, the conquerors seem to have begun gathering yanaconas as personal servants, perhaps from the retinues of defeated Inca lords, perhaps by more direct seizure or attraction. The processes remain undefined. In 1539, only seven years after the capture of Atahualpa, the bishop of Cuzco characterized yanaconas as servants of Spaniards; and in 1541 the emperor Charles V declared their liberty and noted their attachment to the Spanish.[2] Josep M. Barnadas considers that liberty and closeness to Spaniards were precisely the distinguishing traits of yanaconas in early colonial years. This seems a better-considered view than that put forward by another student of early Peruvian labor, Marie Helmer, who, on the strength of a *cédula* of 1533, considers yanaconas to have been essentially slaves of the Spanish.[3] It is true that this cédula, given at Zaragoza on 8 March 1533, permitted purchase, sale and use of yanaconas as if they were chattels; but the crown clearly realized by the late 1530s, perhaps as a result of accounts received of the native status of yanaconas, perhaps in view of their rapid and useful association with the Spanish, that it had erred, and so clearly defined yanaconas' liberty in 1541.[4] Yanaconas were also exempt from the Spanish tribute to which hatunrunas were liable; possibly the Spanish here followed Inca antecedents, since in preconquest times too the yanaconas had provided no tribute. But apart

---

2. Bishop Valverde to crown, Cuzco, 20 March 1539; and real cédula of Charles V to Licenciado Cristóbal Vaca de Castro, Fuenzalida, October 26, 1541, containing the words ". . . anaconas [sic] los cuales son libres y que ellos por ser aficionados a los españoles de su voluntad muchas veces viven con ellos y los sirven . . .:" both quoted by Barnadas, *Charcas*, p. 286, notes 255 and 256.

3. Helmer, "Notes sur les esclaves indiens au Pérou (XVIe siècle)," *Travaux de l'Institut d'Etudes Latino-Américaines de l'Université de Strasbourg (TILAS)*, vol. 5 (April 1965), p. 686.

4. Barnadas, *Charcas*, p. 286.

from this exemption, and possession of freedom, the juridical status of yanaconas in early colonial years is still vague. The legal
standing of the bond between them and their masters needs to be
defined, if possible. James Lockhart refers to the master-servant
link as "semi-legal" and adds that during the rebellion of Gonzalo
Pizarro in the mid-1540s "the rebel authorities granted to some
Spaniards legal title to possess such Indians."[5] But this was an
exception.

It was in 1545, during that insurrection, that Potosí's silver ores
were found. The first laborers were, it seems, largely yanaconas,
sent or taken there by their Spanish masters. According to one
report made not long after the event, over seven thousand yanaconas were soon to be found working at mining or smelting silver
ores in Potosí.[6] A goodly number of these probably served Gonzalo
Pizarro himself, and most of the rest, his adherents, since Potosí
was deep in rebel territory. These yanaconas reportedly had to produce two marks of silver a week for their masters.[7] Anything they
refined beyond that amount, they might keep for themselves. The
result was that even after paying the inflated prices for food that
quickly became common in Potosí, they made minor fortunes of
up to 3,000 *castellanos* (equivalent to some 5,000 pesos corrientes),
and could not be persuaded to leave. Many of these early yanaconas probably came to Potosí from the silver mines at Porco,
which Gonzalo and Hernando Pizarro, with their associates, had begun to work in 1538.[8] So, among the early yanaconas of Potosí, there
were very possibly some who had worked Porco for the Incas.[9]

With the defeat and death of Gonzalo Pizarro in April 1548, and
the restoration of royal rule to Peru in the person of Pedro de la
Gasca, the organization of the Potosí labor force became more

5. James Lockhart, *Spanish Peru, 1532–1560. A colonial society* (Madison 1968),
p. 219.

6. *Relación de las cosas del Perú* (anon., but attributed to Licenciado Juan Polo
de Ondegardo) in *Crónicas del Perú* (ed. Juan Pérez de Tudela, Biblioteca de Autores
Españoles, tomos 164–68, Madrid 1963–98), tomo 5, p. 297.

7. Ibid., p. 297.

8. Barnadas, *Charcas,* p. 36.

9. This continuity was not restricted to yanaconas. The Chucuito Indians in
1567 stated that in pre-Spanish times they had been sent to Porco by the Inca to
extract silver as tribute (and also to Chuquiabo to produce gold). For the past
seven or eight years they had been going regularly to Potosí to earn the cash
they needed to pay tribute to the Spanish king. Some older men undoubtedly

complex. (Some of this complexity, it must be admitted, may only be apparent, resulting as it does from a *de facto*, though not *de jure*, extension of the meaning of "yanacona.")

Gasca naturally deprived the Pizarrist rebels of Indians serving them, and rewarded the loyal by ceding to them those same Indians. These transfers included both hatunrunas in encomienda and yanaconas. In redistributing the yanaconas Gasca did not, however, cede them as out-and-out yanaconas, but—and here the confusion arises—as "yanaconas en encomienda."[10] In late 1548, for example, he transferred to one Padre Alonso Márquez twenty Indians in Potosí who were yanaconas of six men accused of disloyalty, or at least of insufficiently active loyalty, to the crown during the insurrection. The grant reads:

> In as much as you, Father Alonso Márquez, have served his majesty, having the faith and fidelity owed by a good vassal to his king, against the men of Gonzalo Pizarro and those in his rebellion; therefore by this [decree] I entrust *(encomiendo)* to you twenty yanaconas in the town of Potosí, from the yanaconas and youths and servants *[piezas]* of Francisco Hernández and Gonzalo Fernández Colmenero and Enrique Sande (Fleming) and Juan de Alcoba y Montero (carpenter) and from those of Francisco Blanco Dezmero and from those of Father Bartolomé [Sánchez?], deceased, persons who in the late disturbances of Gonzalo Pizarro looked to their own interests and did not serve his majesty; which Indians I entrust to you . . . that you may make use of them as of free people who may go to their fields or lands when they will. . . .[11]

---

did silver-mining work in both places. The Chucuito people were under the direct administration of the crown, and so strictly speaking were neither encomienda Indians nor yanaconas. See *Visita hecha a la provincia de Chucuito por Garci Diez de San Miguel en el año 1567* (transcribed by Waldemar Espinoza Soriano, Lima 1964), pp. 92, 99, 106.

10.   His reason may have been a disinclination, for legal and political purposes, to perpetuate the highly personal yanacona-Spaniard relationship. The notion of Indians in "servicio personal" was by this time counter to the tenor of the law; and the close and permanent tie of the yanacona to his master must, especially in the aftermath of the Pizarrist episode, have seemed politically undesirable; far better to grant Indians in encomienda, which could be revoked.

11.   BAN EP Soto 1549 (Minas catalog No. 1b), cédula of Gasca, December 20, 1548: "Por cuanto vos el Padre Alonso Márquez habéis servido a su magestad, teniendo fe y fidelidad que buen vasallo a su rey debe, contra los de Gonzalo

The odd point of this grant lies in the final line quoted here, which declares the Indians ceded to Márquez to possess freedom of movement to an extent that not only, of course, contradicts any suggestion of slavery, but also exceeds the measure of liberty often associated with encomienda (and certainly the liberty possessed by the normal run of encomienda Indians in Potosí, as will shortly be seen). This anomaly undoubtedly arose from the imprecision of yanacona status itself, as puzzling to the authorities then as it is now to historians.[12]

In 1550, the crown, mindful of the freedoms that it had already declared, by its cédula of 1541, to belong to yanaconas, ordered Gasca to stop distributing yanaconas in encomienda. The particular legal basis given for this order was not, however, the decree of 1541, but clause 22 of the New Laws of 1542, which declared that nobody should use Indians as *naborías* or *tapias* against their will.[13] These were classes of workers in preconquest Caribbean and Middle American society who strongly resembled yanaconas in various ways. It is a measure of the home administration's growing

---

Pizarro y los de su rebelión, por ende por la presente vos encomiendo veinte yanaconas en el asiento de Potosí en los yanaconas y muchachos y piezas de Francisco Hernández y Gonzalo Fernández Colmenero y Enrique Sande, flamenco, y Juan de Alcoba y Montero, carpintero, y en los de Francisco Blanco Dezmero y en los del Padre Bartolomé [Sánchez], difunto, personas que en las alteraciones pasadas de Gonzalo Pizarro . . . estuvieron a la mira y no sirvieron a su magestad, los cuales os encomiendo . . . para que os sirváis de ellos como de personas libres que puedan irse a sus labranzas o tierras cuando quisieren. . . ."

12.   Another interesting point in this grant is the use of the word *pieza*. James Lockhart, in a direct communication to the author, points out that the term was often used in early Peru to indicate an Indian attached to a Spaniard—apparently, therefore, as a synonym of yanacona. The word is translated here simply as *servant*. Its general connotation in colonial Spanish America, of course, was *slave* (generally black). Various notarial mss of 1548–49 refer to piezas working mines in Potosí; and references also occur to *esclavos*. See, e.g., BAN EP Soto 1549, ff. 32v.–33v., and ff. 116v.–117. Taken together, these pieces of evidence indicate that slaves of some sort were at work in Potosí at this early date, but whether Indian or black is unclear. Blacks were certainly present. For instance, Juan Albertos, a mine owner, complained in 1551 that yanaconas, blacks, and others had stolen much ore from him. See BAN EP Soto 1551, f. 39–39v. (Minas catalog No. 22a).

13.   "Ninguna persona se pueda servir de los indios por vía de naboría ni tapia, ni otro modo alguno, contra su voluntad." For this order, a cédula from Valladolid, March 3, 1550, see BAN Reales Cédulas No. 3 (Minas catalog No. 21).

familiarity with Andean native society that in 1550 a connection was made between yanaconas and their northern analogues, whereas in the New Laws eight years earlier yanaconas were not specifically mentioned. It is possible that Gasca, being almost totally unfamiliar with colonization in Middle America and the Caribbean, had failed to make that connection himself, and had therefore seen no obstacle in clause 22 of the New Laws to yanaconas' being distributed in encomienda.

On the other hand, it may just have been that Gasca, faced with urgent demands for labor from prospective miners at Potosí after the end of the wars, had no choice but to issue yanaconas to those who had served the royal cause. It certainly appears that the immediately postwar years of 1548 and 1549 were the time of the first great rush to Potosí;[14] and it is only to be expected that with the increased demand for labor that ensued, yanaconas would lose some of their previous freedom. Despite this, and possibly in part as a result of the crown's ruling of 1550, it does seem that yanaconas in succeeding decades retained a position in Potosí that was preferable in most respects to that of the regular hatunruna, encomienda Indians who also labored there.

One outcome, indeed, of the rush to Potosí in 1548–49 was that regular, tribute-paying encomienda Indians appeared on the scene in large numbers. Despite the general opposition of earlier legislation to putting encomienda Indians into mines, legal precedents for doing so existed in Peru. In 1539, for instance, the *factor* of the royal treasury office in Lima, Illán Suárez de Carvajal (the same man whose murder in 1544 by Blasco Núñez Vela had much to do with sparking off the Pizarrist rebellion), allowed the Pizarros to use encomienda Indians in their silver mines, and also sanctioned gold mining in general by such Indians.[15] The mine ordinances of Licenciad Cristóbal Vaca de Castro, governor of Peru from 1541 to 1545, did not alter these rulings.[16] The Pizarrists, naturally, during the rebel years used encomienda Indians in mines; and in December of 1548 Gasca allowed the loyalists to whom he had

14. Barnadas, *Charcas*, p. 264.
15. Ibid., p. 263, n. 169.
16. Marie Helmer, "Notas sobre la encomienda peruana en el siglo XVI" (*Revista*, Facultad de Derecho y Ciencias Sociales, Instituto de Historia del Derecho Argentino y Americano, Universidad Nacional, Buenos Aires, tomo 10 (1965), pp. 124–43), p. 127.

granted Indians to employ them in Potosí.[17] The result was, as Gasca himself described it in July of the following year, that encomenderos from all over Peru despatched their Indians to the town—from La Paz, Arequipa, Cuzco, Huamanga, Lima, Huánuco, Trujillo and even Chachapoyas, to list the towns in order of increasing distance from Potosí. (Cuzco lies some 950 kilometers to the north-west, Chachapoyas 2,000 kilometers, as the crow flies).

But in 1549 Gasca was obliged to qualify his approval of mining by encomienda Indians, in response, probably, to a crown ruling of February 9 of that year banning such use of native workers.[18] Whether this order was also intended to embrace yanaconas is unclear; they are not mentioned specifically, but could be included under the wording. In any case, Gasca chose to tackle only the question of the *encomendados*, and furthermore interpreted the emperor to mean that these Indians should not work in mining against their will—which is a condition laid down in prior legislation, though not in the order of 9 February 1549. Gasca accordingly issued a *cédula y provisión* in Lima, on July 24, 1549, addressed to the *corregidor* of La Plata and Potosí, Licenciado Juan Polo de Ondegardo, commanding him to identify the encomienda Indians in Potosí, tell them they were free, and send them home if they wished. In January of 1550 Polo carried out the enquiry. The record of it has most fortunately survived, and provides the first information on Indian labor in Potosí from which generalizations on working conditions can be drawn.[19]

Polo called before him, in the presence of various civic and ecclesiastical Spanish dignitaries, the Indians from seventy-two encomiendas in the provinces of La Paz, La Plata and Cuzco. These workers were in the service of 130 encomenderos.[20] The curaca,

17. Ibid., p. 127.

18. *Recopilación*, 6, 9, 22, given at Valladolid.

19. AGI Justicia 667, No. 1, ramo 2—beginning with Gasca's *cédula y provisión* of Lima, July 24, 1549. Marie Helmer gives an excellent summary of this document, and the related ramo 1, dispassionate in contrast to some of her later writing on labor in Potosí, in "La encomienda à Potosí d'après un document inédit," *Proceedings of the XXXth International Congress of Americanists* (Cambridge, England, 1950), pp. 235–38. The first ramo is the record of a similar enquiry carried out in Potosí in May 1550 by the succeeding corregidor of La Plata, Licenciado Esquivel. The following discussion is based largely on Polo's investigation.

20. Helmer, "La encomienda," pp. 235–36.

or some other leader, in each group spoke for it; but ordinary hatunrunas accompanied him in most cases. Only in some cases, unfortunately, is the number of Indians in Potosí from a particular encomienda stated. Helmer calculates from these data that the total number of encomienda workers in the town at the time was some five thousand. The curacas' answers show that the workers had their families with them; so that the total number of Indians being brought to Potosí by the encomienda may have been between 20,000 and 25,000. Counting Indians alone, therefore, Potosí had become a populous place within five years of its first settlement.

In only a few cases did the Indians complain about Potosí. None of the sixteen groups from the province of La Paz voiced any discontent. Five of the twenty-three originating in the Cuzco jurisdiction did complain. After being three years in Potosí, the Indians from Musca in the province of Aymaraes said they were tired, and would leave soon. The Indians of Calla, near Cuzco, after one year in Potosí, said the same. Those from Asángaro stated that the mine they were working had ceased to give much silver, so they found themselves in need. Another group, from various communities (Quispicanche, Quispallata, Acos, Acopia, Cangalla, Llampa) in encomienda to Capitán Juan de Saavedra, a *vecino* of Cuzco, said they feared their master, who was with them in Potosí, that some of their number had already fled, and that they wanted to go home. Finally, the Quechuas, from north of Cuzco, said they were more used to mining gold than silver, which they did not know how to extract; and that their lands, which held gold deposits, were warmer than Potosí. All these groups, Polo told to leave forthwith. The manuscript does not say if they did.[21]

Nearly all these encomienda workers, however, expressed satisfaction at being in Potosí. Some even said they would not leave if they were ordered to do so. Many groups declared they ate better in Potosí than at home. The Guaqui group, for instance, said they had *quinua, chuño,* maize, potatoes, meat, and fish in Potosí, "and everything they want," including coca; whereas at home (Guaqui lies at the southern tip of Lake Titicaca) maize would not grow, and even potatoes were destroyed by frost in some years.[22] This abundance of supplies, which the statements of other groups con-

21. For these groups, see AGI Justicia 667, No. 1, ramo 2, ff. 21, 24, 26v., 27.
22. Ibid., f. 7v.

firm, some of them mentioning clothing also, is clear evidence that Potosí had already become a great commercial attraction, drawing in the produce of surrounding regions. Again, most groups said that Potosí's climate suited them, and that they greatly preferred it to the heat they had suffered when sent to extract gold in the low-lying deposits of Carabaya and Simaco. This is quite plausible, since with one exception the Indians questioned by Polo came from the altiplano or the high Peruvian valleys. The exception was the Quechua group, which, as noted, actually declared a preference for gold mining. One of the crown's objections to encomienda Indians' being sent to Potosí was that it inflicted an unfamiliar climate on them. On the whole this was not so, as Polo's investigation shows, though Potosí was somewhat higher and colder than the more northerly Indians were used to. The emperor was similarly worried about the natives' health in Potosí, which had been reported as suffering from the supposed climatic change, and also from the conditions of mining. Most of the groups, however, asserted that they enjoyed better health in Potosí than at home. This would not seem improbable, if indeed they could buy more varied and abundant food there than in their encomiendas. Their women bore many children, they reported, and the children grew sturdily.[23]

The rather rosy picture painted by the encomienda Indians of their life in Potosí should, of course, be viewed with some scepticism. The record of Polo's investigation is, in fact, a document posing intriguing problems of interpretation.[24] To begin with, the Indians gave their statements through a Spanish interpreter, and while facing a group of Spanish notables, headed by the corregidor, Polo. Polo was himself a mine owner, and so had an interest in seeing that his enquiry should produce results favorable to Potosí. In the background always lurk the figures of the encomenderos: not literally, because there is no mention of their presence at the questioning, and the Indians' replies suggest that normally the encomenderos did not go to Potosí, preferring to entrust the mine workers to agents. But obviously the wrath of the encomenderos

---

23. E.g., ibid., f. 4—the Indians of Capitán Alonso de Mendoza, vecino of La Paz: ". . . el año pasado se ha muerto mucha cantidad de indios en su tierra, y aquí se han muerto pocos de los que vinieron de allá . . . y que los niños se crían bien aquí, y paren las mujeres como en su tierra y mejor. . . ."
24. See Barnadas's treatment, *Charcas,* pp. 266–72.

at any interruption of mining would have been in the workers' minds. One of Polo's questions was whether the Indians had been intimidated into replying as they did; and they denied it. On the other hand, a clerical writer on Potosí in 1550, the lascasian friar Domingo de Santo Tomás (subsequently Bishop of Charcas, from 1562 to 1570), alleged to the *Consejo de Indias,* apparently in reference to Polo's enquiry, that the Spaniards did dictate the workers' answers, and that the Indians were so lacking in spirit *(pusilánimes)* that they spoke as they were told. Besides, said Santo Tomás, they had no concept of liberty, and so to inform them that they were "free" to work in mining or not was meaningless to them. This must surely be an exaggeration, since the workers' replies to Polo's questions seem to show that they understood his meaning perfectly well when he informed them of their freedom to leave.[25]

Nevertheless, the circumstances of Polo's enquiry were certainly such as to make it unwise for the historian to accept the Indians' evidence at face value. A further reason for scepticism is that the curacas did most of the answering, and doubt always arises, even at this early date, over the curacas' fidelity to the interests of their people. In this case they bore much of the responsibility for seeing that their Indians produced silver for the encomenderos. For their own well-being they would naturally incline to enthusiasm over Potosí. Santo Tomás raised this point in the report just mentioned, and on it he was very probably right.[26] On the other hand it is far from impossible that many of the encomienda Indians did find mining in Potosí profitable. In those first years rich ores abounded, close to the surface, and therefore were easily and cheaply extracted. The Indians used their simple guayras to smelt them, and probably had little difficulty in producing more silver than was

25. AGI Lima 313, Fray Domingo de Santo Tomás to Consejo, Lima, July 1, 1550, f. 4v. This is the often quoted letter beginning with the dramatic statement that Potosí was a hellhole which many people entered every year "whom the greed of the Spaniards sacrifices to their God." Santo Tomás's account of Potosí in this letter tends toward such hyperbole. He describes hungry Indians, unable to afford the high cost of food in Potosí, grubbing up "like hens" the grains of maize falling from mangers; though this he confesses knowing from witnesses, not from personal observation. I am grateful to Elinore Burkett for pointing out the ms of this letter to me.

26. After asking the standard series of questions of the Indians, Polo in each case told them they were free to leave Potosí whenever they wished. At this, the curaca of Calamarca "said, in tears, that he does not want to go home until the next batch of workers arrives, because he wishes to be in this mining town seek-

demanded in tribute by the encomendero. So, on balance, these Indians' expressions of satisfaction with Potosí can probably be regarded as in part genuine, and in part the result of their giving Polo the replies that they supposed he wished to hear. Other replies that they made, however, show quite unequivocally that satisfaction with Potosí, in the form of the abundance of food and clothing that their extra silver would buy, was not the central allure that the place held for them. The root of the attraction was that mining provided them with the tribute that their encomenderos demanded, and that this tribute was difficult to produce elsewhere. There is a refrain running throughout the replies—one whose burden there seems no reason to doubt: the Indians' llama herds and food stocks had been destroyed by the raids and seizures of Pizarrists and loyalists in the recent civil war. Few sources of tribute remained in the native communities. The Indians were therefore content to be sent to Potosí to produce silver. Their acceptance of the desirability of this is striking. No hint emerges from their replies that being uprooted from their villages and despatched over great distances to dig for silver was anything but logical, reasonable, and even welcome. To judge by this document, the long conditioning of the Andean populations to tribute paying under the Incas, and perhaps especially the precedent of the Inca mita, which did displace people for a time, made the Spaniards' exaction of tribute that much easier. A very few groups complained, it is true, that their encomenderos demanded too much silver of them. In these instances, Polo ordered reductions. But there was no complaint at all about the principle of tribute.[27]

Taken together, the replies to Polo's questions suggest that the

---

ing some silver for his master and for himself" ("dijo llorando que no quiere ir a su tierra sino cuando viniere la otra mita porque él quiere estar aquí en este asiento para buscar alguna plata para su amo y para sí"). AGI Justicia 667, No. 1, ramo 2.

27. The amount of tribute demanded weekly from each worker varied. Most reported paying 2 *pesos (de oro en plata),* equivalent to about three of the later standard pesos corrientes. A few others reported higher demands, up to 2 marks (one pound of silver) in one case (Sicasica), or almost 15 pesos corrientes. This very high rate applied only, the Sicasica leaders said, to Indians working in the mine their master had bought for them; others of the group paid only 2 pesos de oro en plata. What exactly they meant by that is not clear. Polo in general ordered reductions of the high rates to 1.5 pesos de oro en plata, or some 2.25 pesos corrientes.

encomienda Indians were indeed forced into mining, but that the coercion was a good deal more complex than the crown and Gasca thought. It was not a simple matter of the grasping encomenderos' despatching hapless natives to distant mines, for the natives seemed willing enough to go, and expressed at least some satisfaction with their lot in Potosí. It was, rather, the Indians' general circumstances that were coercive: their ingrained acquiescence to the notion of tribute (and it is worth recalling that the Incas had demanded tribute in labor), the Spanish notion (shared, of course, by the crown) that hatunrunas should yield tribute, the hunger for bullion of both Spanish individuals and the Spanish state, and the destruction of other forms of native wealth by the infighting among the Spanish. All these together constituted a *force majeure* that these encomienda people of 1550 seem to have found so powerful and enveloping that they scarcely thought it worthwhile resisting, allowing themselves to be swept by it even as far as Potosí.

One further revelation of Polo's enquiry demands mention. The replies show that encomenderos were sending their workers to Potosí in relays, and these relays the Indians themselves termed *mita*. This was, of course, the Quechua term for the periodic rote labor required of Inca subjects in preconquest days. The word means *time* or *turn*. Barnadas argues that there is no true continuity between the Incaic and Spanish mitas, since in Inca times the rote worker *(mit'ayuj*, Hispanized to *mitayo)* served and produced for an economic system and a society of which he was a part, whereas under the Spanish he created wealth for a system extrinsic to him.[28] An economic and perhaps psychological distinction does exist. But the fact that the workers themselves used the same term for the Spanish rote system as they had for the Incaic one surely suggests that they, at least, perceived an institutional and practical continuity between the two. And it seems highly likely, as already suggested, that this perception facilitated the working of a Spanish draft.

The mita of encomienda Indians in 1550 clearly foreshadowed what can be called the "classic" mita organized by Viceroy Toledo for Potosí in the early 1570s. Both drew on communities far to the north of Potosí—although Toledo's catchment area went no farther north than Cuzco. Toledo's mita was far larger, however, in

28. *Charcas*, p. 262.

numbers, and regulated by far more rigid rules on how many men might be taken from each community, and how long they should serve. In 1550, of course, no uniformity on these matters had yet appeared. The encomenderos sent on average some forty men each to the mines. The period spent by each group in Potosí was normally several months, though a few had already been there three years. Some Indians who were adept at mining, and who therefore perhaps stood to gain most from it, seem to have stayed on indefinitely, while the less skilled and enthusiastic came and went.[29]

To sum up: by 1550 two fundamental types of Indian labor operated at Potosí—yanacona and encomienda. The line between the two is not as clear as could be desired, partly because of Gasca's practice in the late 1540s of assigning yanaconas in encomienda. Nevertheless, the distinction is undeniable, and denotes the start of a dual system of labor in Potosí that was to persist in one form or another throughout the colonial era. Difference in degrees of coercion marked this duality. In the early years being discussed here, the yanaconas endured less coercion than the mitayos. They did not owe a regular tribute to their masters. Clearly they worked for his profit, but the evidence (admittedly from rather later years) is that they also profited considerably themselves. Second, they belonged to no native community, so in Potosí they were not under the control of any native figure of authority (who, in the case of encomienda Indians, might use the workers for his own profit as well as that of the *encomendero*). Third (and again here the evidence is from somewhat later—the 1560s), yanaconas had in practice considerable freedom of movement; they are often reported as leaving Potosí, having grown dissatisfied with their mining gains, to work in the surrounding farming valleys. Encomienda Indians, on the other hand, were clearly under greater constraints. They were shuttled back and forth between their homelands and Potosí in groups, at the order of their masters. It is true that according to Polo's enquiry of 1550 this was not seen as a great burden, for rea-

---

29. The group from Oruro, for instance, stated that their replacements would come in two months, but "those who are good Indians who know how to get silver will stay here, and the others will go. . . ." ("los que hubiere buenos indios quedarán aquí de aquéllos que saben sacar plata, y los otros se irán . . ."). AGI Justicia 667, No. 1, ramo 2, f. 25v.

sons that have been set out. But none the less there is a qualitative difference between the more or less regular despatch of a group of encomienda Indians to Potosí by their master, under the control of a curaca or other native authority, and the mining labor of the yanaconas, with their relationship of personal service to a master. It also seems likely that the enthusiasm over Potosí expressed by the encomienda workers in 1550 stemmed in part from the early richness of the mines. Quite possibly a good proportion of common workers did profit from their labor in those first years. As the 1550s and 1560s passed, however, and mines grew deeper and ores poorer, the commoners must have seen their gains shrinking.

Specific information on labor in Potosí for the two decades after 1550 is hardly more abundant than for the years before then. No new enquiry resembling Polo's was made. The development of work organization can be followed only through references, sometimes oblique, in administrative reports, and through legislation. It does seem, however, that the initial dual organization of encomendados and yanaconas persisted, despite the royal ban on forced mine work by encomienda Indians already cited, and others added later. These prohibitions naturally raised immediate and vehement protests from the encomenderos; and while complaints and appeals were being made, the existing practices continued. In 1564, for example, the treasury officers of Potosí reported that encomenderos still sent Indians from Huamanga, Cuzco, Arequipa and La Paz to the mines.[30] And yanaconas are constantly mentioned throughout the two decades. In fact, it seems likely that the numbers of yanaconas grew, so that the preponderance of encomendados existing by 1550 was reversed over the following two decades. There is no numerical information to support this suggestion, but descriptive documentation does seem to point to it. The growth in the number of yanaconas to which writers refer in the 1560s was perhaps in part a reflection of a loosening in the meaning of the term. Over the years numerous Indians who had not been yanaconas before the conquest attached themselves as servants to Spaniards, who broadly termed them *yanaconas*. By the 1560s, *yanacona* appears to have lost all its Incaic connotations

30.   AGI Charcas 35, ms 12, reales oficiales to Consejo de Indias, Potosí, March 6, 1564.

except that of servant. In 1578 the royal treasurer of Potosí, Diego Bravo, declared simply that yanaconas were the domestics who served Spaniards.[31] One important result of the growing imprecision of the term was that an Indian who for some reason wished to escape from his encomienda might simply attach himself to a Spanish employer, begin to call himself the yanacona of that Spaniard, and immediately put himself beyond challenge—unless he were unlucky enough to be identified by his curaca or encomendero. With Potosí drawing many hopeful Spaniards to itself every year, there was no lack of eager employers. And for the Indian there was one good and obvious reason to make the move—to avoid tribute. Yanaconas did not pay tribute until Viceroy Toledo, reacting precisely to their proliferation and the resultant loss of tribute income to the crown, obliged them to do so in 1572.[32]

The economic attraction of Potosí for Indians, as well as the demand for labor from the growing Spanish population there, may have contributed to the increase in numbers of yanaconas in the town. An Indian who came initially as part of an encomienda labor gang, once having acquired some mining or refining skill (as Polo's enquiry of 1550 indicates some did) might well then have chosen to stay in Potosí to use that skill in profitable work as a yanacona. Evidence can be found of this sort of absconding from encomiendas, which naturally disturbed the encomenderos. But as time passed, fewer and fewer of the mine owners were encomenderos, so that the latters' complaints weighed ever less heavily against the miners' desire for workers, and, in the colonial administration's view, against the silver that was produced through the yanaconas' labor.[33] Finally, the multiplication of yanaconas owed something

31. ". . . los domésticos que sirven a los españoles. . . ." Diego Bravo to crown, Potosí, January 1, 1578, f. 2v.. AGI Charcas 35, ms 28.

32. AGI Lima 28B, tomo 2, f. 332, Toledo to crown, Cuzco, September 24, 1572, "Hacienda," para. 19. For a general discussion of the postconquest transformation of hatunrunas into yanaconas, and the remarkable growth of the proportion of yanaconas in the native population, see Nathan Wachtel, *Sociedad e ideología. Ensayos de historia y antropología andinas* (Lima 1973), pp. 148–57.

33. Bad treatment by curacas, high tribute, and the Spaniards' persistence in abstracting *(sonsacar)* Indians from encomiendas, along with the Indians' fickleness (". . . es una gente muy fácil y se hace y muda muy de ligero. . .") were the reasons given in 1563 by the Audiencia of La Plata for the hatunrunas' transfor-

to the acculturative influence of Potosí itself. As the town grew, it became a powerful motor of hispanization. Yanaconas were, through their close contact with Spanish masters, partly hispanized Indians. The more of them were present in Potosí, the more incoming Indians were likely to be "converted" to yanacona status. Some of these points are illustrated in a plaintive request directed to Viceroy Toledo by an Indian administrator of the mita in 1575. The applicability of his remarks to the period before Toledo is clear. The official, Don Juan Colque, asked Toledo to rule that any Indians coming to Potosí to trade should associate only with people of their own districts and towns "because when they fall in with strangers, they get involved with Indian women of different origins from their own, and so . . . do not want to return to their homes and wives, and go around as idlers, getting drunk, and become yanaconas so as to live in full liberty. . . ."[34]

One aspect of the yanaconas' hispanization in the 1550s and 1560s is clearly seen in the manner of their participation in mining and refining. As the basic labor force, they were of course central to the production of silver. But their importance went beyond that. They were the first mining entrepreneurs of Potosí. Various accounts indicate that Spaniards, during the first twenty-five years of silver production in Potosí, had a small part in the extraction and processing of ore. Many simply held title to claims, and provided themselves with knowledgeable Indian workers to produce silver from them. Most, if not all, of these skilled men were clearly yanaconas. Those who actually performed the mining were known as *indios varas*, because the mine owner assigned to them a certain length of his claim—a certain number of varas—to work. The fun-

---

mation into yanaconas (". . .se huyen de sus repartimientos y se van españoles [sic] a les servir, y se vuelven yanaconas. . ."). Audiencia to crown, La Plata, February 6, 1563, in Roberto Levillier, *La Audiencia de Charcas* (3 tomos, Madrid 1918–22), tomo 1, p. 89.

34. PBN ms B511, f. 359v., provisión by Toledo, Potosí, February 12, 1575. Colque's Spanish, or the translation into Spanish of his request given in the ms, is awkward, especially because of the shift of tense in midpassage: ". . . porque en irse con extranjeros, se envuelven con indias ajenas y a esta causa . . . no se querían volver a sus tierras y mujeres y andaban hechos holgazanes, emborrachándose y se hacen yanaconas por vivir en toda libertad. . . ." Toledo did, in fact, issue the order that Colque requested.

damental nature of the transaction was a lease of part of a mine by the owner to the indio vara, as the following account by a first-hand observer shows.

These Indians called varas took with them their crowbars and candles, and made the ladders and repairs in the mines, and hired Indians to work with them, all at their own cost, without the owner's spending one *real*. And when this indio vara struck rich ore suitable for smelting by guayra, which is sometimes called *cacilla* ore, his master [the owner] took the best of it and sold it to the same indio vara who had extracted it, or to another Indian; and gave to the indio vara the ore found surrounding the richest part, which is called *llampo* ore. And with the llampos, which were abundant, and with what he made from the rich ore by [selling or] smelting it, it seems that the vara got a return on his labor and covered his costs. Hence this rich ore came to be called cacilla ore, because cacilla in the Indians' tongue means something given freely or for nothing; and as these indios varas paid their master for the rich ore that he sold to them, this ore that they had extracted, at no cost to the master, was called cacilla ore, as something given for nothing. Then afterwards the poorer ores called llampos and the rich ore itself were refined by [some of the mining] Indians in their guayras or smelters; though others (the majority) took it for sale in the *gato* [ore market], and there it was bought only by the smelting or *guayrador* Indians who refined it on the large scale your Excellency has heard spoken of as having existed in this town before mercury refining began. . . .[35]

35. This is a rather free translation of a passage from a letter written by Don Diego Cabeza de Vaca, *teniente de corregidor* of Potosí, to the viceroy, dated Potosí, April 8, 1581 (SBN ms 3040, f. 49v.): "Estos indios llamados varas llevaban sus barretas y candelas y hacían las escaleras y reparos de la minas y alquilaban indios que las labrasen, todo a su costa, sin que el dueño de ellas gastase un real; y cuando este vara topaba en metal rico para guaira, que por otro nombre se llama metal de cacilla, su amo tomaba la yema y lo mejor del metal, y lo vendía al mismo indio vara que lo había sacado o a otro, y al indio vara le daba el metal que salía alrededor de lo rico, que llaman metal llampo, y con estos llampos, que eran muchos, y con lo que ganaba en el metal rico o en su fundición , parece que se satisfacía de su trabajo y de la costa que había hecho; y de aquí vino este metal rico [a] llamarse metal de cacilla, porque "es cacilla" en lengua de indio dice cosa dada graciosamente o de balde; y como estos indios varas pagaban a su amo aquella plata que se les vendía, el metal rico que sacaban, sin haber él costeado nada, le llamaron metal de cacilla, como cosa que la daban de gracia, pues luego este metal más pobre llamado llampos y el mismo rico, unos indios lo beneficiaban en sus

This account was written in 1581, some years after the practices it describes had come to an end, and may well be something of a simplification. But its essentials are confirmed by Capoche.[36] According to him, the amount of rich ore or *cacilla* expected of the *indio vara* differed, as would be expected, from mine to mine; and the price paid by the *indio vara* to buy it back from the mine owner also varied, in accordance with the precise quality of the ore. Capoche records that owners did provide crowbars, although the *indio vara* had to tip and sharpen them. Doubtless other variations occurred in the precise conditions of the transaction. But Capoche says nothing to contradict the notion that this was in essence a lease of the mine, or a part thereof, to the *indio vara*, who in exchange for exploiting the ores gave the owner the rich *cacilla* (or more exactly the cash he paid the owner when repurchasing the *cacilla*). Under this system, Capoche remarks, the Indians possessed the wealth of Peru.[37]

It seems likely that most *indios varas* were yanaconas, since yanaconas possessed both the technical skill and the freedom that would seem necessary for successful mining enterprise. The earliest of them were probably miners with experience from Inca times; but as yanaconas became more common in Potosí, and as the scale of mining grew, others who had mastered the appropriate techniques entered the ranks of the varas.[38] Their yanacona status is indirectly but strongly confirmed by Capoche, when he describes them as "indios ventureros."[39] The adjective is not easy to trans-

---

guairas o fundiciones, otros y la mayor parte lo traían a vender al gato y de aquí lo compraban sólo los indios fundidores o guairadores que lo beneficiaban en la grosedad que vuestra excelencia habrá oído decir que estuvo este pueblo antes que hubiese beneficio de azogues. . . ." (Some punctuation has been added to this passage). Cabeza de Vaca's observations are supported by those of the royal treasurer Diego Bravo in a letter to the crown, from Potosí, January 1, 1578 (AGI Charcas 35, ms 28, f. 2v.); by Licenciado Castro, in a report to the crown from Lima, January 18, 1568 (in Roberto Levillier, *Gobernantes del Perú* (14 tomos, Madrid 1921–26), tomo 3, pp. 288–89; and by Viceroy Toledo in clause 10 of the title "De los desmontes, trabajo y paga de los indios" in his code of La Plata, February 7, 1574 (Levillier, *Gobernantes,* tomo 8, p. 235).

36.   *Relación,* pp. 108–9.
37.   ". . . los indios poseían la riqueza del reino. . . ." *Relación,* p. 109.
38.   See *copias de provisiones,* f. 3, in AGI Charcas 16 ms 29—quoted in Barnadas, *Charcas,* p. 287, n. 262.
39.   *Relación,* p. 108.

late economically—with perhaps the nearest equivalent being *free-lance*. The implication is that there were Indians who moved about freely, taking up work when and where they wished—traits typical of yanaconas under the Spanish.

A central aspect of mine operation by the indios varas, but not one fully illuminated by contemporary sources, was their hiring of Indian laborers. Some of these may have been encomienda men. A report of 1563 by the Audiencia of La Plata does suggest that encomienda Indians hired themselves out, or were hired out by their curacas, for mining tasks.[40] Quite possibly others were yanaconas who were not yet sufficiently skilled or enterprising to become indios varas. And finally there are references by about 1570 to large groups of Indians in Potosí who were apparently considered by the Spanish neither yanaconas nor encomienda men. For instance, in early 1571 the *cabildo* of Potosí issued an edict forbidding the removal from the town against their will of yanaconas engaged in mining, and of "the other Indians from various places who have spent over six years in the said mines, even though they may put others in their place."[41] It would be instructive to know the origins of these people. It seems likely that they were Indians from encomiendas who had stayed on in Potosí after their term of service had ended. Toledo discovered a number of such people in the town in 1572, as will be seen. Very probably, if they had remained long enough there, they would have ceased to be associated with their encomiendas and have become regarded as yanaconas. Whatever their status, the cabildo's concern that they should not be removed indicates that they possessed useful mining skills; and they may be seen therefore as a possible source of hired labor for the indios varas.

Though yanaconas acting as indios varas certainly seem to have been the main developers and exploiters of mines in the first two and a half decades of Potosí's history, it would be an exaggeration to deny any activity at all to the mine owners. It is only necessary to recall the efforts of various Spaniards to cut adits in the cerro,

---

40. Levillier, *Charcas*, tomo 1, p. 89.
41. ". . . los demás indios de diversas partes que hayan estado seis años en dichas minas, aunque pongan otros en su lugar. . . ." BAN Minas catalog No. 122, acuerdo of cabildo, Potosí, March 16, 1571.

from the mid-1550s on, to disprove any such contention.[42] And Capoche, after describing the doings of the indios varas, goes on to say that not all owners could take advantage of these workers, since they were attracted only to mines of known wealth. As time passed, the richness of the earliest workings faded, and other, less well-endowed mines were opened up by newcomers to Potosí; so that little by little, if Capoche is correct, the indio vara system must have lost its dominance. The owners then, he states, took to working the mines at their own cost, using hired Indian labor (the source of which is not identified), or workers distributed to them by the Potosí authorities (a matter that will receive attention shortly).[43] Further evidence for a decline in activity by indios varas emerges from a report of the Audiencia of La Plata in 1563 stating that mining yanaconas were leaving Potosí (and Porco) to go and work for Spaniards on farms supplying food to the mining towns. In this exodus went some who had struck firm roots in Potosí: "they had their houses and businesses there, with their wives and children. . . ."[44] The audiencia, after much debate of the problems resulting from hatunrunas' becoming yanaconas, and yanaconas' leaving mining, simply ordered that mining and agricultural yanaconas should stay where they were (no attempt being made, as the curacas and encomenderos wanted, to send them back to the encomiendas as hatunrunas), and that present hatunrunas should not leave their encomiendas.[45] It is doubtful that this order had any effect. In the same letter, the audiencia also remarked that many Indians were now coming as yanaconas to Potosí not to work in mining, but in "a thousand types of business" that they found profitable. The audiencia did not specify; but these occupations were possibly freighting, sale of food and clothing, cutting wood for fuel, charcoal making, and the like. Again there is the sense that mining was not as attractive to the yanaconas (and hence indios varas) as it had been; and that mine owners were beginning to have to cast around for other types of labor. One solution

42. See Introduction.
43. Capoche, *Relación*, p. 109.
44. ". . . tenían allí sus casas y asuntos, con sus mujeres e hijos. . . ." Audiencia to crown, La Plata, February 6, 1563 (Levillier, *Charcas*, tomo 1, p. 90).
45. Ibid.

was the hiring of workers already alluded to; but paying wages must have been an unwelcome burden on many owners.

There was probably, therefore, no coincidence in the appearance, also in the early 1560s, of suggestions and opinions from colonial administrators that some sort of forced Indian labor in mines should be officially organized. Up to that time, it should be emphasized, the colonial government had not attempted to create any labor system for Potosí. It had merely tried to control whatever arrangements had arisen, and particularly to apply (though without great effect) the crown's injunctions that Indians should not be put into mines against their will. But by the early 1560s, as a result of various causes—the decline in Potosí's output, the crown's demand for greatly increased income from Peru,[46] the threat of instability of labor as yanaconas drifted away, and possibly the rising cost to miners of hiring workers in Potosí—certain officials in Peru (not, it should be stressed, in Spain) seem to have begun contemplating the need for more active administrative intervention in labor arrangements for mining in Potosí. In direct contradiction, indeed, of the tenor of the crown's earlier rulings, notions now began to be put about of the desirability of a formal and compulsory Indian labor system. The genesis of Toledo's mita of a decade later lies partly among these arguments and proposals.

The crown itself took no initiative in the matter. In fact, it always showed strong reluctance to acknowledge that any circumstance might justify an official scheme that forced Indians into mines. Toledo himself never received royal approbation or even confirmation of his mita organization, however strongly he might argue that it was essential to the production of the silver on which the crown so avidly gathered its taxes. It was as if the crown were never quite willing to accept the moral responsibility for forced mine labor. This being so, it is no wonder that the officials in Peru who began to contemplate such arrangements in the early sixties first set out arguments designed to make the work seem advantageous to the Indians. In February of 1563 the Audiencia of La Plata assured the king that in the mining towns of Charcas (Potosí and Porco), Indians enjoyed good health and produced many children—

46. Barnadas, *Charcas*, pp. 253–54.
47. ". . . todos finalmente andan lucios, gordos y bien tratados. . . ." Audiencia to crown, La Plata, February 6, 1563 (Levillier, *Charcas*, tomo 1, p. 90).

"in fine, they are resplendent, fat and well treated."[47] Echoes of
Polo's enquiry of 1550 are obvious here; and possibly there was
some validity to them, though in 1563 Potosí can hardly have been
producing the surplus from which Indians might profit that it had
yielded thirteen years before. Other official declarations of Indian
wellbeing in mining appear in these years. Several of the points
commonly raised are contained in a questionnaire drawn up in 1565
by a *regidor* of Potosí, Antonio de Mesa. The questions were addressed to Spanish respondents, who were asked to confirm that
the native workers were very healthy in Potosí and were spared
many ills that they suffered elsewhere; that they came to Potosí of
their own will and stayed there to enjoy the profits they made from
mining; that they ate, drank, and dressed much better than at
home; that they had a township at the base of the cerro, composed of very good houses ("casas muy buenas de sus viviendas"),
whence they could go up to the mines with the greatest of ease.[48]
Again the echoes of Polo's questions are clear; and again there may
be truth in the points raised by the questionnaire, though the truth
was likely to have been less complete in the mid-1560s than in 1550.

A companion argument to such assertions of Indians' prosperity in Potosí was sometimes presented. This argument held that
Indians were too stupid to see the advantages of working in mines,
and should therefore be forced to do so. The proponents of this
view advanced it in all seriousness, apparently not appreciating
the contradiction between it and their rosy accounts of the workers'
lives. If mine work brought health, wealth, and children to the
laborers, surely little persuasion, let alone force, would have been
needed to draw even foolish men to Potosí? An example of this
thinking is supplied by the Audiencia of La Plata in 1563, which
first declared Indians to be "incapable and lacking in perfect under-
standing," then added that they were weak, and concluded that
they should be forced to work in Potosí because they were better
off there than anywhere else in Peru.[49]

From these arguments founded on the benefits to Indians of

48. AGI Charcas 32, ms 12, ff. 24–27, "Sobre que los indios que viven en la
Villa para el beneficio y labor de las minas, viven sanos," Potosí, September 18,
1565.
49. Audiencia to crown, La Plata, February 6, 1563 (Levillier, *Charcas*, tomo
1, p. 91).

mine work, some advocates of forced labor went on to the much
solider rationale of economic necessity. This was well put by the
Viceroy Conde de Nieva (1558-64) in 1563. The king, he said, had
ordered working of the mines. But Spaniards would not work
them, since they would "rather die of hunger than take a hoe in
their hands."[50] Neither could blacks be employed, since they died
in the cold highlands where the mines lay. (Both these statements
were dramatizing simplifications, but served the viceroy's purpose.
For blacks in Potosí, see Appendix 1). So, considering that "if there
are no mines, there is no Peru," Indians must be forced to work in
mines—not under severe compulsion, Nieva hastened to add, nor
without good treatment and wages. But experience showed they
would not work voluntarily, being naturally lazy; so obligation was
unavoidable.[51]

An official proposal for forced Indian mine labor came from the
Audiencia of La Plata in early 1564—with a suggestion to the crown
that the shortage of mine workers in Potosí could be met by bringing Indians from the provinces of Cuzco and Chucuito. (As will
shortly be seen, Chucuito was already sending a yearly contingent
of workers to Potosí). The audiencia did not say how this movement might be organized. The king would have none of it, however, as a marginal note to the letter indicates.[52]

The first suggestion for an official labor draft on the scale that
was later to characterize Toledo's mita came from the *procurador*,
or official representative, of Potosí, Alonso de Herrera, in the
mid-1560s.[53] He proposed that some four or five thousand Indians should be taken (*sacados*) from the towns between Quito and

50. ". . . antes morirán de hambre que ninguno tome una azada en la
mano. . . ." AGI Lima 28A, ms 39, Lima, August 31, 1563, Viceroy Conde de
Nieva to Licenciado Valderrama, "del Consejo de su magestad." The argument
of the economic necessity of Indian mining work is, of course, often repeated,
and not only in Peru but in other mining regions of the empire. For other examples in Peru in the 1560s, see Barnadas, *Charcas*, p. 280.

51. "Si no hay minas, no hay Perú." Nieva to Valderrama, as in n. 50 above.

52. Audiencia to crown, La Plata, February 9, 1564 (Levillier, *Charcas*, tomo
1, p. 130).

53. AGI Charcas 32, ms 11, Alonso de Herrera to "muy poderoso señor," nd,
1565?

Potosí, and sent to Potosí to work. They should stay there permanently. To encourage permanence, Herrera proposed that they should be accompanied by their wives. The Indians were to come from encomiendas; they were to send back cash contributions to their communities' tribute liability. This scheme fell, it seems, on deaf ears. But it is noteworthy for the geographical breadth of its conception. Even Toledo went no further north than Cuzco in assigning Indians to Potosí. Herrera proposed going over twice as far.

While these proposals were appearing, but failing to produce any response from the home government, practical developments in the supply of labor to Potosí were taking place that also foreshadowed what Toledo later did. Among the most striking of these was the annual despatch from the province of Chucuito of five hundred Indians for mining and other work in Potosí. This custom had begun, according to one curaca, in the late 1550s, and was a means by which the province paid its tribute. The five hundred men in Potosí normally earned enough to cover the roughly 30,000 pesos (18,000 pesos ensayados) owed in tribute by Chucuito each year. (Those staying at home produced the rest of the tribute due: 1,000 pieces of woolen clothing). What is particularly significant in this arrangement for the development of an official mita for Potosí is that Chucuito was a royal province, directly under the control of crown officials rather than private encomenderos. In a real sense, therefore, its regular despatch of a large group of workers to Potosí each year constituted a mita officially approved at the local level, at least.[54] By the end of the 1560s, or the early 1570s,

---

54.   Information summarized here is from the *Visita hecha a la provincia de Chucuito . . . 1567*, pp. 19, 32, 46. Nonmining work performed in Potosí by the Chucuito people included freighting of firewood and charcoal; sale of meat; building walls and houses; making candles and chicha. Although the yearly despatch of a contingent from Chucuito may have dated back only to the late 1550s, people from Chucuito had been present in Potosí, at least intermittently, from the very beginning. A trial of 1548 shows that Chucuito had sent a contingent of workers, under crown control ("en cabeza de su magestad"), to Potosí in 1545 to work, under the direction of one Francisco de Zúñiga, a mine that Zúñiga had claimed for the crown, and to construct a treasury building *(casas reales)*. PBN ms A547, "Proceso hecho a pedimento de la Hacienda Real contra Francisco Zúñiga sobre las casas," Potosí, April 26, 1548, ff. 2, 16v.

official dispatch of Indians to Potosí may have extended beyond
Chucuito to areas both north and south of it.[55]

In the early 1570s some variety of regular distribution of mining
labor within Potosí itself was clearly in existence. For instance, an
order issued in late 1571 by the visitor of the Audiencia of La Plata,
Lope García de Castro, refers to Indians who were assigned *(dipu-
tados)* for work in the cerro, and also to Indians distributed *(re-
partidos)* to Spanish mine owners. The appearance of the term
repartir—the standard verb used in sixteenth-century Spanish America to describe an obligatory and official distribution of Indian labor
for works of public utility—would in itself suggest that a fairly insti-
tutionalized allocation among employers of at least the Indian
workers in Potosí existed by this date. What is especially striking
in García de Castro's order is that it not merely recognized the existence of the labor distribution, but actually sought to make it more
efficient. Its burden was that the treasury officers of Potosí, who
were the senior royal bureaucrats permanently resident there,
should see that Indians worked in the cerro—especially those "di-
putados" for such labor; in particular, the officials should try to
eliminate drunkenness among the workers, which García de Castro saw as the main impediment to labor (an early sounding of
what was to become a familiar note).[56] There can be no plainer
demonstration that at the level of the local audiencia, if no higher
in Peru, approval now had been bestowed on an official or at least
semiofficial forced distribution for mining of Indians actually in
Potosí. Another piece of Toledo's labor mechanism was taking
shape, though its form was still rough.

García de Castro's wording makes it appear that the curacas had
charge over the distribution of workers. But a decision of the cabildo of Potosí a few months later, in May 1572, clearly states that
for some time the corregidor of the town had been assigning Indi-

55. SBN ms 3040, ff. 46–50v., Potosí, April 8, 1581, Don Diego Cabeza de
Vaca to "excelentísimo señor" (Viceroy Don Martín Enríquez de Almansa?). Cabeza
de Vaca writes of Indians from the Cuzco district, the Collao, Chuquiabo, and all
pueblos of Charcas, being told to live in Potosí. The context implies that this was
by official order, rather than by the encomenderos' command; but the expression is not wholly clear.

56. PCM CR 30, f. 72, "La orden que se ha de tener en hacer trabajar a los
indios en el cerro." Clause 13 of "Instrucción para los oficiales reales," La Plata,
November 24, 1571.

ans for mine work in both Potosí and Porco. The Indians resident in Potosí, however, had recently secured from the Audiencia of La Plata a decision forbidding the corregidor to do this, until Viceroy Toledo, who was still engaged in the suppression of Túpac Amaru I, should arrive on the scene. The ban naturally irked the cabildo, in which the mining interest was strong. A resolution was adopted to appeal against it, especially because of the urgent need of labor that had recently developed with the introduction of amalgamation—an innovation that had restored the profitability of abandoned mines.[57]

And so it is evident that by the time Toledo came, in December 1572, strong precedents for the mita—for whose entire creation he is usually held responsible—were already in place. The despatch of native workers from regions very far to the north for a spell of labor in Potosí dated back to the late 1540s, as encomenderos sent contingents of their people for specific, though varied, terms of work. In its organization, though not in its economic nature, this early rote labor was a continuation of the Incaic mita, and was so perceived by the Indians. By 1560, while the encomenderos continued to send their private groups to Potosí, there had also appeared a rote labor of Indians in the direct administration of the crown, with five hundred Chucuito men moving annually to Potosí for mining and other tasks. And by the early 1570s the corregidor of Potosí was distributing Indians among miners for extracting ore. Much remained for the viceroy to do, of course. He changed the mita into a wholly official system, functioning under the supervision of royal administrators. The burden of mita work came to be distributed more or less equally among native communities. In its final form, Toledo's organization of the mita sought to standardize much that had doubtless been variable before: length of stay in Potosí, wages, conditions of work. But, on balance, Toledo's mita should be seen as the formal culmination of many preexisting practices and notions, not as a new creation.

Finally, the concentration over the past few pages on the genesis of the Toledan system should not obscure the existence in Potosí, also from the earliest years, of a tradition of freer workers. Their presence is clearly the result of a demand for skilled labor. From the beginning, possession of mining and refining abilities

57. BAN Minas catalog No. 129, acuerdo of cabildo, Potosí, May 5, 1572.

could give an Indian both greater freedom and greater material rewards in Potosí than were available to the normal run of laborers. Preceding, and then working alongside, the early encomienda mitayos were yanaconas, men who in some cases probably possessed preconquest mining experience at Porco, and freer agents than the encomendados—though the details of their employment are unknown. These yanaconas became the first indios varas, who were apparently given a free hand by Spanish mine owners in the exploitation of ores, to the point that they hired and supervised other Indian laborers. Much remains to be known about the indios varas, however. As yanaconas they presumably owed allegiance to some Spanish master. On the other hand, their independence of operation—the "venturero" quality remarked on by Capoche—suggests that this allegiance may have been a tenuous one. It is reasonable to suppose that some of them worked mines belonging to their masters; while others, perhaps, worked those of other Spaniards, paying some part of their profit to their master. One thing does seem quite clear: the number of indios varas increased as long as the production of silver with the guayra smelting technique remained widely profitable. When it ceased to be so, as a result of depletion of rich ores, they began to drift away from Potosí and on to surrounding farms. The evidence suggests that their departures became frequent enough to be noticeable around 1560. Some, of course, did stay in Potosí throughout the following decade, and even longer, probably becoming the nucleus of the minga (hired man) work force, which was the the group that continued the line of voluntary mine work after Toledo's reforms.

3

Toledo

Y estaban los caminos cubiertos que parecía que se mudaba el reino."

(Capoche, *Relación*, p. 135 , on the first influx of Toledo's mita to Potosí.)

Don Francisco de Toledo was sent to Peru in 1569 as fifth viceroy, charged, under his instructions of November 30, 1568, with instilling royal government into this distant, huge, diverse, and hitherto often unruly viceroyalty. Rectitude of church and civil government, evangelization of the native population, subjugation of rebels (whether Spanish or Indian), regulation of the treasury—these were some of the main issues with which he should concern himself. Reform and control could not come without adequate knowledge of what the viceroyalty contained. Toledo, therefore, was to make in person a general survey *(visita general)* of his territory. This task he actually accomplished to a remarkable degree, inspecting at least the heartland of colonial Peru in the central Andes, where the main towns and sources of wealth lay, between October 1570 and November 1575. He was the only viceroy of Peru to undertake such a journey; the five years it lasted were indeed as long a period as the whole span of office of some of his successors. And while it is doubtful that Toledo did impose, or even could have imposed, on Peru the efficiency of royal control that Philip II sought, nevertheless his firsthand knowledge of the land, the masses of regulations that he threw off as he moved here and there, and the hauteur with which he treated all preexisting authorities, from cabildos to audiencias, combined to engrave his memory in the collective mind of the colonial administration, so that later vice-

61

roys habitually sought a Toledan precedent before pronouncing on this or that problem of their day.

Among the changes associated with Toledo, the mita of Potosí has traditionally been given much emphasis. That much of the organization already existed has not been widely realized. (Nor has it been remembered that in many parts of Spanish America the 1570s saw a marked shift in labor arrangements toward draft systems—as, for example, in Viceroy Enríquez's regularization of *repartimiento* in New Spain). The Potosí mita, furthermore, has brought down on Toledo much criticism from those who have taken the Indians' side, both contemporaries, mainly churchmen, and later historians—not to mention polemicists. And while the mita is certainly good cause for moral onslaught, it is not just that the whole of that attack should fall on Toledo, as a brief sketch of his initial approach to the question of mining labor will show.

The crown was still far from being fully persuaded, by the time Toledo left Spain, that forced Indian mine labor was needed or justifiable in Peru. Consequently, Toledo's orders on this point were indistinct. In instructions of late September 1568, for example, the king left the matter very much up in the air. First, Philip reiterated observations by the Viceroy Conde de Nieva in 1563: Spaniards refused to work in mines, and black slaves were unsuited to the coldness of the mining territories. "And so," wrote the king, "it is unavoidable that they [the Indians] should occupy themselves [in mining] and although it is ordered that no force or compulsion should be applied to them, they must be attracted by all just and reasonable means, so that in the said mines there may always be the number necessary for working them; and for this purpose, it seems that a very careful attempt must be made to establish large Indian settlements in the lands and farms closest to the mines, where, with greatest ease and comfort, and with even greater security of health, avoiding changes of lands and climates, the said Indians may undertake the working of the said mines."[1] This was a

---

1. SBN ms 3040, ff. 23-25, "Carta del rey nuestro señor a don Francisco de Toledo en materia de minas:" ". . . y así es forzoso que se ocupen [los indios] como quiera que esté ordenado que no se les haga fuerza ni compulsión deben ser por todos los medios justos y razonables atraídos para que en las dichas minas haya continuo el número necesario a la labor de ellas, y para este efecto parece

masterly piece of kingly ambivalence. The first section implies that despite the principle that Indians should not be forced into mines, circumstances in Peru might oblige Toledo to use something very close to compulsion—the key, but vague, word, being "attracted." But surely Indians would not have accepted such wholesale transfers voluntarily? And even supposing Toledo could have "attracted" Indians to new towns, how could he then have "attracted" them down into the mines?

Toledo was perplexed. In a letter of early 1570, written some two months after his arrival in Lima, he tried to bring the king to some resolution by setting out the basic logic, as he saw it, of Peru's existence as a Spanish territory. Mining was the key occupation. Without the resulting silver, Spaniards would not stay. Then there would be no evangelization of Indians. And the king, of course, received a fifth of silver production in royalty, and still more through the duties on trade that mining generated. Various royal orders forbade the use of Indians in mining against their will; but it was extremely difficult to find any Indians to work in the mines voluntarily. The king must choose: do without silver, or force Indians into the mines. Toledo hastened to argue that forced labor, if chosen, could be moderated with regulations providing for sufficient pay, supply of clothes and food, and good treatment. Workers would not be moved from one climatic zone to another. Finally, in what seems a clear case of special pleading, he promised the king that permission for forced mining labor would not be regarded as a general license, but would be used selectively in places where no other option existed.[2]

The king, however, sent no decision on the question. In fact, according to Toledo's later statements, he had still not faced up to the problem in the closing years of the viceregency. So Toledo began a tentative advance of his own toward bringing in forced mine work, with the initial intent that once royal approval arrived

---

que se debe procurar con gran cuidado que en los sitios y estancias más cercanas a las minas haya y se hagan gruesas poblaciones de indios donde con más facilidad y comidad [sic] y aun con más seguridad de su salud, excusando la mudanza de tierras y climas, podrán los dichos indios entender en la labor de las dichas minas y ocuparse en esto."

2. Toledo to king, Lima, February 8, 1570 (Levillier, *Gobernantes*, tomo 3, p. 328).

everything should be ready in Peru. In October of 1570 he con-
voked in Lima a meeting attended by the archbishop, Licenciado
Castro (the former governor of Peru), the oidores, fiscal, and alcaldes of the audiencia, and the leading Dominicans, Augustinians,
and Jesuits of the colony. To this company he addressed a lengthy
discourse designed to secure approval of draft Indian labor in
mines. His argument—in brief, the need for funds to sustain Philip's
defense of the faith in the Old World and the New, the providen-
tial placing by God of gold and silver in Peru to attract Spaniards,
the setback to evangelization of the natives that would follow if
Spaniards were *not* so attracted, the disinclination of whites and
the unsuitability of blacks for mine labor, the legal principle that
people might be compelled to do work necessary to the public good
(though why this should apply to Indians and not to Spaniards he
did not venture to explain); and the antecedent of forced labor in
mines under the Incas—all this proved persuasive. The dignitaries agreed, without recorded dissent, that Indians could be forced
to work mines of known wealth without danger to the conscience
of either king or viceroy.[3] Toledo then delegated the archbishop,
Don Fr. Jerónimo de Loaisa, and Dr. Gregorio González de Cuenca
(one of the oidores), together with the heads of the three orders,
to draft ordinances governing forced mine labor—which they did,
presenting thirty-five clauses to the same company six days later.
The ordinances were approved.[4] They have points of interest, especially on matters of Indian welfare, where they foreshadow later
regulations by Toledo himself; but there is no evidence that they
were much invoked, doubtless precisely because they were quickly
superseded by the much more comprehensive rules that Toledo
began issuing two years later.

So all was ready in Peru. The leading religious and administrative figures had approved of draft mine work. But still no consent
came from the king; and without it, Toledo seems to have been
unwilling to move further, at least in sending Indians to Potosí

3. AGI Patronato 238, ramo 1, Lima, October 7, 1570, no title, f. 5: ". . . las
minas de que se tuviese noticia y experiencia que había en ellas riqueza, se debían
labrar, y que su excelencia podría sin cargar la consciencia de su magestad, ni
suya, y por las causas que estaban referidas, compeler y apremiar a los naturales
a la labor de ellas. . . ."
4. Ibid., ff. 5v–8.

and other mines of precious metals. In early 1571 he did, it is true, begin assigning 2,500 workers to the mercury mines of Guamanga province.[5]

In mercury may lie the clue to Toledo's resolution, taken finally at the start of 1572, to organize a draft for Potosí. To a degree, mere impatience perhaps led him to act then. But it seems a plausible speculation that the successful introduction and rapid spread of silver refining by mercury also provided a powerful stimulus for his decision. Mercury processing was clearly spreading in 1571, and was the obvious solution to the problem of falling silver production at Potosí, caused by deteriorating ore quality, since it could handle profitably ores that were too poor for smelting.[6] Toledo was perhaps perceptive enough to see that this technological gain could be exploited to the full only if abundant labor were available.

The topics of draft labor and amalgamation are indeed treated at length and in close association by Toledo in two letters he wrote to the king from Cuzco on March 1, 1572. In one he sets out further justification for a mining draft. His reasoning is much less solid than that presented to the eminent gathering in Lima in October 1570, and that is perhaps a measure of his frustration at the king's silence. The commonplace theme of the natives' innate idleness had cropped up in his earliest references to labor. But now it was decorated with some strangely discordant ornaments. Indians would not work voluntarily, he wrote, "because they are of their nature and inclination idle, and because of the low condition and the little honor and covetousness they possess . . . and their lack of inclination to acquire possessions or to have any inheritance for their children."[7] This curious assemblage of criticisms certainly lacked something in accuracy, since, as Toledo well knew, many Indians *had* worked voluntarily out of "covetousness" at Potosí, but had stopped doing so precisely because their profits no longer matched their expectations. It was precisely those profit-oriented

5. .Toledo to king, Cuzco, March 25, 1571, in Silvio Zavala, *El servicio personal de los indios en el Perú, tomo 1 (extractos del siglo XVI)*, (Mexico City 1978), p. 70.

6. Bakewell, "Technological change in Potosí," passim.

7. Toledo to king, Cuzco, March 1, 1572: ". . . por ser como son de su naturaleza e inclinación holgazanes, y por su bajeza y poca honra y codicia que tienen . . . y no tener inclinación a adquirir hacienda ni a dejar heredados sus hijos. . ." (Levillier, *Gobernantes*, tomo 4, p. 108). (JHR)

workers whom Toledo wanted to replace with draftees. The problem was anything but lack of covetousness: rather, an excess of it.

In the other letter of the same date, before making an extensive report to the king on the progress of experiments in processing by mercury, Toledo announced that he had resolved to force Indians to work in the mines, with their treatment and wages being regulated by ordinances.[8] The resolution and ordinances referred to seem to be those of October 1570 in Lima. So as to decide how many Indians were needed, he had ordered Alonso Muñoz, "the miner whom your Majesty sent me," to make an inventory of all mines so far located in Peru; this volume was indeed being sent to the king along with the letter.

Using, presumably, the information gathered by Muñoz to estimate the numbers required, Toledo began assigning laborers for Potosí in October of 1572. It was on the fifth of that month that he left Cuzco to travel southward to Potosí, where he arrived on December 23. As he moved along, he ordered that a proportion of the tributary population (males between eighteen and fifty) of the encomiendas that he crossed should go to Potosí, though he limited this draft to those encomiendas that had habitually sent Indians to the mines. No list of the places Toledo called on has yet come to light. The proportion to go from the encomiendas between Cuzco and Chucuito was 7 percent of the tributary population, as counted by Toledo's inspectors; but to this percentage were to be added any Indians from these same areas already in Potosí. That raised the number considerably, as will be seen. From the royal encomienda of Chucuito he ordered the despatch of five hundred men to Potosí, to join the five hundred already there. From the district of La Paz he sent thirteen hundred additional men to Potosí (and five hundred to the Machaca mines in the Berenguela district). He also drafted men from the province of Charcas. Although he did not say how many these were, his descriptions suggest that the proportion was 8 to 9 percent of tributaries. Certainly, in his later assignments, a slightly higher levy was placed on areas close

8.   AGI Lima 28B, tomo 4, ff. 245v.–50, "Hacienda," Cuzco, March 1, 1572.
9.   Information on Toledo's first draft is from two of his own accounts: Toledo to king, "Gobierno," Potosí, March 20, 1573, f. 22v. (AGI Lima 29, tomo 1); and the preamble (ff. 435v.–42v.) to the "Repartimiento general que el excelentísimo

to Potosí, doubtless on the principle that undertaking a longer journey merited some relief in numbers.[9]

The total contingent of extra workers ordered to Potosí in those two months or so of late 1572 was about 4,300. Toledo found a slightly larger number already there. There were first some 4,200 men from encomiendas between Cuzco and Potosí, either living in the town permanently and sending their tribute payments back home, or rotating on a yearly mita. Then there still remained about 900 yanaconas. And finally Toledo found an undeclared number of Indians from Cuzco, neither encomendados nor yanaconas, whom he termed "Incas." Adding his new draftees to the laborers already in Potosí, Toledo announced a grand total of 9,300, which is rather less than the sum of the individual categories just given. A good round figure to take for this first great mita is probably 9,500.[10]

The newly drafted men began to arrive in Potosí in early 1573. Toledo provides little detail on his initial organization of the large labor force he was assembling. Some of his writing suggests that he ignored the yanaconas' special status and threw them into the general mass of workers; but other evidence is against that. No detailed record of his allotment of Indians to silver producers in 1573 has yet appeared. In later years—1575 and 1578 in Toledo's case, and subsequent dates in that of other viceroys—it became standard practice to make precise distributions (repartimientos) of workers to mine and refinery operators in accordance with their competence, their labor needs, and their record of treatment of Indians. Such repartimientos are recorded in documents showing the exact numbers of men assigned to each operator, and their place of origin. But nothing of the sort has appeared for 1573. Toledo provides some gross numbers, stating that with labor need as his guide, he assigned to mining 1,430 men, and to refining, 2,308. In addition he allotted 1,000 among those who were building new refineries, for construction work. So the total distributed

---

señor don Francisco de Toledo, visorrey de estos reinos, hizo de los indios que han de venir a la labor y beneficio de las minas y azogues de la Villa Imperial de Potosí," Arequipa, October 10, 1575 (PBN ms B511, ff. 435v–70v.).

10. Figures in this paragraph are from PBN ms B511, "Repartimiento general," ff. 437v.–38.

in 1573 was 4,738; or about half the whole labor force, if the 900 yanaconas are counted in it.[11]

Toledo intended that the other half of the 9,500 should at any time be resting *(de huelga)*. They were not, though, to be idle, but to pursue profitable activities, such as freighting, selling goods they had brought with them, and especially refining silver on their own account, both by smelting in guayras and by amalgamation. The wages that Toledo set for draft workers in 1573 were to be paid in ore, to enable and encourage those who were de huelga to produce silver. What is not at all clear is how often the halves alternated or how long their spell of work was. Nor is the length of stay in Potosí specified; presumably it was a year, since by the 1570s that seems to have been the period for which encomienda Indians served their mita in Potosí. Finally, the precise rôle of the native authorities whom Toledo had ordered to come with each draft from the encomiendas is also undefined.

The viceroy left Potosí in April or May of 1573 for La Plata, remaining there almost a year before setting off on his ill-judged and ill-fated punitive foray against the Chiriguanaes. He passed through Potosí again in early 1575 on his way back to the coast and to Lima, finding that the mining industry had grown fast. With it had grown demand for labor. But the actual number of Indians arriving in Potosí under the 1573 draft was some 2,000 fewer than expected. The reasons for this are not explained. Two possible causes are the reluctance of encomenderos to release their people, and a decline in native population since the original assignments were made. The outcome was that some Indian curacas had been forced to supply more men than Toledo had assessed—occasionally, more than the encomiendas in question contained. This was particularly so with some groups who were found to be notably skilled and tractable. Demand for labor had also led to men being taken from their rest periods, and the Indian leaders' being severely punished for failure to produce more hands. Indians had been paid in low grade silver, not in ore. The corregidor of Potosí and his servants had connived at all this, and so were to be punished. But clearly the only adequate solution to the problem was to increase labor supply. And this Toledo proceeded to do, with a new levy

11.   Ibid., ff. 438v.–39.

on the Indian population and a distribution of the workers among silver producers that declared exactly how many each should receive. The plan was issued from Arequipa on October 10, 1575.[12]

Under these new provisions, 17 percent of the tributaries from the district of La Plata, 16 percent of those from the district of La Paz, and 15 percent from that of Cuzco, should go annually to Potosí (with the exception that the Canas y Canches province in Cuzco should send only 13 percent, the reason for this privilege not being explained). Toledo added the qualification that the Uros, who were to be found in all three districts, should be drafted at double the rate of the other Indians—that is, at 30 to 34 percent of tributaries—since they were generally held to be primitive and therefore less useful. The new percentages may seem startlingly higher than the 7 to 9 percent of 1573; but the figures are of course not directly comparable since the 1573 proportions referred only to workers newly drafted and did not include Indians already in Potosí, who were slightly more numerous than the draftees. In reality the absolute number of workers given in 1575 was not vastly larger than in 1573: 11,494, as opposed to some 9,500.[13] It is curious that Toledo himself, in describing the levy of 1575, gives the total as 9,313, and the gain over 1573 as 928.[14] Whether this is a case of guesswork before all the figures were in, or simply bad arithmetic, cannot be known. There were, finally, presumably still some hundreds of yanaconas in mining in 1575, outside the mita; but if so, Toledo made no allusion to them.

Instead of splitting the mita into two, a working half and a resting half, as before, Toledo now made a threefold division, with two-thirds being de huelga at any moment. The working third became known as the *mita ordinaria*, or current mita, as opposed to the *mita gruesa*, a term signifying the total number of workers assigned to Potosí for the year. The 1575 distribution (repartimiento) shows that Toledo assigned 3,615 Indians among 234 individual silver producers: owners of, or partners in, mines and refineries, or people building or planning to build refineries. In addition, the crown, which at this time held three mines and two refineries,

12. Ibid., ff. 435–70v.
13. Ibid., ff. 443–59.
14. Ibid., f. 441v.

received 128 Indians to work them; and the Mercedarians in Potosí were granted 8 men for a mine belonging to them. These allotments came to 3,751. Of this number, 601 were given for construction of refineries. So the total to be employed in current silver production was 3,150 (though Toledo in his preamble to the repartimiento gives a figure of 3,113: 2,498 workers to refineries and 615 to mining). The assignment to mining was greatly cut from the 1,430 given in 1573. Toledo stated as reasons for this the need to divert more labor to refinery building, and the illicit use for other work of many Indians previously assigned to mining.[15] Dr. Vázquez, the physician of the Indian hospital, received 60 men in lieu of a cash income; and the town of Potosí was allotted 50, for purposes undeclared. Thus the grand total of the mita ordinaria was 3,861, or almost exactly a third of the mita gruesa of 11,494.

Again, no explicit statement appears that the draft should spend a year in Potosí, although it is a reasonable assumption that it did so. Nor is there a specific regulation about the frequency of rotation in Potosí. An order on the payment of wages does suggest, however, that the normal pattern was one week of work followed by two weeks de huelga.[16] Toledo also provided in 1575 at least a general outline of the hierarchy of control that Indian authorities were to exercise over the draftees in Potosí. A ruling group of six leading *principales*—curacas in their own right of groups from various points of the draft area—was appointed and given administrative authority *(gobierno y superintendencia)* over all other curacas and Indians in the mita. The six were to be entitled captains *(capitanes)*. Their duties were first, as might be expected, to ensure that the due number of workers appeared; but then in general to oversee the administration of the draft in Potosí, to look to the workers' interests, and to collect from lesser Indian officials tributes due in Potosí from commoners.[17] Although Toledo stated that he had

---

15. Ibid., f. 442–42v.

16. Ibid., f. 468v., Toledo, Arequipa, October 10, 1575: Indians in mining should be paid every Sunday; but those in refineries, which at this early date were mainly in the lower valleys outside Potosí, should be paid monthly because it was unreasonable to make them travel into the town each week to receive their wages. (Wages were to be distributed in Potosí itself because Toledo had declared that officials should supervise payment).

17. Ibid., ff. 459v.–60.

named six captains, only five appear in his account. Don Juan Colque, *cacique principal* of the Quillacas and Asanaques, should control men from the Urcosuyo province of the district of the city of La Plata—that is, from the southern and western part of the district.[18] Don Martín Ochane, *cacique* of Paria, was to supervise those from the Omasuyo province of the La Plata district—the eastern and northern section. Don Diego Sorope, *cacique* and *principal* of the encomienda of Caquiavire, was to be captain for the district of the city of La Paz. Don Bernardino Cari, whose personal position is not stated, was appointed captain of men from what is loosely described as the province of Urcusuyo (a term that may plausibly be taken to refer to the area north and west of Lake Titicaca). And finally, Don Juan Calpa, *cacique* of Hatuncolla, should be captain for Indians from el Collao, in the district of the city of Cuzco—the northernmost part of the mita area. These leaders were chosen for their mental ability *(razón* and *entendimiento)* and their authority. Colque appears to have become the spokesman for the captains.

Less than three years after the 1575 repartimiento, Toledo found it necessary to issue another, his third and last. It is dated in Lima, August 6, 1578.[19] His reasons for this revision were similar to those advanced in 1575, and included expansion of mining at Potosí; the inflow of new producers deserving labor; and unauthorized distribution by the corregidor of Indians from the huelga, so that workers served half the time rather than a third. On top of this, Licenciado Juan de Matienzo, now president of the audiencia in La Plata, had, without Toledo's permission, made a new repartimiento (or a partial one) of his own in late 1577 or early 1578. Toledo objected, doubtless on grounds of insubordination, but also because Matienzo had assigned "for his own private ends and considerations," as Toledo darkly put it, three thousand extra Indians. This was an excessive burden on them, Toledo thought,

18.   For the meaning of Urcosuyo (and Omasuyo) see Catherine J. Julien, *Inca administration in the Titicaca basin as reflected at the provincial capital of Hatunqolla* (Ph.D. dissertation, University of California, Berkeley, 1978), p. 17 ff.

19.   "El repartimiento general que su excelencia hizo de los indios que se han de ocupar en la labor de las minas y beneficios de los ingenios y lamas y relaves, con las ordenanzas que en ello se han de guardar. Fecho en la Ciudad de los Reyes por el año de 1578." (PBN ms B511, ff. 666v.–85).

exclaiming that not all the Indians in Peru would satisfy the people of Potosí. Unhappy viceroy, perplexed by Indians wanting greed and Spaniards overcharged with it! Matienzo denied having actually added any Indians to the draft, though he admitted to drawing on the huelga in order to fulfil Toledo's allotments; and he had apparently made some changes in these, though not, he asserted, without the approval of both Indians and Spanish.[20]

For all his criticism of Matienzo's increased distribution, Toledo found little choice but to follow suit. The draft of 1578 swelled the number of mita Indians assigned to Potosí from 11,494 to 14,181. The rates of levy on the three main provinces were kept as before: 17 percent from Charcas, 16 percent from La Paz, and 15 percent from the Collao (embracing the same area as that described in the 1575 repartimiento as the district of the city of Cuzco). For Charcas and La Paz, and for much of the Collao, the 1578 list of tributaries and draftees due from encomiendas reads very much as in 1575. Evidently no new general count of tributaries was made, though some adjustments up or down were applied to individual encomiendas. Some eighteen encomiendas listed in 1575 in the Cuzco district fail to reappear in 1578. All but five of these had had very small populations, which possibly vanished in the interim, or were combined with some neighboring encomienda in the *reducción* process being implemented in these years.[21] In only one case did Toledo make a drastic change in the previous levy: Chucuito now had to provide exactly double the number of draftees called for in 1575— 2,202 instead of 1,101. The draft on the Canas province in Cuzco he raised by about a third, from 406 to 619. For most of the rest of

20.   BAN Minas catalog No. 175, acuerdo of audiencia, La Plata, June 23, 1578. The oidores of La Plata here contradict Matienzo's assertion that he had made no more than adjustments to the scheme of 1575. It was, they said, a new allotment, and much complained of by the Indians. When they heard of Matienzo's proceedings in Potosí, the oidores sent him orders that Toledo's arrangements should be left alone. But he snatched these instructions from the messenger, and, apparently, destroyed them. This seems a classic case of an audiencia's taking the opportunity to snipe at its president. Allegations on both sides must be regarded with suspicion. For Toledo's objection to Matienzo's activities, see Toledo to king, Lima, April 19, 1579, in Levillier, *Gobernantes*, tomo 6, p. 132.

21.   The five larger encomiendas in the Cuzco district that failed to reappear in the 1578 list were: Quispallata (302 tributaries), Chicacupa (310), Hatuncana (922), Caporaque (187), and Omachire (180).

the 1578 increase, Toledo drew on Indians hardly touched by the mita before: the "provincia de los Condes de la ciudad del Cuzco y Arequipa," which sent 495 draftees instead of the previous 63; and the province of Arequipa itself, whence no Indians had come before, but now 795 were taken.[22] Small local adjustments provided the balance of the overall increase of 2,687. One final though minor point of interest in the 1578 draft is that the Uros were now spared the double levy imposed on them in 1575. The reason for that had been an alleged incapacity for work. But this, happily for them, had proved a false judgment, at least in Toledo's view. He noted in 1578 that "in working they are commonly more capable than the Aymaraes" (that is, the rest of the draft), and consequently dropped their contribution to 17 percent from Paria and only 11 percent of the other Uros in encomiendas in La Paz and Charcas provinces.[23] This favorable opinion on the Uros was not, however, to become commonplace in Charcas.

Once more, two-thirds of the total draft of 14,181 were to be de huelga at any moment. The working third was allocated among different production activities as follows (the allocations of 1575 are given in parentheses): to mining 1,118 (615), to refineries, 3,055 (2,498), and to reprocessing of tailings from amalgamation (*beneficio de lamas y relaves*), 228 (0).[24] Toledo thought it worthwhile setting aside Indians specially for this reprocessing because it recovered useful amounts of mercury. In addition, two hundred men were to be supplied as hands for hire each month. The mita captains were told to place a group of this size in the main plaza on the first Monday of each month. Any employer needing extra labor for silver production, or some other task, could hire it there for thirty days—no more, no less. Wages should be at least those paid to regular mita workers. It is not clear whether these men were to form part of the mita ordinaria, or whether they were to be taken from the huelga. They quickly became known, for obvious reasons, as *indios meses*.[25] If they are included in the mita ordinaria, Toledo's

22. "Repartimiento general" of 1578, PBN ms B511, f. 674–74v.
23. ". . . en el trabajo comunmente son para más que los aymaraes." Ibid., f. 668v.
24. Ibid., ff. 678, 681.
25. Ibid., f. 683.

allocations in 1578 came to 4,601, or 32.4 percent of the total draft of 14,181: slightly under a third.

A final modification in the 1578 scheme, not of great importance, but worth mentioning because it suggests a growing care in organization and a willingness to respond to the lessons of experience, was to make allocations to individual employers of Indians from a single encomienda, as far as that was possible. This, in fact, had been done by Matienzo in his redistribution, and was the only feature of it to find Toledo's approval. It should have brought advantages. The men would know each other and perhaps work together more effectively; and awkward divergences of custom, dialect, or language that might possibly arise between groups from opposite ends of the mita catchment area would be avoided.

The constant and successful expansion of the mita—a remarkable administrative feat both within and without Potosí, even considering the numerous antecedents—might suggest that Toledo overcame his early qualms about the morality of forced mine labor: not so, however. His letters to the king on the subject in the late 1570s are an exasperated and querulous mixture: arguments that Peru would be nothing without silver, and that there could be no silver without Indian labor; pride in his own achievement in supplying that labor; condemnation of the miners' insatiable demand for Indians; extreme unease over the forcing of Indians into the mines; and complaint that the king had not, still, confirmed or rejected Toledo's action in creating an official mita.

> I do not wish to say here what is entailed in sustaining this business [of mining], since it is some five years since I wrote, as I have continued to write, that if there were no reply on the matter of sending these Indians to the mines, I would remove them, carrying as I do such a heavy burden on my shoulders in order that the affairs of this kingdom shall not collapse; as your majesty may well believe would have happened, both with respect to taxes and to the royal fifth, whence emanates prosperity for all. [But] hoping daily to kiss your majesty's feet, I have suspended it" [removing the Indians].[26]

26. "No quiero decir en ésta lo que va en sustentar este negocio, pues ha cerca de cinco años que tengo escrito y voy escribiendo que si no se responde a haber enviado estos indios a las minas, los quitaría yo de ellas, trayendo esta carga tan pesada en mis hombros porque no diese al través todo lo de este reino,

Doubtless Toledo's annoyance over the king's silence on the matter of Indians was exacerbated by the crown's disregard of another of his requests, which was clearly brought out at the end of this quotation. He had been asking for years to be released from duty and allowed to go home; but to no avail. This further complaint perhaps added shrillness to his remarks on the mita. But there seems no good reason to doubt that his uncertainty was deeply rooted. It further seems grossly unfair of the king, indeed a grave dereliction of duty on Philip's part, to have thrust all responsibility for the mita onto Toledo. The initial instructions were vague. Toledo was charged with making a success of mining, but it was perfectly obvious to the king that to do so he would have to violate a long series of edicts opposing forced mine labor. Such a change of direction was properly a matter for central policymakers. Viceroys, no matter how much local discretion they might be allowed, should not have had to make such decisions in isolation. Less excusable still was the crown's silence after 1573. Toledo, ever since, has had to bear the responsibility and opprobrium of creating the mita. It is true that he was its prime mover. His responsibility may nevertheless be lessened to some degree by the fact that a good part of the organization had already developed; and to a much greater degree by shifting the burden onto those to whom it properly belonged—the king and the Council of the Indies.

At the beginning of his organization of the mita, in 1572 and 1573, Toledo found some alleviation of his moral qualms in the hope, indeed the expectation, that the Indians he was sending to Potosí would benefit from being there. This hope lay behind his insistence from the start that the draft workers should have time de huelga; and also behind his anger whenever Indians de huelga were taken for extra work. This time off was intended not only for rest, though that was certainly part of its purpose, but also to allow the Indians to do other diverse work which, in the bustling center of activity and thriving market that Potosí was even in the early 1570s, would bring them substantial gains. His greatest hope was

---

como en efecto crea vuestra magestad que lo hubiera hecho así en las contrataciones y derecho como en los quintos, donde emana la grosedad para todos. Esperando cada día besar los pies de vuestra magestad lo he suspendido." Toledo to king, Callao, February 18, 1579 (Levillier, *Gobernantes,* tomo 6, p. 99). In a similar vein, see Toledo to king, Callao, April 19, 1579 (ibid., p. 134).

that Indians would reassume the large part in silver refining they had played in Potosí's first quarter century. At Toledo's order the guayras on the cerro were counted, and 6,600 left in place so that Indians should smelt high-lead ores during the windy winter season. This, though, was merely a supplementary measure. Toledo was as aware as anyone else that the reason for so many Indians' having left Potosí was precisely the growing shortage of ores rich enough for profitable smelting by guayra. Some ores of adequate quality did continue to be found, and it was well to preserve a proven means of refining them, especially if this would benefit the Indians.[27] But the natives' true profit, as Toledo saw it, would come from their adoption of the new mercury process. It was a reasonable assumption. The Indians had shown themselves to be skilled refiners before—more skilled than the Spanish, on the whole. Would not their obvious proficiency in things metallurgical enable them to adapt quickly and effectively to the new technique? The answer, in purely technical terms, was yes. By March of 1573 Indian masters in amalgamation, instructed on Toledo's orders by Pedro Fernández de Velasco, were being installed in public training centers in each Indian parish, where the new workers arriving daily under Toledo's first draft should learn to refine silver ores with mercury. It was largely with mercury processing in mind that Toledo in 1573 ordered that the draftees' wages should be paid in ore.[28]

The Indians, however, did not profit from amalgamation as Toledo had hoped, if at all. He was probably correct in his assessment of their technical capacity; but what he did not foresee, and perhaps nobody could have foreseen except those who had witnessed the earlier introduction of amalgamation into Mexico, was

27. Capoche (Relación, p. 111) records that by the mid 1580s most of the guayras remaining around Potosí were dilapidated and in disuse. He gives the maximum number of guayras ever existing there as 6,497—a figure that, despite its suspicious exactitude, suggests that Toledo exaggerated in claiming to have preserved 6,600 on the cerro alone.

28. ". . . les hago hacer en cada parroquia una casa pública con indios maestros de los que ya han aprendido en la casa de Pero Fernández de Velasco, que fue el que yo envié aquí a alumbrar este beneficio a todos. . . ." Toledo noted that the Indians were beginning to understand the profit (ganancia) they could make with the amalgamation process, refining the lower quality ores (metales de llamperías) in which he had ordered their wages to be paid. Toledo to king, "Hacienda," Potosí, March 20, 1573, para. 21 (AGI Lima 29, tomo 1).

the scale of investment that amalgamation demanded, and which the Indians had no chance of achieving (if, indeed, they held the mere notion of capital investment). As has been pointed out, guayras were cheap and simple structures of clay or stone. For successful smelting in them, it was sufficient to crush ores with handheld hammers or the *quimbalete*. Amalgamation, on the other hand, required mechanical crushing mills if it were to be practiced on an economic scale. As the technology of ore dressing advanced rapidly in Potosí during the early 1570s, from small human-powered ingenios to larger animal-powered machines, and then to massive water mills, Toledo's potential amalgamators in the mita were left behind. There is, indeed, no evidence that they tried to compete in this extraordinary process of formation of fixed capital. Toledo's vision of off-duty mitayos amalgamating their way to wealth rapidly faded. Perhaps this is an explanation for his growing inclination in the middle and late 1570s toward cash wages for mita workers. By 1578, in fact, he had *banned* payments in anything but cash: the best hope for the workers' being properly paid lay in specifying wage levels in fine silver. Perhaps, also, recognition of the Indians' failure to profit from amalgamation added to the guilt that Toledo felt over draft labor, and is to a degree responsible for the vehemence of his protests in the late 1570s at the king's failure to sanction the mita. (As a practical matter, however, it has to be said that his arrangements for training mitayos in amalgamation techniques must have generally promoted silver production in Potosí by providing a pool of refiners on which the owners of ingenios could draw).

Toledo, finally, gave much thought to the wages that his draftees should receive. He took it for granted, as of course did the king also, that if there were to be a draft, adequate wages must be paid. His earliest wage orders have not appeared. Clause 7 of the regulations on draft labor that he ordered to be drawn up in Lima in October of 1570 laid down that Indians must receive an adequate salary in silver and food, but it did not specify how much the salary should be. Rather, "the disposition of each province" should govern the rate.[29] This same clause also established the

---

29. AGI Patronato 238, ramo 1, untitled ordinances, Lima, October 13, 1570, f. 6.

principle that Indians should be paid for their journeys to and from
the mines: a point of contention between officials and employers
for many decades to come. Toledo must, however, over the the
course of the next year or so, have given some definite rates for
Potosí, because in April of 1572 the town's cabildo, dominated naturally by miners, began what was to be a long series of protests
over the allegedly excessive levels set by the viceroy.[30] Toledo
allowed Potosí to appeal, but only to the king, perhaps believing
that only the king had the authority to rule on the question, and
perhaps hoping that the appeal would oblige Philip to concentrate
his mind on the whole matter of forced mine labor. Spain was also
conveniently distant. An answer would be long in arriving. (No
evidence has appeared that any ever did.) Meanwhile, Toledo
could continue to insist on what he thought was adequate pay.

The first known pay rates that Toledo set specifically for Potosí
are of April 1573. The basic rate for mine workers was 11 *tomines* a
week—that is, 1.375 pesos ensayados, or about 2.25 pesos corrientes. Workers were not, however, to receive this in cash, but
rather, as has been noted, in ore, so that they could profit from
refining. In 1573 he seems to have tried to achieve this aim by
preserving, for those Indians who wished to take advantage of it,
the old system of mine working by indios varas. He ordered (and
this was repeated in his central series of mine regulations of February 1574) that mine owners should assign a quarter of each mine
to the Indians. These, indeed, might choose the quarter they preferred. At the end of each week they might buy back from the
owner a third of the rich ore (cacilla, though Toledo did not use
the word) that they had extracted from their quarter of the mine;
and this third they would refine at a profit, if Toledo's intentions
were realized. In case of disagreement over the price, one of the
two inspectors *(veedores)* of mines was to adjudicate. If, however,
the workers preferred not to follow this procedure, they were to
be given for a week's work the equivalent of 11 tomines in ore,
which again should be assessed by a veedor.[31] These arrangements were obviously exceedingly cumbersome. If nothing else,

---

30.   BAN Minas catalog No. 127, acuerdo of cabildo of Potosí, April 20, 1572.
31.   Toledo's "Instrucción y ordenanzas hechas para los veedores de las minas
e ingenios," Potosí, April 18, 1573 (PBN ms B511, ff. 153v.–60), clause 3 (ff.
154v.–55); and clause 10 of the title "De los desmontes, trabajo y paga de los

the amount of adjudication required of the veedores would have been beyond the capacity of two men. There is no evidence that quasi-renting of a portion of a mine to Indian workers on the old pattern was perpetuated by Toledo's arrangements. Capoche makes no reference to it in the mid-1580s. What is clear, however, is that Indian miners used their unequaled knowledge of individual workings to make profits beyond their wages. In early 1575 the cabildo of Potosí, in another of its petitions to Toledo to cut wages, complained that Indians took from the mines bags full of the best ore, for smelting, often before the owner or overseer of the mine knew that such ore had been found.[32] This was a problem for mine owners all over Spanish America, and one that was never solved. In most cases illicit extraction of small amounts of good ore came to be seen as inevitable. They are best regarded as a supplement to statutory wages (and possibly often a supplement more valuable than the wage).

By early 1574, when he issued his comprehensive mining code, Toledo had clearly accepted that cash wages would prevail. Several reasons for this change of mind may be suggested: the failure, or rather inability, of Indians to adopt amalgamation; the unworkability of payments in ore; the rising general quality of silver as amalgamation became more common in Potosí; and the imminent availability of good quality small coin from the mint that Toledo was having built in the town. The last two developments reduced the risk of Indians' being cheated when paid in cash. So clause 9 of the title in the code dealing with wages declared that those mitayos who elected not to work a quarter of a mine could be paid either in cash or in ore, at the rate of 3.5 reales a day (again, about 2.25 pesos corrientes for a week of five days).[33] This rate for workers in mines was confirmed by regulations accompanying the repartimiento of 1575, in which Toledo also declared what wages other workers should receive: 3 reales a day for Indians freighting ore from mines to refineries (some undoubtedly using llamas, but

---

indios" of his mining ordinances of La Plata, February 7, 1574 (Levillier, *Gobernantes*, tomo 8, p. 235).

32. "Auto que el señor don Francisco de Toledo hizo del salario y jornal que han de dar a los indios que trabajan en las minas y beneficio de los azogues e ingenios que se reparten en la plaza de Potosí para el servicio de ella," Potosí, January 8, 1575 (PBN ms B511, ff. 355–57).

33. Levillier, *Gobernantes*, tomo 8, pp. 236–37.

others still carrying ores themselves); and 2.75 reales daily for refinery workers.[34] Toledo confirmed his rates of 1575 when he issued his new repartimiento in August 1578, but with the interesting proviso that wages were now payable in coin alone.[35] As suggested before, this clearly signals his renunciation of earlier hopes that drafted Indians would continue to be important and semi-independent refiners of ore. Despite his best intentions, the logic of economies of scale had delivered refining into the hands of those who possessed and understood capital, and had cast the thousands of new draftees into the rôle of manual laborers supplying and tending the booming machinery of the ingenios strung out along the Ribera.

34. PBM ms B511, f. 466v.
35. PBN ms B511, f. 682.

4

Mingas

. . . el señor Don Francisco de Toledo, que todo lo previno. . . .

(Don Juan de Carvajal y Sande, 1633*)

Toledo expanded, standardized, and gave official shape to a draft labor system that had already developed to a considerable degree in response to demand for mine workers. He claimed to have tripled the labor force available to Potosí miners during his administration,[1] partly by increasing the area subject to draft, and partly by applying roughly equal labor levies across towns and territories from which workers had previously been despatched in a far more piecemeal fashion. The largely private organization of the pre-1570s mita he replaced with one regulated by a mass of ordinances; and he established the principle that the colonial government was responsible for the proper functioning of this official draft, even though royal approval of it had not yet been granted.

It is perhaps a measure of Toledo's organizing energies and skills that only minimal attempts were made by the Spanish administration, either at home or in Peru, to change his mita organization during the rest of the period treated here. Toledo's mita remained for officialdom the chief source of labor for mining in Potosí. No

---

*Don Juan de Carvajal y Sande, councillor of the Indies and visitor to Potosí, in the preamble to his repartimiento of the mita, Potosí, September 3, 1633— referring specifically to Toledo's regulation on the sale of mita Indian labor. Carvajal was not, moreover, a man to extend undue respect to his predecessors. (AGI Lima 45, tomo 1, No. 1, f. 12v.)

1. Toledo to crown, Callao, February 18, 1579 (Levillier, *Gobernantes*, tomo 6, p. 91).

effort was made to create any other system, though in fact the late decades of the sixteenth century saw the spontaneous growth of a broad system of hired wage labor, again in answer to demand, alongside and to a degree replacing the mita.

A central reason for the stability of Toledo's arrangements was that the fundamental question he had so pointedly raised—should Indian welfare be preferred to silver production, or not?—continued to perplex both the crown and its colonial officials; and the ultimate consequence of their perplexity was inaction, or something very close to it, so that Toledo's choice of silver over Indians was never in practice seriously questioned.[2]

That does not mean to say, however, that the mita was not the subject of intense and occasionally agonized debate during the decade after Toledo created it. The home government, viceroys, ecclesiastical authorities, and corregidores of Potosí all, at one time or another, gave keen attention to the draft labor system of Potosí. The twistings of those deliberations, hardly less anfractuous than the mines of the cerro themselves, have been carefully traced by Jeffrey A. Cole.[3]

Two viceroys deserve particular mention for the concern they showed over the mita. The first was Don Luis de Velasco (the younger—1595–1603), who, in addition to issuing a series of ordinances for the mita in 1599, in 1603 set in motion a considerable debate on the question of draft labor in mining. This he did in response to a well-known order from Philip III of November 24,

2.   In 1589, eight years after Toledo left Peru, the crown finally made the statement that he had waited so long, and in vain, to receive. Writing to the Viceroy Conde de Villar (1584–88), Philip II declared that despite former orders to the contrary, Indians in Peru might be obliged to work in mines against their will, provided that religious teaching, justice, food, good wages, and hospital treatment were given to them. Toledo's labor ordinances for Huancavelica and Potosí should serve as models for arrangements that Villar might make in sending Indians to the recent and numerous mine discoveries he had reported—discoveries that were, in fact, the reason given by the king for this approval of compulsion. Toledo was vindicated: his forced labor regulations were accepted and even held up as a model. Approval came too late, however, to afford him any satisfaction or relief; he had died in April 1582. For Philip's order to Villar, see AGI Patronato 238.1.8., crown to viceroy, January 10, 1589; also *Recopilación* 6.15.1.

3.   *The Potosí mita under Hapsburg administration. The seventeenth century* (Ph.D. dissertation, University of Massachusetts, Amherst, 1981).

1601. As a monarch who had come very recently to the throne, Philip may have been particularly conscious of the crown's duty to protect native Americans. His order to Velasco in 1601 expressed a desire to relieve the Indians of hardship *(molestia)* and to furnish them with liberty and evangelization, although this should be done with attention still being given "to the holy labor and increase of the land and working of the mines."[4] Drafts of Indians for mining labor should continue for one more year only, during which time miners should provide themselves with black slaves or some other sort of worker. If one year proved insufficient for the change, then the viceroy might, after consulting the archbishop in Lima and other religious and secular leaders, grant an extension of a further year.[5]

Velasco replied in May of 1603 with a distinctly dismissive rejection of the king's orders. The points he made were hardly original, but no less telling for that: miners were too poor to buy the requisite numbers of blacks, who were, in any case, unsuited to the altitude of the mining areas; and Indians were much more adept *(ágiles)* than blacks at producing silver. Despite the firmness of the refutation, Velasco nevertheless, also in 1603, complied with the king's will by seeking views on the orders of 1601 from six important ecclesiastics in Peru; and, in October of that year (the month he retired from his viceregency), and following in part the recommendations of these advisers, he issued a series of regulatory reforms of the mita, the most important of which had to do with procedures for gathering the mitayos and delivering them to Potosí.[6] These measures were of at least potential significance, and reflect Velasco's honest concern over the mita; but they were a trivial conclusion to what appears to have been an attempt by the king

---

4. ". . . se acuda al santo [sic] labor y acrecentamiento de la tierra y beneficio de las minas." SBN ms 19,282, ff. 128–30, real cédula to Velasco, Valladolid, November 24, 1601.

5. The same order was sent concurrently to New Spain. For the full text, see Richard Konetzke (ed.), *Colección de documentos para la historia de la formación social de Hispanoamérica, 1493–1810* (3 tomos in 5, Madrid 1953–62), tomo 2, parte 1, pp. 71–85.

6. Cole, *The Potosí mita*, pp. 111–12. See also pp. 105–13 for a more precise account of Velasco's reaction to the 1601 order.

to do away with the mining mita altogether—the only such attempt, moreover, made during the period examined by this book.

The second viceroy in the pre-1650 period to give notably close attention to the mita was the Conde de Chinchón (1629–39). He was particularly perturbed over the mita assigned to mine mercury at Huancavelica—undoubtedly the most invidious and dangerous mining draft of them all, since the workings were liable to collapse, noxious fumes often filled them, and the product, mercury, was itself a potent poison. Chinchón also strongly disapproved of the Potosí mita. One result of his opposition to it was to reject a plan put forward by the *azogueros* to extend the standard mita work period from a week to two months. The object was greater efficiency, since less time would be lost in the actual distribution of workers to mines and refineries. Chinchón acknowledged the potential gain, but foresaw a number of unacceptably adverse consequences for the workers: they would lose the opportunity to lodge complaints against their curacas and employers, supply of water and food to the mine workers would be complicated, evangelization would become more difficult, and "the slight comforts that these miserable people enjoy through raising a few chickens and domestic animals would disappear, since sale of these things would be impossible."[7] Later in his administration, Chinchón wrote that he had always tried to ensure that mitayos went to Potosí in the numbers established by the levies, but had found this a hard task because the mita "is grounded in a rigorous servitude of such horror and loathing to the Indians. . . ."[8]

Chinchón's hostility to the mita found its most practical expression in his attempt to make a new and fairer distribution of laborers among the miners and refiners of Potosí. This task he entrusted to Don Juan de Carvajal y Sande, who came to Peru in 1633 as a royal *visitador* of the Audiencias of Lima and La Plata. Chinchón instructed Carvajal to use a criterion of previous good or bad use

7. "Que las cortas comodidades de que los miserables gozan criando algunas gallinas y animales domésticos, no las ternían porque se les imposibilitara el modo de su venta." Chinchón to king, "Gobierno y hacienda No. 33," Lima, June 6, 1932. (AGI Lima 43, tomo 3).

8. ". . . se funda en una rigurosa servidumbre de tal horror y aborrecimiento de los indios. . . ." Chinchón to king, "Gobierno No. 23," Lima, October 14, 1638. (AGI Lima 49).

of mitayos by silver producers as his main guide in reallocating workers among them. This was not a new principle, having indeed been established by Toledo in the 1570s (Ch. 3 above); but Carvajal applied it with a rigor unfamiliar to the producers, actually depriving twenty-nine refineries of all mitayos. The owners' vehement protests went back to Chinchón in Lima, and in due course to the Council of the Indies. The argument was still rumbling on when Chinchón's term ended in 1639, and was left for his successor, the Marqués de Mancera (1639–48) to adjudicate. The Council had suggested a completely new repartimiento to replace Carvajal's; but Mancera's doubts and caution in arranging this resulted in its not coming about during his term. And indeed, no new repartimiento was drawn up until 1689, when the Viceroy Duque de la Palata sent orders for a new distribution to Potosí. The bureaucratic fumbling, the politicking, and the doubts of certain viceroys about the morality of the mita that lie behind this enormous delay fall largely outside the chronological scope of this book, and have in any case been followed in detail by Cole.[9]

Despite the best and clearly sincere efforts toward reform by Velasco and Chinchón, the form of the mita continued very much as Toledo had created it. The most daring suggestions of those viceroys hardly amounted to more than hand wringing when set against the practical functioning of the draft. Truly drastic action was almost unimaginable. Universal opinion held that to remove draft labor from mining would at best cause a severe drop in silver output. Equally accepted was the fact that such a drop would be intolerable to the state. Indeed, administrators believed it was their duty to promote silver production wherever they could; and a viceroy's performance, or that of some lesser official in an area that yielded silver, was in part judged by the amount of metal forthcoming during his term of office. Still, it can be said—and the point is not trivial—that attitudes and opinions such as those of Velasco and Chinchón did constitute some sort of barrier to further deterioration of the draft Indian's lot.

The day-to-day working of that draft is not easy to discern. Much quickly became routine, and so was not recorded; though the evi-

9. Cole, *The Potosí mita*, p. 189 ff., and chs. V–VII passim.

dence available certainly suggests that the routine had its origins in Toledo's regulations of the 1570s.

One respect in which this is clearly true was that of the area from which the mita was drawn. This area was not expanded between Toledo's repartimiento of 1578 and the mid-seventeenth century. The 1633 repartimiento by Don Juan de Carvajal y Sande, the last before 1650, shows Indians being assigned to Potosí from the same areas as those chosen by Toledo in 1578. The one exception is that the Arequipa men whom Toledo added in that year do not appear. Their stint in the mita was, indeed, short. Arequipa was excused from sending mitayos to Potosí by Viceroy Enríquez (1580–83) after the severe earthquake that struck southern Peru in 1582.[10]

Responsibility for collecting mitayos in the contributing areas, and sending them off to Potosí, lay fundamentally with the Spanish district officers—the *corregidores de indios*. By the end of Toledo's time, few mitayos went to Potosí from encomiendas—an outcome of the well-known policy of the Spanish crown in the mid-sixteenth century of replacing encomienda with corregimiento, encomenderos with corregidores, who were district officials directly in the royal employ.[11] In the particular matter of the mita, this change

10.   Capoche, *Relación*, pp. 136–39; on Arequipa, p. 145. For a comparison of the 1578 and 1633 mita source areas, a 1643 copy of Carvajal y Sande's repartimiento has been used: "Apuntamiento general hecho por el Señor Don Dionisio Pérez Manrique, presidente de la Real Audiencia de La Plata, de los indios efectivos que acuden a la mita del Cerro Rico de Potosí por el repartimiento hecho por el Señor Don Juan de Carvajal y Sande. . . ." Potosí, November 7, 1643 (AAGN, sala 13, cuerpo 23, ms 10–12).

11.   This process, an important matter that nevertheless lies outside the scope of this book, was set in motion by Governor Lope García de Castro in 1565, and was carried forward in the 1570s by Toledo, who in 1574 issued regulations for the corregidores de indios. See Guillermo Lohmann Villena, *El corregidor de indios en el Perú bajo los Austrias* (Madrid 1957), libro primero (pp. 3–93). According to this account, the main purposes of the change were to bring Indians more quickly into a Spanish style of polity, with the aim of eventual Indian self-government; to evangelize them more effectively; to suppress crime among them and check any threat of revolt against the Spanish; and to curb extortion by curacas of their own people. Lohmann hardly suggests the notion that creating the corregimiento system may have been a conscious attack on the power of the encomenderos; though it very possibly was so, just as the installation of corregidores in New Spain had been there thirty or more years before. See also Robert G. Keith, *Conquest and agrarian change: the emergence of the hacienda system on the Peruvian coast* (Cambridge, Mass., 1976), pp. 53–54.

seems unlikely to have caused much difference. The corregidores, as salaried employees of the crown, should clearly have been more assiduous in sending the required numbers of mitayos to Potosí from their jurisdictions than the encomenderos, who were private citizens dependent for their livelihood on those same workers. But the corregidores were in due course so often accused of withholding Indians for their own use that it seems likely that the corregimiento system yielded no better delivery of the mita than the encomenderos would have provided if they had remained in charge of the Indians.

Some notion of the procedure and atmosphere of the gathering of Indians bound for Potosí emerges from an account of the despatch of the Chucuito contingent of 1600. This may well have been a more formal affair than would have been found elsewhere, since the province of Chucuito was exceptionally populous and was run by a fully fledged royal governor rather than by a mere corregidor. Moreover, Viceroy Velasco had issued special orders in 1596 designed to curtail the Chucuito mitayos' practice of not returning home after their term, but rather of seeking refuge in remote places. For this purpose he required that all those going to Potosí should be gathered in one place and carefully counted. This count *(padrón)* should specify the name, ayllu, *parcialidad* (moiety), and pueblo of each mitayo. It should state how many women and children, and freight llamas, each man took. The padrón was then to be sent to the corregidor of Potosí, who should check that all those sent actually arrived; and that those who arrived, returned. Exempted from mita service (and this was standard practice) were curacas and principales, and men who performed certain church functions (singers, sacristans, treasurers, and schoolmasters); nor might unmarried Indian women, or anyone not liable for tribute, go to Potosí with the mita.[12]

---

12. This last prohibition was directed mainly at males under eighteen and over fifty. Unmarried girls might accompany their parents. See BAN Rück collection, item 2, ff. 135–39 (Minas catalog No. 468): provisión by Viceroy Velasco, Lima, November 1, 1596. Besides the exemption granted to men with church tasks, another was apparently taken informally by Indian craftsmen. This was the subject of another provisión from Velasco, of 1603, which noted that the number of Indian craftsmen had increased beyond the needs of the pueblos precisely because the status of *oficial* was thought to confer immunity from the mita. Velasco ordered that in towns of fewer than 200 people, exemption should extend only

To carry out these procedures, the governor of Chucuito in 1600, Don Luis de Guzmán, gathered his people together in late July to early August at the southern tip of the province—on the flatlands where the River Desaguadero leaves Lake Titicaca. The river, now the boundary between Peru and Bolivia at this point, was then also an important natural marker, separating the two provinces of Chucuito and Pacajes. The level, marshy area through which the river crawls is still an important gathering place. These days it provides space for a regular and well-attended contraband market. It was an ideal place for assembling and counting the mitayos. Guzmán, or rather his lieutenant governor, Lope de Burzeña (since Guzmán had to stay in the town of Chucuito to receive his successor), gathered the people on the west side of the river, not allowing them to cross the bridge. The active figures in the operation were principales chosen to go to Potosí from each of the moieties of the seven towns of the province: Chucuito itself, and Acora, Cepita, Ilavi, Juli, Pomata, and Yunguyo. How the principales were selected for the job is not stated.[13]

Assembling and counting the mitayos took, it seems, rather more than three weeks. Guzmán's first order for gathering the people was given on July 21, 1600. The mita was not sent off by Burzeña until August 14. The count was actually taken by one Don Pedro Cutipa, who came apparently from Ilavi, and who had been appointed, presumably by the governor, to be capitán of the whole mita from the province. He was assisted by four other Indian officials, two of whom were to return from Potosí within two months bearing documents confirming that the full quota of mitayos had been delivered there. The other two were to stay in Potosí as aides *(segundas personas)* to Cutipa.

The number of mitayos actually despatched on August 14, 1600 from the province of Chucuito was 1,749. In addition to these,

---

to one tailor, one shoemaker, one wool dyer, and one chairmaker. Other *oficiales*, whether previously excused or not, should go to the mita. BAN Rück collection, item 2, f. 168, *provisión* by Velasco, Lima, December 5, 1603. A later law, given early in the reign of Charles II, did specifically exempt all Indian master craftsmen from mita service. *(Recopilación*, 6.5.11, Don Carlos Segundo y la R[eina] G[obernante], nd.

13. See PCM CR 72, ff. 1–90, *padrón* of the Chucuito mita, 1600, beginning Ciudad de Chucuito, July 21, 1600.

however, the province's contingent included 399 who were already in Potosí. Lists of these were sent back to Chucuito by the Indian leaders in charge of the previous contingent. The total number was therefore 2,148—a figure remarkably close to the quota of 2,200 assigned to Chucuito at this time. There is no indication of how many years had passed since these mitayos last served. By regulation, of course, each served one year in seven. In view, however, of the population decline and out-migration afflicting Chucuito along with other mita-yielding areas by 1600 (to be discussed shortly), it is likely that town leaders had to enlist many who had served much more recently. Slightly over three-quarters of the mitayos were married (1,629, or 75.8 percent). Of the rest, 418 (19.5 percent) were bachelors, and 101 (4.7 percent) widowers. Allowing each married man a wife and two children (purely a "guesstimate"), the total shift of population, excluding curacas and other leaders, would be on the order of 7,000.[14] Each parcialidad of the seven towns (sixteen in all, since Juli had four) sent two or three leaders; so the total number of Indian supervisors was thirty or forty. The mitayos took with them no fewer than 11,703 llamas, or some five per man, each bearing a load of food (*carga de comida*) for consumption on the way. The curacas' llamas numbered 435, or an average of some 9 to 14 each, similarly loaded.

Although the organization of this despatch of mitayos may, for the reasons already mentioned, have been more formal than was usual, it may nevertheless serve as a guide to corresponding procedures elsewhere.[15] The complexity of the operation is clear—the collection of people parcialidad by parcialidad, their congregation at a central assembly point, the counting of men and animals, the

14. This total is confirmed by a statement of Alonso Mesías, in his memorial to Viceroy Velasco, "Sobre la cédulas del servicio personal de los indios," (*DII*, tomo 6, pp. 118–65, nd, but clearly between 1601 and 1603), p. 140.

15. Viceroy Velasco, indeed, singled out the Chucuito mita organization for special praise, comparing the lists of workers made in this case favorably with those supplied from other districts. He ordered district corregidores to be sure to make a count (padrón) of those men despatched, and to send them under the command of a capitán, who should be responsible for returning as many as he took. See BAN Rück collection, item 2, ff. 182–83 (Minas catalog No. 453), provisión of Velasco to corregidores of repartimientos supplying mitayos, Lima, June 30, 1601.

solicitation from Potosí of lists of those already there, again parcialidad by parcialidad. Capoche refers to the use of the *quipu* by
the Indian leaders in keeping track of mitayos,[16] but the Chucuito
document of 1600, some fifteen years later, clearly implies a written list *(memoria)*, as does Cañete in his *Guía de la Provincia de Potosí*.[17] The active and central part given to Indian leaders, both principales and segundas personas, is very clear in the 1600 document;
Spanish officials seem to have taken a largely supervisory rôle.

Chucuito was among the most distant of the mita-supplying
provinces, about 500 kilometers from Potosí as the crow flies.
Cañete states its distance at 130 leagues over the ground (from
the Desaguadero). There were four still more distant towns that
served as assembly points for mitayos: Tinta and Pomacanche at
180 leagues, Azángaro at 170, and Llampa at 160.[18] Little direct
information has come down to indicate how long the mitayos took
to reach Potosí from their various starting points. A report of 1620
compiled by the Viceroy Príncipe de Esquilache (1614–21) on the
matter of paying mitayos for time spent on the journey proposes
that they could be expected to advance three leagues a day, a distance suggested originally by the president of the Audiencia of La
Plata.[19] At that rate, mitayos from the most distant region (Tinta)
would have traveled for sixty days, and the average journeying
time would have been a little more than a month.[20]

The question of whether mitayos should be paid for time they
spent on their way to and from Potosí was one that arose early. In
1563 the crown issued a standing order that Indians should be paid

16.   *Relación*, p. 139.
17.   Quoted in Alberto Crespo Rodas, "El reclutamiento y los viajes en la 'mita'
del Cerro de Potosí," *(CIM*, tomo 1, pp. 467–82), p. 474.
18.   Cañete, *Guía*, pt. 1, ch. 6, para. 6.
19.   AGI Charcas 20, "Copia de una carta que el Virrey Príncipe de Esquilache
escribió a su Magestad en 29 de abril de 1620," f. 2v.
20.   A comment by Alonso Mesías suggests that a daily march of three leagues
was more than could be expected. According to him, the mita from Chucuito
took two months to reach Potosí because general progress was slowed down by
children—who were made to walk from the age of five upwards. If, as Cañete
states, Desaguadero lay 130 leagues from Potosí, then the rate of progress according to Mesías was only a little more than 2 leagues daily. See his "Sobre las cédulas
del servicio personal de los indios," p. 140.

while traveling to draft labor.[21] Nevertheless nothing suggests that such payment was made to Potosí mitayos in the latter part of the sixteenth century; and clearly none was made for much of the first half of the seventeenth. In 1618, Viceroy Esquilache, in response to royal orders, told employers receiving mitayos in Potosí to pay travel costs *(leguaje)* at a rate of 2 reales per day per person for journeys to and from the town.[22] This met with much opposition, as would be expected, and by 1627 nothing had yet been done. The crown again ordered compliance,[23], and in 1634 Viceroy Chinchón reported with some jubilation that his visitor to Potosí, Don Juan de Carvajal y Sande, had indeed managed to persuade the employers to pay leguaje.[24] But it is doubtful if this innovation persisted, especially in view of the employers' fierce hostility to the visitor.

Once they arrived in Potosí, the supreme authority over mitayos was the corregidor of the town. Indeed, the corregidor had wide executive powers over the mita throughout the area from which drafted men were drawn. This rankled with the presidents and oidores in La Plata, who regarded themselves as the senior royal representatives in Charcas, as indeed they were in jurisdiction. But control over the mita came early to be defined as a matter of administration *(gobierno)*, and only infrequently did the audiencia, in the period here in question, exercise gobierno in Charcas. It was the viceroy who had direct executive authority over the province, and hence ultimate control over the mita—a control delegated by him to the corregidores of Potosí.[25] This did not prevent interference

21. *Recopilación* 6.12.13, issued by Philip II at Monzón de Aragón on December 2, 1563, and repeated with specific reference to mining mitas in 1594, 1595, 1597, 1618, and 1627 (*Recopilación* 6.15.3).

22. AGI Lima 39, tomo 5, Esquilache to crown, "Gobierno No. 5," para. 8, Lima, April 29, 1620.

23. BAN Minas tomo 143 (Minas catalog No. 655), real cédula to Viceroy Guadalcázar, Madrid, January 13, 1627.

24. AGI Lima 45, tomo 1, Chinchón to crown, "Gobierno No. 2," Lima, April 9, 1634.

25. A real cédula of Madrid, February 15, 1567, conferred administrative power for the provinces of Peru solely on Licenciado Castro, the then governor of Peru. The same order denied the audiencias of Charcas and Quito even the faculty of hearing appeals on administrative decisions. Any such appeals should go before the Audiencia of Lima alone. See BAN Minas catalog No. 620. The rul-

in mita matters by presidents and oidores of La Plata from time to time; and in fact they were sometimes ordered to take part in the organization of draft labor, as, for example, in the case of Don Diego de Portugal, president of the audiencia, whom the Viceroy Marqués de Guadalcázar (1620–28) instructed to make a new *repartimiento general* in 1625.[26] In general, however, the ruling that the mita was a matter of gobierno, and therefore the corregidor's preserve, was observed, despite the audiencia's protests.

With rare exceptions, though, it seems, on available evidence, that corregidores were generally not notably active in either procuring or distributing mitayos, or in other aspects of mita regulation. They delegated these tasks to subordinates. The district corregidores were the crucial figures outside Potosí, since theirs was the responsibility for gathering mitayos and despatching them. The actual performance of these tasks, as has been pointed out, they passed on in large degree to local Indian authorities. Nevertheless, they were accountable to the corregidor of Potosí in mita affairs, and he was empowered to put pressure on them if they failed to deliver their men. An order from Viceroy Velasco in 1597, for example, authorized the corregidores of Potosí to send out agents to gather up missing mitayos at the expense of the corregi-

---

ing of 1567 is quoted in a provisión of Viceroy Guadalcázar of Lima, January 31, 1625. Gobierno should be exercised by audiencias only by reason of the death of a viceroy, according to a real cédula of March 19, 1550 directed to New Spain and Peru. In Peru, only the Audiencia of Lima should have gobierno, according to a royal letter to Viceroy Villar of October 19, 1586. (For the 1550 and 1586 orders, see BAN Rück collection, tomo 3, ff. 68v.–9, real cédula to Audiencia of La Plata, given at El Pardo on November 20, 1606, repeating that gobierno of Charcas devolved, in the absence of viceroy, onto the Audiencia of Lima.) Despite such orders the Audiencia of La Plata did briefly assume gobierno after the deaths of Viceroy Enríquez in 1583 and Viceroy Monterrey in 1606—and was reprimanded for doing so. An example that the mita was a matter of gobierno is clause 25 of Viceroy Velasco's ordinances accompanying his repartimiento of the mita given at Lima on August 31, 1599 (in AGI Charcas 134). For delegation of authority to the corregidores see, e.g., Viceroy Velasco to the Audiencia of La Plata, Callao, June 30, 1605, which also declares that in most cases the viceroy, not the audiencia, should hear appeals from mita decisions made by the corregidores. See BAN Minas catalog No. 491.

26. Portugal to crown, La Plata, March 25, 1625, in AGI Charcas 20.

dores to blame for the shortfall.[27] This, to judge from other documentation, was often done; although the cost ultimately passed over the district corregidores and on to the local Indian officials, to add to their already heavy financial burdens.

The role of local Indian leaders in the mita both outside and inside Potosí was clearly crucial. The manuscripts surveyed for this study do not, however, give a complete view of their functions. The case of the Chucuito mita of 1600, already described at some length, shows plainly the importance of native community leaders in gathering mitayos and families and in escorting them to Potosí. Once there, the mitayos fell under the supervision of a number of Indian capitanes. Six of these had been appointed by Toledo in 1575, and endowed with administrative powers over the mitayos. By the time Capoche wrote, a decade later, the number had grown to eleven (Viceroy Enríquez adding one, and the Audiencia of La Plata four more), almost all of whom were senior men, leaders of the large cultural groups that the Spanish identified as *naciones*.[28]

Evidence on these leaders' treatment of mitayos in their charge is mixed. On the one hand, it is perfectly obvious that the leaders, in order to keep up the numbers of mitayos they were expected to deliver under usually outdated quotas, abused their people. As early as the 1590s there are reports that caciques, faced with mitayo quotas they could not meet because of depopulation of their provinces, were substituting cash payments for workers; and since their own resources were quickly exhausted, they exacted funds from Indians in their jurisdictions. Another money-raising practice of mita leaders was to supply workers on demand (*indios de ruego*) to the corregidor and other high officials of Potosí, in return for goodly (though unspecified) cash payments, and presumably political favor.[29]

27. AGI Charcas 266, ms 24f., provisión of Velasco, Lima, February 2, 1597.
28. *Relación*, pp. 136–39.
29. AGI Indiferente General 1,239, two undated mss, certainly from the 1590s: "Lo que resulta de los pareceres de Luis Osorio de Quiñones y Sancho de Valenzuela sobre la reducción de indios de Potosí. . . ," and Luis Osorio de Quiñones to unidentified "muy poderoso señor." Alonso Mesías writes of a curaca who in

On the other hand, records do show that mita leaders sometimes came to the defense of their Indians, and successfully. In
1601, for instance, the captain of the Chucuito mitayos, Don Carlos Visa, at least for a time blocked the assignation of fifty-six of
his men to the Porco mines from Potosí. He simply refused to supply these workers, and when the business was taken before the
Audiencia of La Plata, made skillful use of the categorization of
the mita as a gobierno matter to deny the audiencia jurisdiction in
the case. The audiencia was obliged to ask the viceroy, Velasco, to
take a hand; which he duly did, ordering the corregidor of Potosí
to force Visa to deliver the men. The outcome is not known.[30]
Other similar cases might be cited. The impression given by the
evidence, however, is that the depredations of Indian officials
among their people outweighed the defense they provided for
mitayos.

A mitayo arriving in Potosí found his labor already assigned to
a mining or refining employer. Viceroys, and occasionally others,
made periodic repartimientos of the workers coming from the various mita districts, following the procedures started by Toledo. With
his three repartimientos (of 1573, 1575, and 1578), Toledo was a
more prolific reorganizer than later viceroys. Indeed, with Juan
de Matienzo's additional repartimiento of 1577, the decade of the
seventies saw four distributions made in Potosí. Rapid changes in
mining and refining practices, along with Toledo's propensity for
legislating, were doubtless responsible for these multiple revisions.
The manuscript record shows that succeeding repartimientos were
made at roughly ten-year intervals: 1582 (Viceroy Enríquez), 1591
(Viceroy Cañete), 1599 (Viceroy Velasco), 1609 (Viceroy Montesclaros), 1618 (Viceroy Esquilache), 1624 (Don Diego de Portugal,
president of La Plata), and finally in the pre-1650 period, the distri-

---

1601 confessed to a Jesuit in Potosí that, to provide cash in lieu of the workers
due from him, he had sold his mule, his llamas, and his clothing; had then bor-
rowed money; collected cash from his Indians; and finally pawned (*"empeñé"*) a
daughter to a Spaniard for 64 pesos. Having exhausted all money-raising possi-
bilities, and lacking means to meet the following week's demands, he saw no
solution but to hang himself. "Sobre las cédulas del servicio personal de los
indios," pp. 159–60.

30. BAN Rück collection, tomo 2, ff. 79–80 (Minas catalog No. 455), provisión
by Velasco, Lima, November 24, 1601.

bution of 1633 by Don Juan de Carvajal y Sande, visitor of Potosí by appointment of Viceroy Chinchón.

The purpose of the periodic reassignment of Indians was to ensure as far as possible that active refiners and miners received the labor they needed, while workers should not go to those who did not intend to use them for producing silver. This was a matter of conscious policy, though the policy was far from consistently realized.[31] There was continual complaint from administrators at all levels that recipients of mitayos rented their laborers out to other producers, and that mines and refineries were sold not so much for their own worth, but for the value of the mitayos assigned to them. This buying and selling of mita labor, however disturbing to Spanish governors (because it smelled of slavery), was a natural outcome of the unpredictability of mining fortunes. If a vein suddenly became barren, and its owner's refinery consequently grew short of ore, then the obvious source of income remaining to the owner was his mita laborers.

The mitayo newly arrived in Potosí was likely to be assigned to work among strangers. Little effort was made to keep men of the same origins together. Matienzo in 1577 did try to do so; as also did Carvajal y Sande in 1633. He, indeed, went further, and did his best to distribute Indians from single communities among as few employers as possible. Apart from any simplification of lan-

---

31. See PCM CR 229, "Libro de acuerdos de real hacienda," ff. 83v.–4v., *exhortatorio* of reales oficiales of Potosí, July 16, 1632. Also, AGI Lima 34, tomo 6, Viceroy Velasco to crown, Lima, October 10, 1603, para. 2, explaining how viceroys normally organized the allocation of mitayos. When the viceroy thought a new repartimiento necessary, he ordered the corregidor, alcalde mayor de minas, and veedores of the cerro to examine the mines and refineries, and particularly to assess their productivity. A report was then sent to the viceroy, who, after consultation with experienced people, assigned Indians in accordance with it. Velasco's own repartimiento general of the Potosí mita, dated Lima, August 31, 1599, conformed to these principles. (For it, see AGI Charcas 34). It allotted mitayos to refineries and mines in accordance with the assiduity of the owners. Such comments as "suele traer labor" and "trae siempre gruesa y buena labor" are frequently attached to the names of recipients of mitayos in this repartimiento. Similar comments are found in the repartimiento of Don Diego de Portugal, in Potosí, November 15, 1624. (See PCM CR 201, ff. 269–79v.). *Recopilación* 6.15.16 likewise enjoins the efficient and just allotment of Indians in the repartimientos of Potosí.

guage problems that might be achieved by keeping groups together, Matienzo hoped that Indians would work better under a single master, and that the master, having a work force composed largely of men from one place, would grow better disposed toward them.[32] Carvajal, for his part, hoped that keeping workers together would simplify assembly of mitayos each week for work, since men from the same pueblos lived, according to him, in the same parishes and part of the *ranchería*. A master would therefore be able to lay hands on his entire work force with a minimum of trouble, and "without resorting to the pernicious and wretched abuse of [using] fetchers."[33] Whether this hope was realized is unknown. But at least in making this statement Carvajal provides a small clue about the mechanics of the weekly distribution of mitayos in Potosí—a process which, precisely because it became so deeply embedded in the fabric of the town's life, is barely referred to in extant documents.

Even the broad outlines of the work régime under the mita are unclear. Toledo, in his later repartimientos, divided the mita gruesa coming to Potosí each year into three equal mitas ordinarias, so that no Indian should do mita work for more than four months of the year. This threefold division persisted, but the difficulty is in knowing exactly how the individual worker fitted into it. Some sources, including Capoche,[34] seem quite clearly to indicate that a mitayo worked for four months continuously (save weekends), and then had the rest of the year free of service. This, however, would seem an excessively, even insupportably, harsh working régime; besides which, other sources very strongly suggest that the individual worked in a one-week-on, two-weeks-off pattern.[35] Practice probably lay somewhere between these two systems. The Indian mita leaders in Potosí were obliged to produce each week a set number of men for the mines and refineries specified in the current repartimiento. In practice they probably took for their

32. AGI Lima 45, tomo 1, No. 1, f. 9–9v., Carvajal y Sande's preamble to his repartimiento, Potosí, September 3, 1633.
33. ". . . sin valerse del pernicioso y reprobado abuso de sacadores. . . ," ibid.
34. *Relación*, pp. 135, 144.
35. For example, AGI Charcas 134, item No. 5 in folder of mss "sin fecha": an anonymous, undated (though clearly post-1607) account of the mita system, arguing principally that mitayos should be relieved of paying tribute.

quotas any workers they could find, paying little attention to the niceties of the rotation. Rotation must have been ever harder to maintain as the numbers of mitayos fell—so that individual mitayos would have found themselves working an average of over four months a year (perhaps with some periods of two or three weeks together, and occasional one-week spells for relief) well before 1600.

In addition to the extra pressure of mining and refining work placed on mitayos by their own decline in numbers, obligations to serve in other capacities during their resting (de huelga) periods soon arose. Toledo in 1578 ordered the mita captains to supply 200 indios meses from the mita ordinaria (chapter 3 above). By Capoche's time the 200 were being drawn from the resting contingent, as were some 2,000 others for appointed tasks. Capoche states these as follows:[36]

150 *indios de plaza*—to be made available every Monday in the plaza for service as domestics in the houses of needy people, in those of regidores, in monasteries and hospitals.

80 *indios para los trajines*—to help freighters of food into Potosí.

70 *indios para las salinas*—to mine salt at Yocalla.

100 *indios para los reparos de las lagunas*—to maintain the reservoirs during the dry winter season.

60 Indians—to Dr. Franco, by a grant made by Toledo as a stipend to Franco, the doctor and surgeon whom he had appointed to attend Indians sick in the hospital and in their parishes.

300 Indians—to work at the new silver strike of Guariguari, under a draft made by the Audiencia of La Plata. (Capoche notes these were later withdrawn.)

141 Indians—to accompany the Factor Juan Lozano Machuca and his soldiers as carriers on his campaign against the Chiriguanaes.

100 Indians—to serve various people under grants by the Audiencia of La Plata. (Capoche specifies no particular purpose.)

1,000 Indians—to work at the Porco mines. Two-thirds were to serve at any one time, with the rest being de huelga.

Capoche's account suggests clearly that adjustments were often made in these allocations from the huelga.[37] Clearer still, however,

---

36. *Relación*, p. 142. Capoche's commentary on each group has been summarized here.

37. *Relación*, p. 144.

is the outcome of the allocations: that the fraction of the mita gruesa being permanently employed in draft work grew, as a result of them, to almost a half. Worse still, for the workers, was that this extra labor does not seem to have been paid. Capoche, at least, makes no reference to wages for it.

A manuscript of 1603 corroborates Capoche's figures of drafts from the huelga, showing the following allocations:[38]

indios de plaza	150
indios de mesas [sic]	200
To Porco	800
para las salinas (Yocalla)	75
para los trajines (freighting)	100
for *aderezo de lagunas*	100 (not for a full year)
for hospital and doctor	60
Total	1,485

Apart from a reduction of 200 in the number of men allocated to Porco, and the elimination of special grants, these figures are very close to Capoche's. The same manuscript estimates the mita ordinaria at 4,467 in 1603, so that the total number of Indians drafted at any one time was approaching 6,000—again almost a half of the mita gruesa. Further confirmation of the mitayos' working for half their time in Potosí, rather than the nominal third, comes in 1608 from Felipe de Godoy, a former treasurer of the Potosí mint. Godoy takes it for granted that the standard mita working year was by then six months (and in passing conveys equally clearly that the pattern of work was one week on, then one off).[39]

Most mitayos lived in the main Indian quarter, usually known simply as the *ranchería*, lying between the Ribera and the foot of the cerro. It would appear from the late sixteenth or early seventeenth century *Planta general* of Potosí that other rancherías encircled the Spanish center of the town. But the term *ranchería*, unless

38. SAU, tomo 330/122, ff. 235v.–37, "1603. Relación de los indios que se ocupan en la labor del Cerro de Potosí y en los ingenios y beneficio de metales, así de la mita como mingados," anonymous.

39. BL Sloane mss 3,055, item 4 (ff. 26–73), "Phelipe de Godoy a la magestad de Phelipe 3° en respuesta de una carta que por su orden le escribió Juan Ruiz de Velasco. . . ," La Plata, February 14, 1608. See especially f. 47.

otherwise qualified, meant the native township south of the Ribera. According to the *Planta general*, the ranchería consisted of ten parishes—from east to west, San Cristóbal, La Concepción, San Pablo, San Sebastián, San Francisco de los naturales, San Pedro, Nuestra Señora de Copacabana, Santiago, Santa Bárbara, and San Benito— parishes whose churches still survive today to a greater or lesser degree, and some of which were undoubtedly among the eight added by Toledo to the existing six in 1573.[40]

Toledo tried to impose on the ranchería a gridiron plan; but the pattern was lost as the population grew. Arzáns reports some Spanish vecinos as thinking that the ranchería had a better site than did the Spanish section of the city, since it did not suffer from the excess of springs that made the ground to the north of the Ribera an unstable base for buildings. The ranchería had enough ground water, however, to supply a "multitude of wells." According to Arzáns, "there live in each house . . . twenty or thirty Indians, in rooms so small that there scarcely fit in them a bed, a fireplace, and up to eight or ten jugs of that drink of theirs [chicha], which occupy the best place in that confined space."[41] At present, no clue exists to the ownership of these houses—whether they were the property of Spaniards or Indian leaders, and rented by mitayos; or that of the Indian communities sending workers to Potosí; or even in some cases possibly that of the mitayos themselves. The cost of housing to mitayos is therefore also unknown, and is a large missing element in any calculation of the value of their income.

Up to 1600, or very shortly thereafter, it was the custom for Spanish employers of mitayos to go into the ranchería and other Indians quarters on Monday mornings to seek out the workers assigned to them. The precise mechanism of this collection is not visible. It seems likely that the mita captains delegated the gathering of the men to lesser Indians: town curacas or ayllu leaders. But this system was then abandoned, perhaps because of the "troubles and

---

40. Capoche, *Relación*, p. 169. Capoche does not state exactly which were the parishes added by Toledo.

41. *Historia*, tomo 1, pp. 42-3. " . . . viven en cada casa . . . 20 o 30 indios en unos aposentos tan pequeños que apenas caben tan solamente una cama, un fogón, y hasta ocho o 10 [sic] cántaros de aquel su brebaje, que tienen el mejor lugar en aquella estrechez."

tyrannies" imposed on Indians by the Spaniards that one witness mentions.[42] The procedure was replaced by one in which mitayos were gathered in a single place between the town and the cerro, presumably by their own leaders, and there distributed among the employers. In time an enclosure for this purpose was obviously built, since in 1625 a reference is made to the reconstruction of a *cerca* on Guaina Potosí (the smaller hill immediately north of the cerro, and overlooking the ranchería), where Spanish officials evidently attended to ensure a just distribution of laborers.[43]

Toledo, in his 1574 ordinances, laid down a work week for mitayos of six days.[44] By the early seventeenth century, however, if not before, this was reduced to five days, since Monday was taken up in the collection and distribution of mitayos, and delivery of them to mines and refineries; so that work did not begin until Tuesday. It continued until Saturday evening. The weekly assembly was obviously a drawn-out and somewhat hectic affair. There are occasional indignant references by Spaniards to Indians' Sunday carousals, sometimes continuing till Monday and even Tuesday, which must have slowed matters down.[45] Capoche suggested that the mita captains, if provided with horses or mules, would be able to check their people's excesses more effectively, and also contribute better to the assembly of workers on Monday. But, he complained, the captains were themselves the first to get drunk.[46]

Mitayos, in fact, spent a good part of their Sunday waiting to be paid—again a source of occasional complaint from conscientious Spaniards who disapproved of the Indians' thus being robbed of their rest day. A general ruling existed, indeed, from the beginning of the seventeenth century that all Indian workers, whether

42.   AGI Charcas 51, Carlos Corso de Leca, "En cumplimiento de lo que vuestra excelencia me manda haga relación tocante al repartimiento de los indios de mita. . . ," Potosí, March 1, 1617, para. 2.

43.   AGI Lima 40, Viceroy Guadalcázar to crown, "Gobierno No. 2," Lima, October 31, 1625, para. 7.

44.   ". . . que trabajen toda la semana excepto las fiestas . . .": clause 3 of the title "De los desmontes, trabajo y paga de los indios" in his mining ordinances of La Plata, February 7, 1574 (Levillier, *Gobernantes*, tomo 8, p. 231).

45.   AGI Lima 35, tomo 2, Viceroy Montesclaros to crown, "Minas," Callao, March 28, 1609, para. 12; or AGI Charcas 415, tomo 2, ff. 205–6, real cédula to Montesclaros, Aranjuez, April 20, 1608.

46.   *Relación*, p. 141.

mitayos or voluntary, should be paid on Saturday evening, so that they should have Sunday free for rest and worship.[47] But by that time Potosí had slipped irrevocably into a Tuesday to Saturday working week, with no time remaining for payment on Saturday evening. And there were those in authority who thought that waiting for wages on Sunday at least reduced the Indians' opportunities for imbibing chicha then.

The daily rates of mita pay set by Toledo in 1574–75 prevailed for the next twenty years, until Viceroy Velasco raised them slightly, as follows:[48]

	mine workers	freighters of ore (cerro to refineries)	refinery workers
Toledo	3.5 reales p.d.	3.0 reales p.d.	2.75 reales p.d.
Velasco	4.0 reales p.d.	3.5 reales p.d.	3.0 reales p.d.

Velasco's revision was the last in the period to 1650.

Two obvious questions arise over wages: were they really paid, and, if so, what were they worth? Both are hard to answer with certainty, for lack of apposite information. No sixteenth-century account books for mines came to light during research for this book. But a few such books surviving from the 1630s do suggest strongly that the statutory rates were being paid then: though, of course, the accounts in question refer to a minute proportion of Potosí's mines and refineries.[49] There is, nevertheless, some force in the argument that if wages were paid in the 1630s, a time of general decline in mining, they were likely to have been paid also in the

47.   *Recopilación*, 6.15.9, dating from 1601, and repeated in 1608.

48.   For Velasco's rates, see AGI Lima 39, tomo 5, Viceroy Esquilache to crown, "Gobierno No. 5," Lima, April 29, 1620, para. 3. The date of Velasco's revision of wages is not clear from this document. Velasco assumed office in 1595, and the new rates were in effect by August 1600. (See AGI Charcas 80, untitled ms, headed "Charcas 1600," f. 30v). (JHR).

49.   BAN Minas tomo 9 (Minas catalog No. 720), "1630–1638. Cuaderno 1 de los autos seguidos por Don Rodrigo de Mendoza y Manrique, administrador y arrendatario que fue de las minas y los ingenios del General Don Pedro Sores de Ulloa en el cerro y la Ribera de Potosí, con Doña Francisca Campuzano, viuda y heredera de aquél. . . ," containing account books of an ingenio and a small number of mines in the cerro. These accounts are clearly original daybooks kept by the administrator. There is no reason to suppose they were falsified.

late sixteenth and in the early seventeenth centuries, which were in comparison times of great prosperity. Absence of complaints by Indians of nonpayment is another positive indication. The official protectors of Indians were not inactive, and brought other grievances in mining before the justices. Again, Jesuit critics of the mita, while seizing avidly on multifarious abuses of laborers, made no reference to failure to pay wages.[50] Finally, there is the evidence of witnesses. Toledo himself wrote in his late despatches from Peru in the evident belief that his ordained wages were reaching the workers. There exists also a rather odd questionnaire, with answers, of 1577—odd because its purpose is not apparent—in which several vecinos of Potosí confirm both the wage rates set by Toledo and that those wages were truly disbursed.[51]

On the value of wages the evidence is equally scanty. Hardly any prices are available for Indian staples, whose cost would be the surest measure of the worth of earnings. A *Descripción* of Potosí of 1603 offers some round figures for prices of maize, potatoes, *chuño*, *oca*, and *charqui* (jerked beef). To judge by these, the amounts of the different foods that the three categories of mitayos could buy each week if they earned on the scale set by Velasco, and spent all their mita income on one food alone, would have been as follows:[52]

50. Antonio de Ayáns, "Breve relación de los agravios que reciben los indios que hay desde cerca del Cuzco hasta Potosí. . . ," 1596; and "Pareceres de los Padres de la Compañía de Jesús de Potosí," 1610; both in Rubén Vargas Ugarte (ed.), *Pareceres jurídicos en asuntos de Indias* (Lima 1951), pp. 35–88 and 116–31 respectively.

51. AGI Charcas 40, ms 77, Potosí, December 30, 1577, información by Juan Calvete (JHR).

52. "Descripción de la Villa y minas de Potosí. Año de 1603," in Marcos Jiménez de la Espada (ed.), *Relaciones geográficas de Indias—Perú*, tomo 1, (BAE, tomo CLXXXIII, Madrid 1965), pp. 381–82, gives prices per fanega, in pesos ensayados, thus: chuño, 6; maize, 5; potatoes and oca, 3. Charqui is shown as costing 1.5 pesos per arroba. These prices cannot be confirmed from any other contemporary primary source. But early seventeenth-century records do provide prices for llamas, wine, and coca that closely coincide with those given in the "Descripción" for those items, which suggests that the writer of the "Descripción" stated the prices of his day with some accuracy. Alonso Mesías, in his "Sobre las cédulas del servicio personal de los indios," p. 149, shows the price of charqui as

mitayo	wage for a five day week (reales)	food purchasable (to the nearest pound) in a seven day week				
		potatoes	oca	maize	chuño	charqui
mine worker	20	80	80	44	33	25
freighter	17.5	70	70	39	29	22
refinery worker	15	60	60	33	25	19

In the following table, the quantities of food purchasable with the weekly wage are shown translated into daily kilocaloric equivalents. That is to say, by spending his entire earnings on food, a mitayo could have purchased each day these numbers of kilocalories in either potatoes, or maize, or charqui. The lack of precision of the figures cannot, of course, be overemphasized.[53] They hold, also, only for the opening years of the seventeenth century.

---

3 pesos corrientes per arroba, or about 1.2 times the price given in the "Descripción." The calculations in this table are made on the assumptions (drawn from contemporary sources) that an arroba weighed 25 pounds; and that 1 peso ensayado was worth 425 maravedís, and one peso corriente, 272 *maravedís*. It is further assumed that a fanega was the equivalent of 2.5 U.S. bushels (Stephen Naft, in *Conversion equivalents in international trade*, Philadelphia, nd., p. 336, shows the modern fanega in Chile and Peru as, respectively, 2.575 and 2.36 U.S. bushels, though not giving a value for Bolivia); that the weights of 1 U.S. bushel of potatoes and of maize are, respectively, 60 pounds and 56 pounds (ibid., p. 193); and that (by analogy with Naft's figures) 1 bushel of oca and of chuño weigh, respectively, 60 pounds and 50 pounds.

53. The figures are rounded to the nearest 100. They show the amounts of food purchasable with the wages earned in a working week of five days, spent over seven days. Caloric values of the three foods shown are taken from Table 1 of Catherine F. Adams, *Nutritive value of American foods in common units*, (Agricultural Handbook No. 456, Agricultural Research Service, United States Department of Agriculture, Washington D.C., 1975). This source provides no values for oca and chuño . The values per pound of potatoes, maize, and dried, chipped beef (the closest equivalent in Adams's table to charqui) are, respectively, 454, 436, and 921 kilocalories. It is assumed that the maize on sale in Potosí was pure grain, and that the weights quoted do not, therefore, include the cob. Adams estimates the caloric value of corn on the cob, with the cob constituting 45 percent of the weight, at 240 per pound. The assumption here is that the cob in Potosí at the time in question made up a larger proportion of the total weight (say 50 percent), so that the caloric value for pure corn used here is 50/55 x 240 x 2 kilocalories (= 436).

	kilocalories purchasable daily with mita wage		
	potatoes	maize	charqui
mine worker	5,200	2,800	3,300
freighter	4,500	2,400	2,900
refinery worker	3,900	2,100	2,500

Clearly, assuming that the mita wages were indeed regularly paid and that prices of food were as in the scanty sources recording them, the individual mitayo stood some chance of securing through his earnings the number of calories necessary to enable him to carry out his work. (Three to four thousand kilocalories daily may be taken as enough for a heavy laborer.)[54] If he had a family in Potosí, however, either they or he must have suffered lack of food if the only source of income was the mita wage. A very few passing references appear to women and children's working in tasks connected with silver production. Capoche, for instance, mentions that women and children sieved crushed ore in refineries; and the "Descripción" of 1603 relates that both would search for pieces of ore abandoned on the surface (an occupation described by the verb *pallar*).[55] In all probability, however, wives and children had to work extensively in nonmining tasks so as to buy the food that the man's wage would not cover. And when the extra costs of housing, clothing, tributes and other levies (not to mention the journey to and from Potosí) are taken into account, it is clear enough that a mitayo had no choice but to seek work during his six months in Potosí when he was free of the mita.

This is made quite plain by an estimate of 1608, drawn up by

54.   This estimate is based on the calculation made by Sherburne F. Cook and Woodrow Borah of the daily caloric expenditure of a typical Aztec farmer or *cargador* in preconquest Mexico. Their estimate of 2,785 for a working day has been increased here since the mitayos' work régime seems likely to have been heavier than that of the Aztec laborer considered by Cook and Borah. See their essay "Indian food production and consumption in Central Mexico before and after the Conquest (1500–1650)," ch. 2 of *Essays in population history. Mexico and California. Volume Three* (Berkeley 1979), p. 157. The probable body sizes of central Andean mitayos and of the Mexicans considered by Cook and Borah seem comparable (at 50 to 55 kilograms) (ibid., Table 2.1).
55.   *Relación*, p. 122; "Descripción," p. 377.

Felipe de Godoy, of a mitayo's expenses in Potosí during his six months of obligatory work:[56]

		pesos corrientes
1.	tribute *(tasa)* at 32 pesos a year	16.0.0
2.	*granos* at 0.5 real weekly	1.5.0
3.	hospital	0.4.0
4.	10 fanegas of maize and chuño (combined), bought retail at 12 pesos the fanega	120.0.0
5.	meat, fish, firewood	25.0.0
6.	chile, salt, other extra foods *(chucherías)*	6.0.0
7.	clothing—to replace that destroyed in mine work	5.0.0
8.	candles, supplied at worker's cost	26.0.0
total		200.1.0

For twenty-six weeks' work, at 2.5 pesos (the maximum rate, given to mine workers), the mitayo received 65 pesos. He therefore had to find, according to Godoy's calculations of his costs, 135.1.0 pesos for himself—either bringing that sum with him to Potosí in cash or goods, or earning it during his six months de huelga. Godoy's figures do not seem inflated. The food prices are rather higher than those in the "Descripción" of 1603, but that may be accounted for by retail buying. Granos and hospital costs will be discussed in due course. And, of course, Godoy's estimates here are for an individual worker's expenses. Again, it seems clear that the mita wage, at least in the early years of the seventeenth century, was far from being enough to support a family.

The mitayo's burden was made the heavier by the constant decline in the numbers of drafted men actually appearing in Potosí for work. Though counts of draftees are at best imprecise, and generally suspect because they were made, or rather estimated, by people with points to disprove or prove, there can be little doubt that what was called the *entero* of the mita, or the total number of Indians appearing for a year's service, declined constantly from the time Toledo gave form to his third and largest mita in 1578. Juan Ortiz de Zárate, corregidor of Potosí from 1592 to 1594, asserted that in 1592–93 more than five-sixths of the mitayos supposed to

---

56. "Phelipe de Godoy a la magestad de Phelipe 3°. . . ," f. 46v.

be in the town were indeed there, though in 1594 Licenciado Juan Díaz de Lopidana, an oidor of the Audiencia of La Plata, sent to take control of the mita from Zárate, maintained that scarcely half (6,900 of 13,400) were present.[57] Both estimates seem exaggerated—Zárate's excessively high in view of the recent smallpox epidemic that he himself had stated had reduced the entero; and Lopidana's far too low, in the light of later reports. For instance, in 1622, Alonso Martínez de Pastrana, an official visitor of Potosí, calculated that the entero was about a third below its statutory level.[58] The decline may well have accelerated after then. In 1633, for example, the province of Pacajes was reputedly sending to Potosí only 500 of the 1,300 mitayos annually due.[59] And in 1649, the mita ordinaria was estimated by the corregidor of Potosí to be only 2,800, which suggests a mita gruesa of some 8,500—a figure far below the 12,500 or so who should have been present that year. The number of actual mita workers was still smaller, since the figure of 2,800 also included "Indians in silver"—men for whose presence cash was substituted, by either the curaca or the workers themselves, to enable the employer to hire others in their place. (This practice, and its possible ramifications, will be discussed below.) Indeed, in 1650 the viceroy relayed to the king another report from the corregidor of Potosí stating that only 800 mitayos had appeared in person *(entregados efectivos)* for the mita, while 800 others had been "delivered" in cash. If this was truly so, not only was the mita failing to bring to Potosí some four fifths of the number of workers it should have yielded, but also there had been an immense slump in numbers between 1649 and 1650.[60]

57.   Juan Ortiz de Zárate to ?, Potosí, August-September 1593 (ned), in AGI Charcas 17; vecinos of Potosí to crown, nd (but clearly 1594), para. 2, in AGI Charcas 32 ms 32.

58.   Pastrana to crown, Potosí, March 22, 1622, f. 2v., in AGI Charcas 36.

59.   BAN Minas catalog No. 683, "1633. Don Gabriel Fernández Guarachi, indio, capitán general enterador de la mita en 1634, sobre los trabajos que Don Antonio Mogollón de Rivera, corregidor de La Paz, le opone en el cumplimiento de su comisión," f. 15 (letter of Fernández Guarachi to the Audiencia of La Plata, Pacajes, November 8, 1633).

60.   Don Juan Velarde Treviño to crown, Potosí, July 31, 1649, in AGI Charcas 21; Conde de Salvatierra to crown, "No. 53, gobierno secular," Lima, March 20, 1650, in AGI Lima 54, tomo 3.

While collapse on this scale in the space of a few months stretches belief thin, there is no resisting the conclusion that a general and severe decline in the number of mitayos received by Potosí had come about by the mid-seventeenth century. Several clear reasons for this decline are visible, though it is hard to rank their importance.

One central point should be made clear at the start. The drop in numbers of mitayos at Potosí was to only a small extent the result of reductions in the statutory levies made on Indian communities. With few exceptions, the numbers demanded annually from the native population remained much as Toledo had set them. His mita gruesa of 1578 comprised 14,181 workers. That of Viceroy Cañete in 1591 specified 13,302, as did Viceroy Velasco's in 1599. In 1609 Viceroy Montesclaros provided for a mita gruesa of 12,720; in 1618, Viceroy Esquilache for one of 12,882; in 1624, Don Diego de Portugal (president of the Audiencia of La Plata, acting under orders of Viceroy Guadalcázar) for one of 12,795; and in 1633, Don Juan de Carvajal y Sande, acting for Viceroy Chinchón, for one of 12,354. There was, therefore, an official reduction of only 1,827 in the mita gruesa, or some 13 percent, between 1578 and 1633 (and no further cut before 1650).[61]

The severe fall in the number of mitayos presenting themselves for labor in Potosí was therefore largely the result of quotas' not being filled. One clear reason for that was population decline in the mita area, even though this was not recognized by Spanish administrators until the early years of the seventeenth century. The Viceroy Marqués de Montesclaros (1606–1614), for example, noted in 1610 that in some places the natives were so diminished (*acabados*) that it was impossible for them to send full contingents to Potosí.[62] Ten years later, the Príncipe de Esquilache reported that the decline had so persisted that from several communities around Potosí—Puna, Chaquí, San Lucas, Tocobamba, Potobamba, Tinguipaya, Yura, Visisa, Caiza, and Toropalca, none of which lay

---

61. AGI Charcas 266, ms 3, f. 16, auto of Don Juan de Carvajal y Sande, Potosí, May 15, 1634. Carvajal gives the mita ordinaria in each case. The mita gruesa is obtained simply by multiplying by three.

62. AGI Charcas 54, Montesclaros to crown, "H. Minas de plata y oro," Callao, March 22, 1610, para. 4.

more than twelve leagues from the town—no mita came at all, nor had done so for many years past.[63] Chinchón was sure, in 1635, that those who maintained that no loss of Indian numbers had occurred (as did Don Juan de Lizarazu, president in La Plata, in 1636) were wrong: "the most pious, sensible and safe [opinion] is that their deterioration has been great, and experience so reveals it in the re-inspections and reassessments that are made."[64] An anonymous writer on the mita in the late 1630s asserted that some communities had to send half their tributaries annually to Potosí, so severe was the loss of people.[65]

Modern research on the demography of the period shows that these observations were well founded, if tardy. Numbers of Indians in fact fell from the time of Toledo's general census in the early 1570s—or rather, they continued on a downward track that had begun with or before the conquest. In the area of present Peru, from which much of the Potosí mita came, the fall between 1570 and 1620 was on the order of 50 percent.[66] The decline persisted into the early eighteenth century, though probably at a progressively slower rate.[67] A variety of dismal causes, which are all too familiar to the historian of colonial Spanish America, brought about this slump. Epidemics of European, Asian, and African diseases destroyed people of all ages. Warfare took a toll in the early post-conquest decades—whether Spanish against Indian, or Indian against Indian (through the Spanish use of native auxiliaries), or less directly in conflicts of Spanish against Spanish (as in the Pizarrist-royalist struggle in Peru and Charcas, which may not have killed many Indians outright, but which, as has been seen, brought suffering and mortality through disturbance of everyday life, especially through theft of food and animals). General disruption of economy, society, and worldview may indeed, in the longer term,

---

63. AGI Charcas 54, Esquilache to crown, "Gobierno No. 4," Lima, April 24, 1620.

64. AGI Lima 45, Chinchón to crown, "Gobierno y hacienda No. 46," para. 7, Lima, May 1, 1635.

65. AGI Charcas 134, ms 5 in folder of undated mss.

66. Noble David Cook, *Demographic collapse: Indian Peru, 1520–1620*, (Cambridge, England, 1981), p. 118 (for summary figures) and pp. 247–55 (for a summary of the causes of the decline).

67. Nicolás Sánchez Albornoz, *La población de América Latina. Desde los tiempos pre-colombinos al año 2000* (Madrid 1973), p. 113.

have been as serious a menace to the native population as disease: disease killed people; disruption hindered the conception of children to replace those removed by illness.

Potosí and the region from which it drew the mita certainly suffered from disease. While no special search was made for records of illness, the manuscripts consulted for this book revealed several bouts of sickness in Potosí, its surroundings, and over larger areas of the viceroyalty of Peru between 1570 and 1650. These are combined in the following list with serious epidemics previously identified by Henry Dobyns as having occurred in Peru in the same period.[68]

period	place	diseases
1572–73	Peru	smallpox, measles[1]
1584	Peru (especially Potosí)	unidentified *pestilencia*[2]
1585(D)	Peru, Quito, Santa Fe	smallpox, measles
1589(D)	Potosí	influenza
1590–93(D)	Potosí, Charcas, all Peru	smallpox, measles, influenza[3]
1615	Charcas	unidentified *enfermedades contagiosas*[4]
1618–19(D)	Quito, Lima, central *sierras*, Potosí	measles *(sarampión y alfombrilla)*[5]
1628(D)	Peru	measles
1634–35(D)	Peru	measles

68. "D" suffixed to the date indicates an epidemic mentioned by Henry F. Dobyns in "An outline of Andean epidemic history to 1720," *Bulletin of the history of medicine,* 37:6 (November-December 1963), pp. 493–515. Other sources and information are shown by numbered notes, as follows:

1. AGI Lima 270, tomo 1, f. 418, Don Francisco Manrique de Lara to Juan de Ovando, Lima, April 8, 1573.
2. PCM CR 7, f. 102, acuerdo de real hacienda, Potosí, September 5, 1584. This may be an early mention of the 1585 epidemic pointed out by Dobyns.
3. The early 1590s were a time of particularly severe disease, with various waves of sickness passing over the viceroyalty. For the incidence of these in Potosí and Charcas, see AGI Charcas 32 ms 17, cabildo to crown, Potosí, March 2, 1590 (stating that mortality was not yet high in Potosí); AGI Charcas 17, passim (petitions of curacas of Presto, Tarabuco, Chayanta, Visisa, Chaquí, Tacobamba, Tinguipaya, Potobamba, Sipesipe, all indicating widespread and serious measles and smallpox, with heavy mortality, in Charcas); AGI Charcas 35 ms 79, Diego Bravo, contador of Potosí, to crown, Potosí, March 18, 1593 (relating that during his recent service as corregidor of Porco, he

Potosí's labor force was reduced by these afflictions, as observers of the day realized; but what was not realized by miners and administrators was the grievous possibility that Potosí itself aggravated the ill effects of epidemics and contributed to their frequency. By concentrating population on what was, for the time and place, a huge scale, Potosí obviously exposed larger numbers of people to infection than would have been the case if it had not existed. In addition, the constant to and fro of people in various activities—mitayos, traders, freighters, and herdsmen serving this great market—undoubtedly accelerated the spread of disease across the countryside.

If Potosí exacerbated the effects of introduced disease, it was also a prime cause of disruption of native life. The large movements of people to and from the town, from its earliest days, cannot but have brought interruptions of agricultural cycles. Some of the encomienda-mitayos examined by Licenciado Polo in 1550 said that relatives farmed their lands and kept up their houses while they were away; but it seems unlikely that this was always so, after the expansion of the mita in Toledo's time, and especially as communities became obliged to send ever larger proportions of their members to Potosí in order to meet fixed labor quotas. The degree of disruption added by Potosí to the disorganization caused by the

---

had seen Indians die by the roadside as they brought in their llama trains; and estimating mortality from smallpox at perhaps 25 percent of the population of Peru).

4.   BAN Audiencia de Charcas, libros de acuerdos, tomo 3, f. 118, *parecer* of Audiencia, La Plata, July 8, 1627 [sic]. This may have been a bout of diptheria, beginning in Cuzco, and moving south, mentioned by Dobyns (p. 509).

5.   This began in Quito during 1618, traveled down the coast to Lima, and then entered the highlands, killing many criollos but still more Indians, according to the viceroy—who instructed doctors to prepare prescriptions for simple remedies, which were then printed and sent to all corregidores and parish priests in the sierra east and south of Lima. (AGI Lima 38, tomo 4, Esquilache to crown, "Gobierno No. 22," para. 1, Lima, March 27, 1619). The incidence of disease in Potosí was high between May and August 1619. Sixteen temporary hospitals were set up in the Indian rancherías, attended by the corregidor, the town councillors, and private people—with the result, so the corregidor maintained, that few Indians died. Worms that consumed the intestines "and other parts" were an especially nasty accompaniment to this sickness, though they were successfully combatted with clysters. See AGI Charcas 52, Don Francisco Sarmiento de Sotomayor to "vuestra señoría," Potosí, March 25, 1620; and also to crown, Potosí, March 17, 1621.

conquest in general probably cannot be usefully estimated; but the mere fact that the mita alone shifted annually, according to Toledo's rules, between a sixth and a fifth of the tributaries from a large portion of the central Andean upland serves as an indicator of disruption. Since at least some of the mitayos took wives with them to Potosí (as the despatch of the mita from Chucuito in 1600 shows), and presumably some children also, it is probably not an exaggeration to suggest that the mita drew to Potosí, along with the mitayos, an equal number of dependents. So the annual movement of population resulting from the mita may have reached in some years 25,000. To these must be added a substantial number of non-mita workers, in mining and other occupations. Some of these came and went, but others stayed in Potosí.

The permanent displacement of people that Potosí brought about was, indeed, a further and serious effect that the town had on the native population falling within its ambit. The displacement took various forms. The town itself acted as a great magnet on population. This might seem strange, since the mita was anything but attractive. But many chose, evidently, to stay on after their year of service. The unpleasant prospect of the journey back home (in many cases very long), the hard work necessary to restore houses and bring neglected plots back into production, simple destitution after the expense of the journey to Potosí and passing a year there, in contrast to the attractive wages to be earned as a hired man in mining or some other task—all this combined to make Potosí alluring to some mitayos at the end of their turn. No official count of the Indian population of Potosí was carried out during the first hundred years. But such estimates as were made suggest strongly that the permanent native population outstripped that of the mitayos by far. In a very early seventeenth-century report, a vecino of the town, Alonso Mesías, gives the Indian male population as between 50,000 and 80,000, though he stresses the imprecision of the estimates.[69] Taking the lower figure, Mesías divides it up thus:

69.   Alonso Mesías to Viceroy Velasco, nd, but clearly soon after 1601 (*DII*, tomo 6, pp. 145–47). Mesías's total is confirmed by the "Descripción" of Potosí of 1603 (*BAE*, tomo CLXXXIII, pp. 372–85), where, after estimating the total number of Indians engaged in mining and related tasks at 30,000, the author adds: "y están avecindados [the 30,000] en sus casas, mujeres e hijos a vueltas, con más

mitayos, 12,600; craftsmen *(oficiales)* and servants of Spaniards, 10,000; hired men in mining and refining, 8,000; transients 8,000 to 10,000; and 10,000 others, to the total of 50,000, assigned no particular occupation. If just the 30,600 mitayos, hired men, crafts-men and servants had, on average, only one dependent, the total number of native people in Potosí would have been some 80,000. For comparison, it is worth pointing out that N. David Cook esti-mates the tributary (that is, adult male) population of the central sierra and southern sierra regions of Peru in 1600 at 118,413.[70] While Potosí drew Indians from Charcas as well as from the Peru-vian regions, these figures undeniably confirm that it exerted a strong attraction on Indians. A certain irony is apparent here. Min-ers bemoaned the low entero of the mita—without realizing, or perhaps wishing to concede, that many of the missing mitayos were indeed in Potosí, but as carpenters, tailors, domestic servants, and the like.

Potosí was not always so attractive, however, as to retain all those who chose not to go home. Some tried to avoid all further contact with the place by taking refuge in hidden places. How many did this, it is again impossible to say; though, if their num-ber corresponded to the volume of complaints on the subject in the late sixteenth century, it was large. The documents of that time on mine labor are strewn with the statement (or perhaps more accurately, the cliché) that the *guaicos y quebradas* (ravines and canyons) surrounding the town, which are certainly plentiful, were stuffed with recalcitrant mitayos, whose exact whereabouts were known only to their curacas. The curacas (again in the popular

---

de otros 30 mil indios que hay en esta villa ocupados en diversos oficios y entre-tenimientos, todos necesarios y forzosos, en 14 parroquias que de ellos hay en esta villa." In early 1603, the corregidor of Potosí reported to the king that the town was a "lugar muy grande" with normally over 40,000 Indians [males only, or total native population?], and over 3,000 Spanish males inhabiting more than 1,500 houses. (Don Pedro de Lodeña to crown, Potosí, April 9, 1603, in AGI Charcas 46) (JHR). As corroboration of these early seventeenth century data, it is useful to note that in 1576 the native population of Potosí was estimated at over 30,000, living in some 12,000 dwellings, along with more than 1,600 Spanish males (and other *naciones*). (Don Lope Diez de Armendáriz, president of the Audiencia of La Plata, to king, La Plata, September 25, 1576, in Levillier, *Charcas*, tomo 1, p. 368).
70. *Demographic collapse*, p. 118.

view) profited from this by extortion, threatening to send their people back to the mita if they did not pay to remain hidden.

While some Indians did undoubtedly choose this form of flight, it does not seem likely to have been as widespread as another sort of population shift that clearly had become common by the early seventeenth century. This was the movement of natives not to remote places unknown to the Spanish, but rather the converse: to places where Spanish employers sought their labor—needing it so much, indeed, that they were prepared to protect the Indians from the demands of the mita. This is not a simple matter of people's being displaced by the influence of Potosí. A desire to avoid the mita undoubtedly inclined them to leave their communities; but they were also pulled away by the attraction of work for which they would receive decent wages. This movement of people is, therefore, more than a mere disruption; it is more of a voluntary migration. And it signals the existence of competition for labor between Potosí and other centers of production. This competition is clearly the second main cause, with population decline, of the falling entero of the mita. Indeed, part of what was seen as population decline may well have been migration, since it proved hard to keep track of Indians once they left their home communities.

Competition for labor with other employers was, of course, no stranger to miners in Potosí, even in the early days. Before Toledo, indios varas turned to agricultural work when their mining profits fell. But in post-Toledan times, the first serious rivalry came from another mining center, Oruro, where a long-lived boom began in 1606–07. Oruro received no immediate assignment of mitayos, and under the 1609 ban on issues of forced workers, never received any later either—except during part of the decade 1610–20, when a transfer of 550 mitayos from nearby ailing mining centers was briefly in effect; and that was quickly canceled by the crown. Labor in Oruro, therefore, was almost entirely hired. In 1615 there were said to be from four to six thousand Indian men living there, hiring themselves out for mine work; and this number reportedly rose to ten thousand by 1617–18.[71] Some, perhaps most, of these were

71. AGI Charcas 36, Don Esteban de Lartáun (*tesorero* of Potosí) to crown, Potosí, February 15, 1615; AGI Charcas 415, tomo 3, ff. 20–21, real cédula to Esquilache, Madrid, April 16, 1618, citing Joseph Natero, vecino of Garcimendoza.

men who would otherwise have worked at Potosí. As early as April 1607 the corregidor of Potosí asserted that over a thousand of the most skilled ore cutters *(barreteros)*, all of them wage workers, had left for Oruro. This was a severe blow to Potosí because these workers knew better than anyone else where good ores lay in the cerro. Just as serious, however, was the attraction exerted by Oruro on Potosí's mitayos. Oruro lay directly on the main route *(camino real)* that most mitayos followed to reach Potosí, and so was a very obvious lure to them. In the same report of 1607, the corregidor complained that mitayos were stopping off at Oruro and hiding there, then emerging to take well-paid jobs in the mines, which had the added attraction of being newer and shallower than those of Potosí, and hence more easily worked.[72] Oruro continued to siphon labor, both hired and mita, away from Potosí, though its attraction undoubtedly waned after the 1620s, when its silver output began to fall. On the other hand, prospecting had by then revealed numerous small but often rich silver deposits in various parts of Charcas; and these, too, drew workers from Potosí.[73]

By the time of Oruro's decline, moreover, agriculture had again raised a challenge. The signs appeared in the first two decades of the seventeenth century. In 1611 the corregidor of Potosí, finding absenteeism from the mita very high, sent out officials to chacras in the vicinity with orders to bring in all Indians found on them. Each man was to be identified (surely an impossible proposition), and those found to be avoiding mita service retained in the town. The scheme was never implemented, because the cabildo of Potosí, backed by the Audiencia of La Plata, objected to it—not on grounds of undue interference with chacra Indians, of course, but rather for fear that agriculture would be disrupted.[74] What is significant

---

72. AGI Charcas 47, Don Pedro de Lodeña to crown, Potosí, April 13, 1607.

73. AGI Lima 41, Viceroy Guadalcázar to crown, "Gobierno No. 6," Lima, March 8, 1627.

74. AGI Charcas 19, Audiencia to crown, "No. 15," La Plata, March 1, 1612. The audiencia also judged that the corregidor, Don Rafael Ortiz de Sotomayor, in sending out agents, had exceeded his powers over the mita, which, according to his title of office, enabled him only to compel district corregidores, and curacas, to deliver the quotas due from their jurisdictions. This was a narrow reading of the corregidor's attributes, probably owing to the audiencia's permanent annoyance at being outranked in mita matters by the corregidor.

about the episode for present purposes, in any case, is that mitayos were working in agriculture when they should have been mining.

Though in 1611 the cabildo of Potosí was apparently not greatly concerned about this drift of mitayos into farmwork, it had changed its mind five years later. In 1616 it made great play of the need to recover these workers for the mines, while simultaneously beseeching the king to allow larger imports of black slaves through Buenos Aires—slaves who could take the Indians' place in farming.[75] (No indication has emerged of increased use of black slaves in agriculture as a result of this request.) The movement of mitayos into farming continued, none the less. In 1624 the governor of Chucuito tried to recover missing mitayos due from that province who had gone to the valley of Cochabamba, and others close to it. These places were, as they remain, temperate and fertile agricultural enclaves set in the eastern foothills of the Andes, but lying close to the edge of the altiplano.[76] An agent sent by the governor, Juan de Castillo, found that Chucuito Indians were in the habit of going down to the valleys to fetch food, especially maize, and often taking their families with them. This they did without the knowledge of even their curacas. Once there, they rented land from the Spanish, and settled; with the result that there were Indian towns in Chucuito in which only 200 houses of a total of 2,000 were inhabited. By Castillo's estimate, 2,000 Chucuito Indians lived in the valleys (from the context, this figure seems to refer to men alone); but he had been able to recover only seventy-two of them because of the opposition put up by the corregidor of Cochabamba, Don Diego de Zárate, who had invoked the authority of the cabildo, the municipal attorney (procurador), and the protector of Indians to hinder removal of the farm laborers. Allowing for a certain exaggeration of numbers, this account still clearly shows that migra-

75. AGI Charcas 32 ms 80, cabildo to crown, Potosí, November 30, 1616. Mitayos had gone to small farms, crop and pasture lands ("chácaras, tierras de sembraduras y estancias de ganado"), while the previous inflow of blacks had slowed, owing to the rigorous application of royal restrictions on imports through Buenos Aires by the governor, Hernán Darias de Saavedra.

76. SAU tomo 330/122, ff. 193–94, Juan de Castillo to "excelentísimo señor" (Viceroy Guadalcázar?), Potosí, January 23, 1625. The valleys in question besides Cochabamba itself are not specified, but probably included at least those of Mizque and Aiquile.

tion to the eastern valleys could be a heavy drain on the mita. Castillo recommended forcing the district corregidores to make censuses of Indians in their areas, so that those from Chucuito due for mita service could be found and sent to Potosí. Nothing of the kind seems to have been done, however, in the period before 1650.

A similar situation is recorded, in a document of 1633–34, as having developed in Pacajes—a province extending from the southern tip of Lake Titicaca south and east almost to Oruro. The native official responsible for despatching the Pacajes mitayos, Don Gabriel Fernández Guarachi, claimed to have been able to collect only 500 of the 1,300 due in 1634; and the main reason for the difficulty, he thought, was that so many of his people had moved to La Paz, where they worked for the vecinos of the city.[77] An even more serious conflict developed here between the mita officials and the local government than in the Cochabamba episode. Fernández Guarachi was accompanied to La Paz by an agent of the Audiencia of La Plata, who was to add official weight to the effort of recovering the missing Indians. The agent went so far as to shut up a substantial number of these in the city jail—whereupon the corregidor freed them again, so challenging the audiencia's authority, and apparently with success, since the Indians were not retaken. They, indeed, profited from the lesson to hide themselves with greater care than before. They had already taken the precaution of changing their names, and lying about their parents' names and communities of origin. Fernández Guarachi had no doubt that it was La Paz's need for labor that led the corregidor to defy the audiencia. First, the vecinos tried to bribe the audiencia's agent; then they threatened him and beat up witnesses to the Indians' origins. The agent at one point tried to move some of the Indians he had identified as mitayos from the jail to his residence in La Paz. The corregidor seized the opportunity to free them and assault the agent's guards.

A further cause of declining delivery of the mita was illicit use of Indians within the mita area itself by their own curacas, by parish priests, and by the Spanish corregidores of native districts. Much complaint on this score is recorded from both Indians and

---

77.   BAN Minas catalog No. 683, "1633. Don Gabriel Fernández Guarachi . . . capitán general enterador de la mita en 1634. . . ," especially ff. 1–5v., 15–15v.

those who wanted to see them in Potosí; but once again, the precise loss of mita labor cannot be estimated. A few examples of practices will have to suffice. In the late 1620s curacas of Pacajes were renting Indians to freighters, presumably to work as drivers of mule or llama trains, and keeping the earnings. In Paucarcolla province the corregidor was said to be making small drafts of labor available to local miners.[78] Numerous Indians from Chucuito in the mid-1620s were reportedly living in isolated hamlets *(estancias)*, whose whereabouts were known only to their curacas. Whether these places had been created by the curacas or by the commoners is unclear; but in any case the curacas exploited the situation to demand from these people payments far in excess of the normal tributes, in return for exemption from the mita and other undeclared obligations.[79]

Although the two chief and related causes of the falling delivery of the mita were recognized by the authorities—decline and shifting of the native population—no solution was found for them; and in fact little sustained attempt was made to produce even a policy that might lead to a solution. True population loss—as distinct from apparent loss caused by migration—was in any case beyond the power of the government to remedy. Such official pondering as took place was therefore directed at making available to the mita all those Indians who had in some way escaped from it. A rational first move would clearly have been a census. But this was apparently felt to be neither possible nor desirable until all the people who had left their communities returned to them. Toledo's example here was well remembered by his successors. One of his most remarkable achievements—still not fully studied—had been to concentrate the native population into fewer, and in many cases new, communities. But these people had later found a number of good reasons for leaving their towns; and putting them back where the government thought they belonged proved problematic, indeed impossible. The implementation of a "general reduction" *(reducción general)*, as the process of moving people back to their

78. AGI Charcas 20, Licenciado Don Gabriel Gómez de Sanabria to crown, La Plata, January 18, 1629.

79. SAU tomo 330/122, ff. 193–94, Juan de Castillo to "excelentísimo señor," Potosí, January 23, 1625.

previous homes was called, was made the more difficult by the growth of new economic interests in the labor of those Indians, as the cases of La Paz and Cochabamba, already described, show. Several efforts were made at reduction, none the less, in the decades after Toledo. One of the most promising was that of Viceroy Esquilache, who, having consulted senior advisers, and the audiencias of Lima, Quito, and La Plata on the problem of depopulation of Indian communities, resolved that the best course of action would be to order corregidores of Indian districts to return any immigrants who were then in those districts to their places of origin. This scheme had been in operation for a year, when Esquilache reported it to the king in September of 1617.[80] Clearly, it had one advantage over other possible plans of attack, in requiring little in the way of new officials, and hence new expense, which was always an obstacle. The corregidores were already in place. On the other hand, they had entrenched interests that might make them unwilling to part with the native labor in their areas; and they lacked authority to ensure that Indians returned to distant regions. Esquilache's scheme had no success in the long run. In 1633 Viceroy Chinchón, under order from the king to consider the question of reduction, reported that all previous projects had come to nothing and that he was gathering opinions on the matter from the audiencias and others.[81] No more came of this, either, and the subject seems to have been dropped until after the midcentury.[82]

An interesting general question arises from the matter of "reducing" Indians. How did Toledo contrive to accomplish a task that no other viceroy in the next eighty years could repeat? Indeed, it

80.   AGI Lima 38, with "Duplicado. Gobierno No. 47," Lima, September 16, 1617. For general information on Toledo's efforts at concentration of native population, and antecedents to them, see Alejandro Málaga Medina, "Las reducciones en el Perú (1532–1600)," Historia y Cultura No. 8 (Lima 1974), pp. 141–72.

81.   AGI Lima 44, tomo 4, Chinchón to crown, "Gobierno No. 9," Lima, May 10, 1633.

82.   A census was finally taken of the whole of Peru, Charcas, and Quito, though without prior reduction, at the instigation of Viceroy La Palata, between 1683 and 1688. See Cole, The Potosí mita, pp. 394–99, and Nicolás Sánchez Albornoz, Indios y tributos en el Alto Perú (Instituto de Estudios Peruanos, Lima 1980), ch. 3.

was a greater task, since Toledo managed not only a general reduction, but also a census of Indians. The answer may well be
multiple. In the first place, Indians were more numerous in Toledo's time. This, paradoxically, made his job easier, since there
were correspondingly fewer demands on any one of them from
the colonists (who themselves were fewer), and hence Indians were
less likely than later to be defended from governmental interference by their employers. Similarly, a lighter labor burden meant
that the Indians had less work to escape from, and accordingly
less cause to hide from the authorities.[83] Again, Toledo was in Peru
longer than his successors, so naturally he achieved more. But, all
this granted, still something remains to be explained in the inaction of the later administrations. In part, it can be put down to the
growing complexity and sluggishness of colonial government.
Jurisdictional conflicts multiplied; local interests of officials increased as they became more closely enmeshed with colonial society. More colonials occupied administrative posts, and used their
influence to block unwelcome change. Lastly, though, the sheer
drive of Toledo cannot be ignored. He was an unrepeated phe-
nomenon, perhaps best seen as the final bearer in Peru of the
conquistador's energy—a Francisco Pizarro of a bureaucrat.

Another, less ambitious, scheme existed for making up the shortfall in Potosí's mita—though one that proved unworkable as for-
mally proposed. It did, none the less, come into effect without the
administration's noticing the fact for a long time. The formal plan
was to concentrate Indians in a large new town near Potosí from
which labor could easily and constantly be drawn. This project had
a long history. Philip II, in his first instructions on mining to Toledo
in 1568, suggested the creation of such towns as a general solution to the problem of labor supply for mining. (See chapter 3
above.) Philip III picked up the scheme in clause 20 of the royal
cédula on forced labor of November 24, 1601, and again in an order
specifically directed to Potosí of May 26, 1609. The Council of the

---

83. This is perhaps what Viceroy Guadalcázar meant when he wrote that
reduction had been made more difficult by the growth of the Indians' cunning
("malicia") since Toledo's time; quoted by Chinchón in "Gobierno No. 9" to
crown, para. 3, Lima, May 10, 1633 (AGI Lima 44, tomo 4).

Indies reminded Esquilache of this order in late 1618, with a command to implement it.[84] No new satellite town outside Potosí existed by that time, nor ever did. The difficulties were pointed out in 1620 by Alonso Martínez de Pastrana, visitor to the Potosí treasury. The central problem, he suggested, was one of space and resources. To persuade numerous Indians to move to the vicinity of Potosí, enticements of land and water would have to be provided. But all available sites for twenty leagues around the town were already taken by Spaniards, who had paid heavily for them and farmed them to supply Potosí with food. It would be a great expense, Pastrana declared, for the crown to acquire title to enough of this land to support an Indian population of sufficient size to ensure supply of labor on the mita scale to Potosí.[85] Pastrana did not press the point; but what the scheme in reality proposed was to replace with a single source of labor the dozens of communities spread out over many thousands of square miles of the mita area: an extremely unlikely proposition.[86]

On the other hand, as Esquilache pointed out to the king even before he received the Council's reminder of September 1618, a large Indian town supplying Potosí with labor did in fact exist[87]—in the form of the great ranchería, lying not in some nearby valley, but cheek by jowl with the Spanish city center, between the Ribera and the cerro itself. (See the discussion of Potosí's urban layout in the Introduction.) After Toledo had given the ranchería its initial shape, it had grown, over the final decades of the sixteenth century and the early years of the seventeenth, not in response to any decree, but rather to economic forces. Most of its expansion resulted from movement to Potosí of Indians who saw there the

84. AGI Charcas 54, "Papeles tocantes a la mita de Potosí," Consejo to Esquilache, September 10?, 1618.

85. AGI Charcas 36, Alonso Martínez de Pastrana to crown, Potosí, March 24, 1620, para. 9.

86. In 1625, Dr. Juan de Solórzano Pereira, then an oidor in the Audiencia of Lima, raised similar objections, and some others: disruption of the economy of regions from which the Indians were taken, inadequate evangelization of them in Potosí, the dangers of moving people into the cold climate of Potosí. See BL Additional mss 13,974, ff. 155–56, Solórzano to Don Suero de Quiñones, Lima, March 1, 1625. Quiñones offers refutations of Solórzano's points.

87. AGI Lima 38, tomo 3, ff. 157–58v., Esquilache to crown, "Gobierno No. 4," Lima, April 20, 1618, para. 1.

opportunity to find wage work, in mining and other occupations. This was the place that by 1600 housed many of the tens of thousands of permanent native residents in the town.

Of particular interest here is that the ranchería was home to the mingas, the hired mining and refining workers who came onto the scene in growing numbers in the late sixteenth century. Not nearly as much information is available about the mingas as could be desired. But what there is reveals that they were a highly important part of the mining labor force, and indeed may have played an economic role in Potosí that went far beyond labor itself.

The history of hired Indian labor in Potosí goes back into the earliest years before Toledo. Indios varas, as has been recounted in an earlier chapter, then hired other natives to work for them, and so did Spanish mineowners toward the end of the pre-Toledan period. In the 1570s the record of hired labor seems to be lost in the welter of information on the organization of the mita, though clearly some of the yanaconas remaining in the town continued to hire themselves out, and other Indians still came to Potosí to do so. Various of Toledo's mining ordinances refer to these people.[88] But it is Capoche who, in 1585, provides the first substantial evidence in the post-Toledo years on hired labor, and indeed the first use of the term *indio minga*.[89] He relates that Viceroy Enríquez, in making his repartimiento of the mita in the early 1580s, assigned to ingenios only sufficient mitayos to permit refining on a moderate scale *(un mediano beneficio)*. Refiners who wanted to run their plant at a higher rate had to hire mingas.[90] Toward the end of the *Relación*, Capoche devotes a section to mingas, and there raises a number of provocative points about this category of worker.[91] His main observations are these.

Mingas were much in demand for both refining and mining. Ingenios needed as many hired men again as they had mitayos. For refining work, mingas were hired from among men who were

---

88. See, for example, ordenanzas 5, 6, 7, and 9 of the title "De los desmontes, trabajo y paga de los indios" (Levillier, *Gobernantes,* tomo 8, pp. 232–33, 236–37).

89. *Relación,* p. 109. The word derives from the Quechua *mink'ay,* which, at bottom, means to perform reciprocal labor, to work in exchange for an equivalent amount of work.

90. Ibid., p. 118.

91. Ibid., pp. 173–75.

de huelga from the mita. These would gather in various squares in the town, waiting to be engaged. Capoche was not impressed with their industriousness. They demanded prepayment in cash, and had a habit of taking their money and then going off to rehire themselves to another employer. They worked from 10 a.m. to 4 p.m. only—or even less: " . . .often, once they have hold of their money, they quite shamelessly enter through one door and go out through another."[92] They worked feebly, refusing altogether to do milling, since that was arduous, but not applying themselves energetically either to the process of amalgamation itself. If put to stirring the amalgam, said Capoche, they did it so halfheartedly that the silver was taken up slowly, with a severe loss of time, fuel, and mercury. Finally, they stole silver once it was refined.

In assessing these observations, it is worth emphasizing that Capoche writes, on the whole, in a remarkably pro-Indian vein. In this same section, as elsewhere in the *Relación*, he decries forced Indian labor, and wishes that the mita could be replaced by volunteer work; though those who offered themselves for it would have to work better than the present mingas. Indeed, Capoche is at a loss to explain why the same Indians who work so well in the draft become so idle as mingas: ". . .they seem another people, and they are as bad and as perverse when hired as they are disciplined when forced to work. . . ."[93] A partial explanation might possibly be that something of the old Inca discipline still attached to the mita, but was absent from the individual work pattern brought in by the Spanish.

Unlike mingas engaged for refining, those used in mining were not hired at gathering points in the town, but directly from their houses in the ranchería. Capoche offers no explanation for this difference; perhaps the reason was simply that the ranchería lay at the foot of the cerro, whereas the refineries were in the opposite direction, northward toward the center of the town. It would have been a waste of time to bring mining mingas into town only to send them back through the ranchería to the mines. Capoche

92. ". . . muchas veces como tienen el dinero en su poder, entran por una puerta y salen por otra sin ninguna vergüenza." Ibid., p. 173.

93. ". . . parecen de otra nación, y lo que tienen de corregidos, siendo de cédula, tienen de malos y perversos cuando se alquilan. . . ." Ibid., p. 174.

cites the mine owners' disapproval of the mingas' demands to be allowed ore in addition to their cash wage, but himself thinks this reasonable enough. Without the extra recompense, he argues, the men could earn as much by working in some kitchen. The mingas' cash wages were higher than the mitayos': for mine work, 4 reales a day, plus ore, as against 3.5 reales for mitayos; and for refining, 4.25 reales a day, plus coca in some cases, as against 2.75 for mitayos.

In Capoche's account several characteristics of hired labor in the Potosí industry emerge, characteristics not of his time alone but of later years also. First, the workers offered themselves freely for mine and refinery labor. They could have taken other tasks, but apparently chose mining and refining for the superior rewards that these offered. Their cavalier attitude toward at least refinery work is a further argument against compulsion, if one were needed. Second, mingas were better rewarded than mitayos, though the disparities in earnings between the two classes of workers shown by Capoche were very small compared to what they became a decade or two later. Third, and this is the general point that emerges most strongly, there was a great demand for mingas: a demand which, of course, explains the higher wages and toleration of poor performance. This demand arose form the simple inability of the mita to supply enough men to a rapidly expanding industry. It also arose, though this can hardly be glimpsed in Capoche, from the superior skills of the mingas. It must have been so to a degree in his time as it generally was later—that the skilled ore cutters and refiners were mingas. The more purely physical jobs were left to mitayos.

In stressing that mingas were hired because the mita did not supply enough hands for silver production on the scale desired by mine and refinery owners, Capoche conveys strongly that mingas in his day were extra workers, men employed in addition to the mitayos. The word *minga*, however, came also to have a substantially different second meaning: a worker engaged to substitute for a mitayo. A mita worker who wished to avoid service might hire a minga to take his place; or a curaca might hire a minga to replace a mitayo whom for some reason he could not deliver; or either the mitayo or the curaca might pay an employer the sum necessary to hire a replacement for a missing mitayo. The last practice was known as "delivering in silver" *(enterar en plata)*, or more cynically as giving "Indians in the pocket" *(indios de faltriquera)*.

As mining declined in the seventeenth century, it became increasingly common that employers who received indios de faltriquera chose not to use this money to hire a minga, but merely to keep it, because that was more profitable than spending it on working a depleted mine with a hired hand. The practice of indios de faltriquera was then recognized by morally conscious administrators as an abuse, and efforts were made to remedy it, though with little effect. (The abuse is discussed in more detail in the next chapter.) When the minga served as a substitute, the elements of hire and free choice were still present; but the total labor force was obviously not increased. The precise functioning of this second type of minga organization is a little complex, but worth tracing because it does have important economic ramifications for the silver industry as a whole.

The substitute minga had already appeared on the Potosí scene by Capoche's time,[94] though he does not seem to have yet been common. It is easy to see why the development should have come about. Curacas were already finding difficulties in fulfilling the demands of the mita ordinaria, either because of population decline, evasion of the draft, or because they were obliged to supply mitayos for non-mita work to powerful people. Similarly, mitayos might merely wish to avoid draft work, or have some other work they found preferable. The outcome was predictable: hire a substitute from the huelga or from the permanent native population of Potosí. A striking feature of the transaction was cost. The substitute minga naturally demanded a higher reward than the mita wage; and in fact he received, according to Capoche, even more than the extra-hand minga of the day: 24 reales (3 pesos) a week as opposed to 20 reales (or 21.25 reales in refining). And these 24 reales were merely what he received from the curaca of the mitayo who hired him; in addition he collected a standard mita wage of 13.75 to 17.5 reales for a week of five days. So the total cash wage of the substitute in the mid-1580s averaged around 40 reales (5 pesos) a week. In all likelihood, substitutes in mining also gathered ore.

These rates rose, along with silver production and prices in general, over the final years of the century. By 1600 the rates for

94. Ibid., pp. 174–75.

ore cutters (barreteros) were these: extra hands, 56 to 72 reales (7 to 9 pesos) for the five-day week, depending on skill; substitutes, the same amount from those who engaged them, and 20 additional reales (2.5 pesos) in regular mita wage (Viceroy Velasco having by this time raised the mining mita rate from 3.5 to 4 reales a day). Barretero mingas of either type received extra recompense in ore, which, according to one observer, might be worth as much as the wage.[95] Barreteros normally worked from Monday night to Saturday sunset; but if they had completed the amount of work expected of them by Friday, they might leave the mine then. Mingas who were not barreteros were paid at a lesser rate of 8 reales (1 peso) daily (substitutes presumably receiving mita pay also). But those in ingenios, at least, seem to have done correspondingly less work, since, having started in the early morning, they downed tools at two in the afternoon.[96]

The "Descripción" of Potosí of 1603 confirms these minga wages quite closely, giving a mine rate of 72 reales weekly, and an average refining rate of 7 reales daily, or 35 a week.[97] The years around the turn of the century were in all likelihood those of highest pay for mingas. With the subsequent decline in silver production, along with prices, and probably profits also, the rate tended to ease. The wage of the extra-hand minga in mining was reported at 56 reales in 1615, 60 in 1630, and from 56 to 60 in 1637.[98] The slight variation in these figures doubtless results from differences in working conditions and in the skill of the men in question. Indeed, in 1639, certain mine owners contended that there were some workings in the cerro in which mingas would not labor for under 9.5 pesos (76 reales) a week, because the ore they were allowed to take as sup-

95. Testimony of Alonso Romero, resident of Potosí, August 29, 1600: f. 33v. of untitled expediente of 100 ff. on the mita service demanded of the Indians of Chucuito, headed "Charcas 1600" (in AGI Charcas 80). The wage rates quoted are from this same source. (JHR).

96. Ibid., ff. 41–43, testimony of Hermano Diego de Morales, SJ, Potosí, August 30, 1600.

97. "Descripción," pp. 377, 384.

98. AGI Charcas 36, Don Esteban de Lartáun (tesorero of the Potosí treasury) to crown, Potosí, February 15, 1615, f. 3v. For 1630, AGI Escribanía 865A, f. 1,034v. For 1637, AGI Charcas 56, protector de los naturales de Chucuito to crown (no exact date, but 1637); also, in same ms, the statement of the reales oficiales, Potosí, January 3, 1637.

plementary pay was so poor there.[99] But, on the whole, extra-hand minga wages seem to have stayed notably steady after the first decade of the seventeenth century. And such evidence as exists, suggests that the substitute rate followed suit: hiring a substitute cost the mitayo (or curaca, or employer) from 56 to 60 reales a week.[100]

With this information on wages laid out, the economic outcome of the minga system becomes visible. The substitute minga practice clearly effected a considerable transfer of wealth from the native population to the Spanish operators of mines and mills. Suppose that the cost of the extra-hand minga represented on average the value of his labor to the employer, as it should at minimum have done, since the pay rate was a free-market wage determined by supply and demand. Add that the value of the labor of the substitute minga should have been the same as that of the extra hand. Then, if the employer were presented with a substitute minga at no other cost to him than the mita wage (as happened when a mitayo or curaca hired a replacement), he received, depending on the period in question, 7 to 9 pesos' worth of work in a week, at about 2.5 pesos' cost. (In this statement the value of the ore conceded to the minga, if he were a barretero, is not included, and it may have been considerable. On the other hand, it was not an out-of-pocket cost to the mine owner.) There is even some evidence that, toward the mid-seventeenth century, employers were receiving substitute mingas at no cash cost at all. This is suggested by the "Respuesta del Licenciado Robles de Salcedo" already cited as a source of minga wages (n. 99 above)—a complex document of 1639 recording a dispute between Robles, an oidor of La Plata, and the mining guild of Potosí over precisely the morality of the indio de faltriquera and substitute minga practices. The guild itself stated quite clearly that by this time the employer no longer paid the mita rate to the substitute minga. The minga, rather, received only the

99. AGI Charcas 21, "Respuesta del Licenciado Robles de Salcedo . . . a un exhortatorio que el gremio de los azogueros . . . le hicieron. . . ," Potosí, October 28, 1639, para. 8.
100. AGI Charcas 36, reales oficiales to crown, Potosí, March 20, 1620, f. 2; AGI Charcas 21, "Respuesta del Licenciado Robles de Salcedo. . . ," para. 8.

7 pesos that a mitayo or curaca paid to engage him. So the employer had free minga labor (apart from the value of any ore taken by mining mingas). When Robles remonstrated with them over this, the miners replied with the justification that the practice increased silver production and hence the royalty. How prevalent this practice was cannot be judged. Possibly it did not extend to refining, where most mingas were used, and where there was no extra recompense comparable to ore in mining work. Nevertheless, the evidence available only confirms the argument that employers benefited handsomely from the substitute minga system.

Their precise benefit, of course, could be calculated if proportions of extra-hand and substitute mingas were known; but they are not, nor were they known to contemporaries. Indeed, the total number of mingas was a matter of debate, though some useful guides to it can be found. The earliest of these is an anonymous document of 1603, clearly drawn up to show the difficulties of establishing near Potosí a native town of sufficient size to supply the silver industry with all the workers it needed. Its estimates of numbers of workers, both mingas and mitayos, may therefore be exaggerated.[101] The writer assumes, for example, that the mita ordinaria was fully delivered, at 4,467 men, which is certainly an optimistic view. The number of mingas in refining he calculates at 5,220; and this is very much of a calculation, rather than an actual count, since he arrives at the figure by multiplying the average number of workers in an ingenio by the number of ingenios in operation (assuming that no mitayos worked in refining, which was probably true enough for his purpose). The writer states that each of the seventy-two water-powered ingenios in Potosí and the Tabacoñuño and Tarapaya zones (upstream and downstream, respectively, of the Ribera) employed on average seventy mingas. So the total there was 5,040. Then there were six animal-powered ingenios in Potosí, with thirty mingas each, for a total of 180. Hence a total of 5,220 mingas worked in refining. In mining the writer identifies some *(algunos)* mingas, but gives no estimate of the number. Two or three hundred may perhaps be allowed. If these various estimates are accepted, the mingas directly engaged in sil-

101. SAU tomo 330/122, ff. 236v.–37, "1603. Relación de los indios. . . ."

ver production formed about 55 percent of the mining and refining labor force (some 5,500 of a total of about 9,950).[102]

Another, and independent, source of 1603 also supplies a rough count of mingas—the already cited "Descripción de la Villa y minas de Potosí" of that year. Refining mingas are here estimated at 4,000, and those in mining variously at 600 or 1,000.[103] So the total number directly in silver production lay roughly between 4,500 and 5,000—figures providing surprising confirmation of the first estimate of 1603, if its possible exaggeration is taken into account.

Only one other count of mingas has come to light for the period before 1650—the "Respuesta del Licenciado Robles de Salcedo" of 1639. This manuscript contains a statement by the silver producers that they normally hired 1,600 mingas for mine work, and 1,850 for refining, or 3,450 altogether. They added that the number of effective workers efectivos in the mita ordinaria was 2,800. So the percentage of mingas in the total labor force of 6,250 would be 55, just as indicated in 1603. The true proportion of mingas, however, may well have been higher, since the producers probably followed the habit of their day of counting among efectivos not only workers in the flesh, but also absentees for whom substitute was made in cash.

From these estimates of minga numbers, scant though they are, suggestive calculations can be made about the value of the substitute minga practice to miners and refiners. Although the relative numbers of substitutes and extra hands cannot be known, it seems inherently likely that the substitutes were in the minority to begin with, but became ever more common as time passed. Capoche, as previously noted, implies that extra hands predominated in the mid-1580s, as would be expected: it was a time of general growth of silver production, probably of widespread profit, and certainly of high demand for labor. In the seventeenth century, in contrast, production trended downward, aggregate profitability very proba-

---

102.   The "Relación" of 1603 does, in fact, list some 3,000 more mingas than these. But they are not included in the calculations here because they were not directly engaged in the production of silver; though they are certainly shown as working in related tasks, such as reprocessing of tailings to recover mercury (1,000 mingas), mining and freighting of salt (300), bringing ore down from the cerro (250), manufacture and freight of charcoal (300), candle making (200), and so on.

103.   "Descripción," pp. 377, 384.

bly followed suit, and Potosí's industry generally contracted. In those circumstances it is unlikely that employers were as keen to hire expensive extra-hand mingas as they had been in the 1580s, and so more of the recorded mingas were probably substitutes. An additional argument for this suggestion is that substitute mingas seem usually to have received higher wages than the extra hands: the minga hiring rate, plus the standard mita pay. So Indians wishing to hire themselves out for mining or refining work would naturally have preferred to be substitutes. Suppose, then, that of the 3,450 mingas reported active in 1639, a mere half, or 1,725, were substitutes, and that each of these received 7 pesos from a mitayo or curaca for a week's work (or from an employer spending money received from an indio de faltriquera). The total yearly cost of this labor, which the employer was spared paying, would be 627,900 pesos. This sum was no small proportion of registered silver production of the Potosí district in the late 1630s. Average annual production over the three years 1638–40 was about 4,809,000 pesos. The value estimated here of substitute minga labor is some 13 percent of that amount. A more significant comparison would be one between the estimate for substitute minga cost, and silver production in Potosí itself, since that is where these mingas worked. Just how much of the total production of the district came from Potosí around 1640 cannot be said with with accuracy, since no separate accounting was made. A contemporary estimate was that at the most Potosí gave a half of the district's output.[104] This seems likely, for various reasons, to have underestimated Potosí's contribution. But, in view of high silver production at Chocaya in the second half of the 1630s,[105] it would be reasonable to suppose that mines outside Potosí yielded a third of the district's total. If so, the value of substitute mingas rises to around 20 percent of Potosí's own silver output. The assumptions made in arriving at this figure are many and not demonstrable; but they are conservative. At the very least it can be said that the substitute minga practice saved silver

104. Para. 3 of the "Respuesta del Licenciado Robles de Salcedo. . . ."
105. Many references to Chocaya are to be found in the correspondence of officials in Charcas in the late 1630s. See, for example, Don Juan de Lizarazu (President of the Audiencia of La Plata), to crown, "consulta," Potosí, March 1, 1637, in AGI Charcas 20.

producers a most considerable proportion of their labor costs; or, put another way, it enabled them to produce from mines and mills that otherwise would have been uneconomic. And if previous argument here is correct, savings became greater, in a very convenient fashion, as mines grew poorer.

The question now arises: where did the Indians find money with which to engage substitutes or provide indios de faltriquera? Manuscript sources do not supply direct answers, but several plausible ones are easily imagined, and offer interesting implications. Curacas seeking to replace absentees among the mitayos whom they were due to supply doubtless used their political authority in their communities to secure cash with which to hire mingas. One of the constant themes of the history of Indians in the Potosí mita area is exploitation by their own leaders—exploitation that was at least partly the result of pressure put on the leaders to supply fixed amounts of tribute and labor from their generally shrinking communities; though self-seeking was also present.[106] Where, in turn, might the cash come from that the leaders took from their people? Major sources may well have been the sale of goods (cloth and food) to Spanish settlements, among which Potosí stood very large as a market, or wages paid in such settlements. Again, Potosí was a center of employment. Mitayos, while de huelga, worked in many capacities, including minga labor in mining and refining. So it may well be that the earnings of mingas circulated through the hands of the native leaders back into hiring more mingas. Mitayos' earnings from non-mita work went, of course, even more directly and quickly into hiring mingas when the mitayos provided their own replacements or paid cash for indios de faltriquera to the employer so that he could hire substitutes. And a further interesting transfer of cash suggests itself in this connection. If Indians in Potosí for mita service worked during their periods of huelga in some occupation unconnected with mining, and then used their earnings to hire mingas to replace them during their mita turns, a flow of money took place from the non-mining sector of Potosí's economy into the mining sector. This would be of particular interest because it seems to have been the general pattern of Spanish-

106. Cf. Karen Spalding, "Social climbers: changing patterns of mobility among the Indians of colonial Peru," (HAHR, 50:4 [1970], pp. 645–64), pp. 658–60.

American silver mining that the bulk of mining profit came to rest not in the hands of the miners, but in those of middlemen, such as suppliers of goods and credit, and the *mercaderes de plata*, who bought raw silver from the producers for minting. Perhaps, through the substitute minga practice, there was, at least in Potosí, a countercurrent of cash that in part balanced this tendency. Just how many off-duty mitayos received wages from such middlemen in Potosí it is, alas, impossible to say.

Evidence also can be found suggesting that wealth accumulated by mitayos before their period of draft service went to buying substitutes. A complaint of the Chucuito Indians in 1600 was that each year the mitayos whom they sent to Potosí left home with large herds of llamas and quantities of food and clothing, but returned (if they returned at all) twelve months later with nothing save the clothes on their backs.[107] Exactly what or how much the Chucuito people did sell in Potosí cannot be said. But there is no doubt that the province, an ancient and renowned llama-raising area, did send great flocks of animals with the annual batch of mitayos. The count made at the despatch of the province's mita contingent at the Desaguadero bridge in August 1600 (see the description earlier in this chapter) showed that the 1,749 men actually setting off for Potosí took with them no fewer than 11,708 llamas, all carrying food to sustain the mitayos and their families on the journey. Curacas and principales took an additional 475 beasts. Any food remaining from the journey was presumably consumed in Potosí, or sold there. Sale of the llamas alone at the prevailing price in Potosí of about 6 pesos a head would have brought in a considerable sum—roughly 72,000 pesos, worth 8,000 man-weeks of minga labor, if, as the Chucuito people themselves maintained, income from such sales went to hiring mingas. It seems unlikely that all the llamas would have been sold for that purpose; some must surely have been disposed of to raise cash for tribute,

---

107.   AGI Charcas 80, "Charcas 1600," f. 37v., question 7 of the "Pedimento" of Alonso de Zamudio, protector general de los naturales in Potosí, in name of Don Carlos Visa, *cacique principal* of Acora, Potosí, August 28, 1600. See also f. 48.

or food. Nevertheless, a part of the accumulated wealth of Chucuito did go to filling gaps in the mita ranks, and so was transferred from Indians to mining employers. For other mita groups coming to Potosí, there is no firsthand evidence of this process. But others certainly did bring such animals, food, and saleable goods as they possessed to Potosí to help sustain them and to pay for replacement workers during the mita stint.[108]

A final question about mingas remains. To what extent did they come from a resident native population in Potosí, and to what extent from the part of the mita gruesa that was de huelga? In previous pages both sources have been mentioned, and indeed both existed. Again, it is numbers and proportions that elude precise statement. Capoche implies that most mingas in his time were hired from the huelga, and repeated statements to that effect can be found thereafter.[109] On the other hand, Alonso Mesías, in his estimate of Indian population in the very early seventeenth century (pp. 111–12), wrote of 8,000 men living permanently in Potosí, outside the mita gruesa, who hired themselves out for mining and refinery work. That figure may well be too high, or may include many who did work related to silver production, but not, as stated, direct mining or refining. In 1615, the royal treasurer of Potosí mentioned in a letter to the king that the number of perma-

---

108.   Alonso Mesías, in his "Memorial" of the beginning of the seventeenth century to Viceroy Velasco, p. 148, estimated that from 40,000 to 50,000 llamas destined for consumption as meat were brought into Potosí each year by incoming mitayos, along with 90,000 to 100,000 cargas (roughly 3,450 to 3,850 metric tons) of maize and "comida" (possibly chuño in the main). According to another source, Canas, Canches, and other Indians in 1610 consumed all the provisions with which they left home, either on the journey to Potosí or during their year there. See Manuel Ballesteros-Gaibrois, "Notas sobre el trabajo minero en los Andes con especial referencia a Potosí (s. XVI y ss.)," (CIM, tomo 1, pp. 529–57), p. 534. For Chucuito, see PCM CR 72, padrón of the mitayos of Chucuito, ff. 1–91v., Ciudad de Chucuito, July 21, 1600, and later dates. Finally, John V. Murra, in "Aymara lords and their European agents at Potosí" (Nova Americana 1, Turin 1978, pp. 231–243), refers to two native leaders of the late sixteenth and early seventeenth centuries, one of them a mita captain, who clearly made considerable profits by selling in Potosí the agricultural produce of their extensive personal land holdings.

109.   For example, Viceroy Esquilache to crown, "Gobierno No. 14," Lima, April 20, 1618, para. 3, in AGI Lima 38, tomo 3, ff. 157–58v.

nent native residents of Potosí who took waged mining work was over 2,000. Here the reference seems to be to labor in mines alone.[110]

On the whole it seems likely that resident mingas would form a growing portion of the total minga force. To begin with, the number of mitayos reaching Potosí fell with time, and the periods they had de huelga for minga work also became shorter, as extra drafts from the huelga grew. Second, the strong association of superior skill with the mingas, quite evident in seventeenth-century comments and in the fact that mingas were used for skilled jobs, whereas mitayos tended to be relegated to physical tasks, argues for the growth of the resident wage-labor force.[111]

Besides those mitayos who worked as mingas in silver production during the huelga, there were reportedly others who did so during their allotted mita spell also. Alonso Martínez de Pastrana, while official visitor to Potosí, in 1622 attributed most of the decline of the mita to this practice.[112] Since no wage advantage would seem to have accrued to the mitayo in doing this, as he would have had to pay yet another minga to replace him during the period he should have worked as a mitayo, and the cost of hiring this man would have been as much as he earned himself as a minga in that same period, the reason for avoiding mita service presumably lay among the following: better treatment by employers and overseers as a minga than as a mitayo; better working conditions or lighter tasks (for example, refinery work instead of hauling ore in a

110. AGI Charcas 36, Don Esteban de Lartáun to crown, Potosí, February 15, 1615, f. 7. Lartáun argued for the need to root more Indians in Potosí and in other mining towns, so that they should become more accustomed to, and accepting of, mine work. This he saw as a process for the long term. Children would grow up "with senses formed to the sound of the crowbar" ("hechos los sentidos al golpe de la barreta"), and gravitate naturally to mining. Since Potosí already had a sizable permanent native population by 1615, this was doubtless already happening, and it certainly became a standard pattern in later times, persisting to this day.

111. For example, the accounts of one ingenio from June 1632 to June 1633 indicate the regular employment in it of only one mitayo. See BAN Minas catalog No. 720, "1630–1638. Cuaderno 1 de los autos seguidos por Don Rodrigo de Mendoza y Manrique, administrador y arrendatario que fue de las minas y los ingenios del general Don Pedro Sores de Ulloa. . . ," accounts of the ingenio of Doña Francisca Campuzano, ff. 41–93.

112. AGI Charcas 36, Pastrana to crown, Potosí, March 22, 1622, f. 2v.

mine); and a better chance of recompense in the form of ore allowances in mining.

The development of a permanent minga force, added to the choice of minga work by mitayos in Potosí, some permanently and others during their huelga period, constitutes strong reason to believe that minga labor was in the main voluntarily undertaken. If all mingas had come from the huelga of the mita ordinaria, and if there had been no other work available in Potosí for mitayos in their rest periods, then it could be argued that minga labor was at least informally obligatory: that off-duty mitayos had no option but to work in silver production to earn the cash needed to support themselves and their families, and to pay their tributes—cash that the mita wage alone certainly did not approach supplying. But, given that much other work was to be had in Potosí, and that that work was evidently profitable enough to support families, since thousands existed on it, then the conclusion must be that the many Indians who at any moment were to be found in refineries and in the depths of the mines, and who were not there under the compulsion of the mita, had taken that work of their own volition. This means, therefore, that—to judge from the admittedly rather scant numerical information available—by the beginning of the seventeenth century about half the Indian labor force directly engaged in producing silver in Potosí was voluntary.

That statement clearly and significantly changes the prevailing view of the mining labor system of Potosí: that silver production rested wholly on a peculiarly vicious form of draft labor, the mita. On the other hand, the labor practices subsumed under that statement were anything but simple. Indians chose to become mingas for varied reasons: they could avoid a tiresome and costly return to their communities after a mita spell; they could avoid the future exactions of curacas and priests; above all, they could secure a substantial wage in minga labor. (Felipe de Godoy, in 1608, calculated that a mitayo needed 200 pesos to support himself during six months of labor in Potosí, but earned only 65. [See p. 105 above.] An extra-hand minga of that period, working as a barretero, might earn in six months, according to payrates given above, 234 pesos, and ore besides.) The voluntary minga system hid, however, a substantial transfer of value from the Indian community to the silver producers. Indeed, through the substitute minga practice, another burden was laid on the mitayos, in the form of the cash they had to produce in order to buy themselves out of draft labor. The initial burden fell on the curacas; but these, whenever possible, passed it on to the communities they controlled. In this way, Indian villages in the mita area found themselves supplying not only draft laborers to Potosí, but appreciable sums of money as well. These sums provided the producers of silver with what was, in effect, free, or very nearly free, labor; and not only that, but with free labor that tended to be more skilled, and hence more valuable, than that of mitayos. The minga system suited those who worked within it, and their employers, well. Both groups benefited from it—but at the expense, as always, of the communities that supplied the mitayos.

5

Work in Potosí

Specialization, conditions, welfare

Es un retrato del infierno entrar dentro, porque ver tantas cuevas y tan hondas, y tantas luces por tan diversas partes, y oír tantos golpes de los que están barreteando, es cosa que pierde el hombre el tino y aun el sentido."

(Fray Diego de Ocaña, 1600, on the cerro of Potosí*)

As the scale and technical complexity of silver production in Potosí increased, so also did the specialization and diversification of labor. At the beginning, when the techniques used were predominantly native, the types and specialization of workers were presumably very much the same as in preconquest times. Only one specialist is, in fact, clearly visible in those early decades: the guayrador, the operator of the windblown furnace. Whether the same men also operated the quimbalete beneath which ore was crushed before smelting is not apparent. Similarly, in mining itself, there is no indication of whether any division between cutters and carriers of ore existed. The only specialization that can definitely be glimpsed in ore extraction is that of the indios varas—the native miners to whom Spanish mine owners, in effect, leased portions of workings. These men clearly acted as supervisors as well, possibly, as actual miners. Under them, and hired by them, worked other Indians, probably yanaconas in large part.

These mine laborers were probably soon equipped, or equipped themselves, with Spanish iron picks and bars, in place of their

Un viaje fascinante por la América hispana del siglo XVI (ed. Fr. Arturo Alvarez, Madrid 1969), p. 187.

native implements. But this, though adding to the workers' efficiency, would not have modified the existing organization of labor. Possibly the first native people to become specialists in a Spanish technique were those who learned to use bellows-blown furnaces of the Castilian type at Porco. Just when such furnaces came into use is conjectural; but some seem to have been built by 1549.[1]

It was, of course, the coming of the alien, complex, and many-stepped amalgamation process that brought extensive division and specialization of Indian labor to the Potosí industry. This development was actively accelerated by Viceroy Toledo's efforts to educate Indians in Potosí in amalgamation techniques. For that purpose, as noted before, he set up a school in each parish of the town, where Indians who had already learned the method from Pedro Fernández de Velasco should transmit it to others.[2] Toledo's efforts in that direction were admittedly of little effect. (See chapter 3 above.) So there were few, if any, independent Indian amalgamators. But as the volume of ore extraction increased, to feed the amalgamation refineries, specialization and further sub-specialization of workers appeared.

Various manuscripts of the 1630s show this differentiation in a developed state. Ore was cut by barreteros (Spanish *barreta:* bar), and was carried from the face of the workings on the backs of *apires* (Quechua *apay:* to carry), who dumped it in heaps on the leveled platform, or *cancha,* at the entrance of the mine. There, before being taken to a refinery by llama, it was picked over, and the waste material discarded, by *pallires* (Quechua *pallay:* to gather), some of whom might be women. The mine workings were kept clear for the passage of apires by a number of *siquepiches* (a vulgar Quechua term, signifying roughly "backside cleaners"), whose job it was to gather and carry out rubble; and if the mine needed internal support, inevitably of stonework since large timbers were so dear in Potosí, this was constructed by *pirquires* (Quechua *pirqay:* to build walls). These various specialized workers were directed by a number of Indian supervisors, or *pongos.* The origin of this term is in

1. Cieza de León writes of the smelting of silver in Porco in that year "with fire, [the refiners] having for that purpose their large bellows" ("con fuego, teniendo para ello sus fuelles grandes"). *Crónica,* ch. cix, p. 449.

2. AGI Lima 29, tomo 1, Potosí, March 20, 1573, Toledo to crown, "Hacienda."

the Quechua *punku:* door; and Capoche defines pongos as the door-keepers of mines (some of which might actually have a locking grille over the entrance).[3] But the word's connotation of supervisor was already well established by the time Capoche wrote. Toledo, for example, had so used it in one of his mining ordinances of 1574, eleven years before the composition of the *Relación*.[4] So, for example, there appears in one case an *apirepongo*—the leader of a gang of apires; and ordinances came to state that for every twenty Indians in a mine there should be one pongo.[5] It is clear that these various specialities generally remained distinct; though sometimes a certain overlapping took place, as would be expected. A manuscript of 1634 reveals, for example, that in the mines of one Francisco Gómez Silvestre at Esmoraca, barreteros and apires spent Saturday sorting ores on the surface, so temporarily becoming pallires.[6]

Amalgamation refineries developed a specialization of labor at least equal to that of mining itself. Indian *morteros* fed ores for crushing between the stamps of the mill and its mortar block. They also shoveled the crushed ore onto inclined sieves, returning to the mill any material that was not fine enough to pass through the mesh. Capoche recounts that Indian women and youths were also hired to sieve ores in ingenios, using hand sieves—though to no great effect, he thought.[7] The blending of crushed ore with mercury and other reagents was done by the *beneficiador*, or refiner. This post was the most responsible of any in the ingenio, and was normally held by a Spaniard or mestizo, though manuscripts show

---

3. ". . . son los porteros de las minas . . ." *Relación*, p. 151.

4. ". . . el indio que tiene la mina a cargo, que llaman pongo . . ." in No. 11 of "Ordenanzas del Virrey Don Francisco de Toledo acerca de los descubrimientos, registros y estacas de las minas. . . ." in Levillier, *Gobernantes*, tomo 8, p. 237.

5. This last statement and the types of workers described here are given in BAN Minas tomo 15, item 1 (Minas catalog No. 953), which is part of a suit between Doña Francisca Campuzano and Don Rodrigo de Mendoza y Manrique. The suit spanned several decades, but the evidence drawn on here (ff. 537v.–618 passim) refers to the early 1630s.

6. See f. 28 of BAN Minas tomo 131, item 3 (Minas catalog No. 691), "1634. Visita que el Licenciado Don Mesía de Arriola . . . tomó del ingenio nombrado San Francisco. . . ."

7. *Relación*, p. 122, ". . . y por la falta que hay de indios se mingan las mujeres y muchachos, y les dan a dos reales [daily] y no ciernen casi nada."

140 Chapter 5

at least one case of an Indian beneficiador in the Potosí district.[8]
The ore was then blended with the various other substances employed in the refining process by *repasires* (Spanish *repasar:* literally,
to re-pass, and hence to mix thoroughly). Possibly these men used
paddles for the task, but it was certainly common enough for them
to stir up the amalgamating material by wading in it barelegged.[9]
Once amalgamation was complete, *lavadores* (washers) or *tinadores*
saw to the washing away of waste material in tubs *(tinas)*. The shifting of ore and other substances around the mill was performed by
servires (Spanish *servir:* to serve). Among still more specialized
Indian personnel, an ingenio might employ a *leñatero* to gather fuel
(Spanish *leña:* firewood); a *carbonero* to make charcoal (Spanish
carbón); and an *hornero,* sometimes called a *quemador,* to supervise
roasting of sulfide ores before amalgamation and the production
of magistral by roasting (Spanish *quemar)* pyrites in a furnace (Spanish *horno).* One isolated ingenio in the province of Chichas even
possessed a specialist in making clay hoods for removing mercury
from amalgam.[10]

One variety of refining work that had originally been the province of men seems to have passed into women's hands in the late
decades of the sixteenth century. This was the operation of guayras.
Women not only gleaned neglected pieces of good ore from tailings discarded on the cerro, but also smelted them in guayras. To
their gleanings they added, for smelting, fragments of high-grade
ore taken from mines by barreteros. An early seventeenth-century

8. In 1634, at the ingenio of Nuestra Señora de Guadalupe in the province of
Chichas, the beneficiador was an Indian from Porco named Pedro Hachata. See
BAN Minas tomo 131, item 2 (Minas catalog No. 690a): "1634. Visita que el
Licenciado Don Martín de Arriola . . . tomó del ingenio nombrado Nuestra Señora
de Guadalupe . . ." f. 31v.

9. ". . . en tiempo de fríos y aguas hay cajones que requieren muchas doblas
[repeated mixings] hasta que el pie de los indios los calienta . . .": BAN Minas
tomo 15, item 1 (Minas catalog No. 953, f. 537, para. 35), early 1630s. See also
Capoche, *Relación,* p. 123.

10. A maker of "caperuzas de barro para desazogar piñas." See BAN Minas
tomo 131, item 2 (Minas catalog No. 690a), f. 61. This same ms makes reference
to some of the other refining specializations described here; and further data have
been drawn from BAN Minas tomo 131, item 3 (Minas catalog No. 691), a ms
referring to the early 1630s; and from AGI Charcas 21, "Respuesta del Licenciado
Robles de Salcedo . . ." beginning Potosí, October 28, 1639.

account relates that these ore cutters would climb to the entrance of the mine on Wednesdays (after two days of underground work), receive food that their womenfolk carried up onto the cerro to supply them for the rest of the week, and hand over to the women small pieces of particularly rich ore that had turned up in recent digging. This practice was so general and so much an accepted part of barreteros' behavior that mine owners and supervisors had little choice but to tolerate it.[11] Women, for their part, seem to have become expert not only in refining by guayra, but also in appraising the ores to be smelted. They must have developed a keen eye in order to glean efficiently. And some of the ore that was gleaned, or abstracted from the cerro, circulated through the native ore market of Potosí before processing—a trade that was at least partly in women's hands.[12] Several possible, and probably interconnected, explanations for the entry of women into ore trading, and more interestingly, into the traditional refining practice with guayras readily come to mind. A broad one would be the general effect of acculturation to mining as an accepted way of life that Potosí seems to have exercised on its population. More particularly, the absorption of available male labor by the expansion of Potosí's industry in the wake of amalgamation may have left women as the only potential labor force for guayra operations. Third, as individuals, women clearly sought to supplement their menfolk's wages; and one possible means of doing so was to smelt in guayras.

In general, and with the obvious exception of female workers, the specialized labor in mines and refineries was done by mingas, with the carrying tasks being left to mitayos. The development of an extensive range of specialists indeed both impelled, and was facilitated by, the increase in numbers of mingas in Potosí and the district. The economies available from division of labor inclined employers to seek specialists, and workers possessing some aptitude could more easily develop it if they were employed perma-

---

11. Ocaña, *Un viaje fascinante*, pp. 202–03.
12. Ibid., p. 202. See also, for the Indians' trade, Capoche, *Relación*, p. 150 ff.. For discussion of sixteenth-century debate in Potosí over the licitness (moral and legal) of the Indians' trade in ore, consult Josep M. Barnadas, "Una polémica colonial: Potosí, 1579–1584," *Jahrbuch für Geschichte von Staat, Wirtschaft und Gesellschaft Lateinamerikas*, Band 10 (1973), pp. 16–69.

nently as mingas, rather than sporadically as mitayos. At the same
time, the tradition of permanent, nondraft labor existing at Potosí
from the start encouraged the growth of a specialized and skilled
work force.

A question that follows naturally from discussion of labor specialization is that of the conditions of work, and treatment, of
laborers, both mitayos and mingas.

The forcing of American natives into mines under conditions of
great hardship and danger is one of the most severe moral charges
brought against Spain's conduct of the American empire.[13] This
sort of criticism, while undoubtedly well supported by fact, as will
shortly be seen, nevertheless has something in it of a reflex reaction. Mining and punishment have come to be naturally linked in
the minds of many. And for nearly everyone the very notion of
mining is abhorrent, associated as it is with darkness, wetness,
airlessness, a sense of entrapment beneath threatening masses of
rock, and perhaps yet more elemental fears. Few casual visitors to
even a modern and well-engineered mine can have re-emerged
into the outside air with these apprehensions anything but confirmed; so the impression generally held of conditions in colonial
Spanish mines is understandably one of almost unremitted bleak-
ness. This sort of belief about mining has been made the more tena-
ble by the sparsity of information on the subject. Apart from a few
accounts by writers on late eighteenth-century Mexico, little description is to be found of colonial mining conditions. Fortunately
for the historian, however, the ocean of manuscripts relating to
colonial Potosí occasionally throws up pieces of information on
the subject.

That working conditions below ground, especially for mitayos,
could be atrocious is beyond doubt. The official defender of the
people of Chucuito wrote in the mid-1630s that mitayos from there
were forced to work underground for twenty-three weeks a year,
without rest, day and night "without light, 1,200 to 1,800 feet
down, dragging themselves along adits and over supports, cutting ore with bars weighing 30 pounds, at the expense of blood
and sweat; and the apires, who are those who carry and extract

13.   For example, Stanley and Barbara Stein, *The colonial heritage of Latin America* (New York 1970), p. 79.

the ores, crawl along like snakes, burdened with ore, and when they have to pass through narrow places, they tie their sacks to their feet, exerting greater than human efforts with their bodies, and so, dragging themselves along, they get by; and if they do not do so quickly, the mineros deal them many kicks and lashes with a whip. . . ."[14]

Some obvious hyperbole and special pleading color this account. Nobody could work indefinitely without rest, as the writer clearly states. Nevertheless, it is probably an accurate depiction of what subterranean conditions could be, at or near their worst, for the mita laborer. A document of the 1590s confirms that some mine operators had a habit of whipping Indians for allegedly inadequate performance, and that the apires did sometimes tie their ore sack to a foot in negotiating difficult places or ladders.[15] Again, Capoche recounts an incident of the early 1580s in which an Indian carrier, fleeing back into a mine to avoid the stick with which the overseer threatened to strike him, "on account of his alarm fell, and was dashed into a hundred thousand pieces."[16] Capoche is a balanced witness, notably sympathetic to the native workers in Potosí, but also proud of the great enterprise that had been so quickly constructed there by Spanish ingenuity and effort. The incident he describes undoubtedly occurred; and beating or whipping of native mine workers, especially of mitayos, was probably a common enough practice.

It is Capoche who provides the best single account of under-

14. AGI Charcas 56, anonymous protector de los naturales of Chucuito, on behalf of the curacas and indios naturales of the province, nd, but seen in the Council of the Indies on April 24, 1638: ". . . andando debajo de la tierra sin luz, doscientos y trescientos estados, arrastrando por los socavones y puentes, barreteando con unas barretas de treinta libras a fuerza de sangre y sudor, y los apires, que son los que cargan y sacan los metales fuera de la mina, vienen arrastrando como culebras, cargados con los metales, y cuando han de pasar por partes estrechas, se atan los costales a los pies llenos de metales, haciendo fuerza más que humana con el cuerpo, así arrastrando las pasan, y si no es con toda puntualidad, los mineros con un rebenque les dan muchos azotes y coces. . . ."

15. AGI Charcas 17, *petición*, c. 1594, of Doña Ana de Avendaño y Zúñiga, et al., in "Provisión del Marqués de Cañete . . . para que el Licenciado Lopidana volviese a algunas personas de Potosí los indios que les había quitado . . ." Callao, December 13, 1594.

16. *Relación*, p. 109.

ground conditions. The apires carried their loads from the face of the mines up long ladders. These usually had three heavy ropes of twisted hide for their vertical members, between which were placed rungs, normally of wood in Capoche's time. In effect, each ladder was double, with a shared central vertical. The length might run to some 55 feet (10 *estados*). Ladders were commonly arranged in series, with a wooden platform *(barbacoa)* as a landing between them. Since by Capoche's day some mines measured vertically as much as 1,000 feet (180 estados) from their entrance to their lowest workings,[17] long series of such ladders must already have been necessary. The ore sacks used in the 1580s were simple woolen blankets, knotted across the chest so that the load could be carried on the back, space permitting. The apires, according to Capoche, climbed the ladders in groups of three, the lead man holding a candle in one hand. (Other, later accounts say that the candle might be tied to a little finger or to the forehead, so as to leave the hands freer for climbing.) The carriers naturally arrived breathless and sweating at the mine entrance, "and the refreshment they generally find as consolation for their effort is being called dogs, and being molested for having brought up little ore, or being told that they have been slow, or that they have brought up earth, or that they have stolen the ore."[18]

A visit today to the colonial workings in the cerro confirms the atmosphere of hardship and danger conveyed by Capoche's words. Galleries suddenly open out into great caverns, where a large body of ore has been carved out. Access tunnels in the upper part of the cerro, where most of the early workings were driven, are wide enough only to permit passage of a man—as little as two feet.[19] The cerro, however, did hold for workers two advantages that made it generally less unpleasant a place than many other Spanish-American mines. In its upper reaches there was little flooding, since they lay above the water table. Flooding was a problem mainly of the seventeenth century and later, when the higher mines be-

17. AGI Charcas 35, No. 66, reales oficiales of Potosí to crown, Potosí, February 11, 1585.

18. *Relación*, p. 109.

19. Rivas and Carrasco, *Geología*, tomo 2, p. 77. Ocaña notes graphically that, in the mines, workers going in opposite directions "pasan como culebras cuando van mudando el cuero." *Un viaje fascinante*, p. 136.

came extremely deep and when veins in the lower flanks were attacked.[20] Secondly, the porphyritic rock of the igneous stock of the cerro, in which most veins occurred, is a compact substance. Collapses of mine workings were therefore less frequent than they might have been. To these two natural alleviations of danger and discomfort must be added one manmade technique—the cutting of adits. (See Introduction.) It is impossible to say what proportion of mines in the cerro were served by these; probably not a large one, though it included the main workings on the major veins. But at least a portion of the Indian work force was spared much arduous climbing, wriggling through serpentine passages, and shortage of breathable air, by the existence of adits.

The central question about mining labor conditions are those of the precise danger attached to the work, and the mortality resulting from that danger. The questions will probably never be accurately answered, for lack of the necessary numerical information. By Capoche's report there died every year in the hospital some fifty or more Indians as a result of both mining and refining injuries—people, he said, whom "this wild beast [the mining industry] swallows alive."[21] This figure evidently does not include those who died outright as a result of accidents in mines or refineries. Mining accidents—falls and entrapments by the collapse of workings—were clearly frequent enough. Capoche, himself a miner, called the cerro a "harsh executioner of Indians, for each day it consumes and destroys them, and their lives are made misery by the fear of death."[22] He attributed this high mortality to the Indians' rashness within the mines: they were by nature cowards,

---

20. BAN Minas catalog No. 953, f. 604v., refers to some barreteros of the 1630s on the veta Centeno standing in water while they hacked out ore by touch below water level.

21. *Relación*, p. 159, ". . . que esta fiera bestia se traga vivos."

22. *Relación*, p. 158: ". . . se colegirá . . . cuán riguroso verdugo ha sido este cerro para esta nación, pues cada día los consume y acaba y ellos tienen la vida aguada con el temor de la muerte." Capoche's numbers and observations are closely confirmed by the commentary of Antonio de Ayáns, SJ, in 1596: on average one or two Indian mine workers died weekly in the cerro from falls or injuries caused by falling rocks, while seven or eight suffered less than fatal injuries. In addition, groups of thirty or forty were frequently (*muchas veces*) killed in collapses. Besides these fatalities, others occurred in the cerro that were simply never known about. "Breve relación de los agravios . . ." p. 38, para. 7.

but in the mines they took risks that the most valiant would shun. The two examples Capoche gives to demonstrate his contention suggest, however, that it was pressure from the Spanish mine owners as much as the workers' foolhardiness that led to catastrophe. In one case, twenty-eight Indians perished, and in the other, five, after strenuous rescue attempts.[23]

The scale of the mortality figures given by Capoche, that of other, though admittedly sparse numbers of mining deaths given in manuscript sources, and the absence in official correspondence of commentary on deaths in the workings, taken together, convey the impression that mining accidents, though frequent, and a source of constant fear to the Indians, did not destroy them on quite the scale that the graphic language of the *Relación* would suggest. Officials—viceroys, visitors, members of the Audiencia of La Plata, treasury officers in Potosí—were constantly concerned with anything threatening silver production, including supply of labor. Supply of labor was probably, indeed, their main concern. But in their reports they rarely allude to deaths or injuries in mines as a threat to that supply. This is probably not a case of their covering up a well-known source of abuse and danger to Indians, since they unhesitatingly reported the existence of other sorts of maltreatment: for instance, the overworking of mitayos. So, taken as a whole, the available evidence suggests that deaths from mining accidents were not on a massive scale. A figure of a few hundreds yearly seems more likely than one of thousands: bad enough, to be sure, but not so large as to pose a threat by itself either to the Potosí work force or to the total population on which Potosí drew.

To those who died inside mine workings, or directly as a result of injuries suffered in workings, must be added an unknown number of others who succumbed to diseases brought on by adverse working conditions in various stages of the production of silver. Scarcely any precise information is available on the ills suffered specifically by miners and refinery workers; but it is hardly a risky surmise to suggest that they were probably mainly respiratory afflictions, resulting from breathing dusty air and from passing from high temperatures inside the workings into the freezing exterior air at the top of the cerro. Disease resulting from mining was probably less prevalent than that caused by refinery conditions—particularly by the dust raised when ore was crushed in the stamp

23. *Relación*, pp. 158–59.

mills. Silicosis is a common lung complaint of miners of modern Potosí, engendered by the great amounts of dust raised by pneumatic drilling apparatus. But colonial ore-cutting technique with bars and picks would have produced rather little dust. Blasting, introduced in the second half of the seventeenth century, would, it is true, have given rise to hazards from dust.

Regulations on mine safety were few. The authorities were certainly aware of the dangers and of their duty to protect Indians from them, but apparently placed reliance on the owners' self-interest in the survival of the work force to safeguard the lives and limbs of the men. Neither in the 1561 mining ordinances for Potosí, which were an assemblage of new and earlier regulations, nor in Toledo's series of 1574, which both drew on the 1561 code and became the basis of most subsequent regulations until the late eighteenth century, is much consideration given to safety. Only two clauses, Nos. 20 and 21 of title 2, in a total of ninety-four given in 1561, and the three constituting the title "De las labores y reparos de las minas y ruinas que suceden en ellas" in a total of ninety given by Toledo, refer specifically to safety. Toledo's three safety rules, repeating and elaborating points made in 1561, are as follows. The first bans opencast mining, because of the dangers of collapses, and orders that supports *(puentes)* of native rock shall be left to shore up underground workings. The second forbids removal or weakening of these supports. And the third orders that ladders shall be sufficiently strong and of specific dimensions—no more than 82.5 feet long (15 *brazas*) and with rungs no more than 16.5 inches (1 *codo*) apart. The mine owners' compliance with these orders was to be checked periodically by an inspector, either the *alcalde mayor de minas* or the *veedor*. By the late sixteenth century, three veedores were regularly present on the cerro. One other regulation of Toledo's has a bearing on mine safety. Ordinance 6 of the title "De los desmontes, trabajo y paga de los indios" states that groups of twenty or more Indian workers in the cerro shall be accompanied by an Indian supervisor; but this was more designed to ensure they worked hard than to keep them out of danger.[24]

---

24. The 1561 ordinances are printed in Guillermo Lohmann Villena's edition of Juan de Matienzo, *Gobierno del Perú (1567)* (Paris and Lima 1967), pp. 139–56. For Toledo's ordinances of La Plata, February 7, 1574, see Levillier, *Gobernantes*, tomo 8, pp. 143–240.

Safety regulations may have been few. Those few, nevertheless, were observed in letter and spirit. Again, precise knowledge is elusive: it cannot be said what proportion of safety offenses was discovered and prosecuted by the alcalde mayor de minas and the veedores; but some certainly were. For example, in the collapse recounted by Capoche that led to the death of twenty-eight Indians, a veedor had declared the mine unsafe and banned work in it. The owner ignored the order, and was subsequently fined 12,500 pesos, of which a part was distributed among the widows of the dead men.[25] This was not an isolated case of punishment, though the fine may have been higher than usual. A series of brief accounts of cases in the 1590s over the death, injury, or mistreatment of Indians in mines confirms that prosecution and punishment of the offender were usually pursued, though sometimes not carried through.[26] This series relates twenty-one such cases. The most common category, with eight incidents, was ill-treatment (beating, whipping, or kicking) of Indians by mine supervisors (*mineros*), even to the point of causing death. Second most frequent (six cases) was injury or death of Indians in collapses of workings. Then, with two cases each, came falls from ladders, unspecified mine accidents, and bad treatment in an ingenio. Finally there was one case of an Indian's being forced to carry a heavy wooden stamp block (a *mazo de soto*) to an ingenio, falling, having his leg crushed, and consequently dying. These cannot have been all the incidents of injury or death befalling Indians in the course of silver production over the several years covered in the document, but possibly the proportions of the different sorts of incidents were typical. Defendants were fined on average some 200 pesos for each death, and were generally made to pay for masses for the dead man. The fines for injuries averaged some 120 pesos, though they varied widely,

25. *Relación*, p. 158.
26. BAN Minas tomo 125, item 13 (Minas catalog No. 859): "1652–1656. Competencia de jurisdicción suscitada entre Don Francisco Sarmiento de Mendoza y el Capitán Pedro de Montalvo, corregidor y alcalde mayor de minas de Potosí. . . ." Despite the initial date given in the title, much of this ms refers to cases of the 1590s, adduced as evidence in a dispute over whether the corregidor or the alcalde mayor de minas had first instance jurisdiction in cases of injury to Indian mine workers.

from 10 to 350 pesos. A portion of the fine, perhaps a half, was paid to the injured man in compensation. Defendants were often briefly jailed, and then banished from the cerro or from Potosí itself. In eleven cases, however (seven of deaths and four of injuries), prosecution was not concluded because the defendant was said to have disappeared. So in over half the instances, no punishment was received.

In general, therefore, the evidence suggests that, despite the sparsity of formal safety regulations for mining, some official inspection of workings took place; and mine owners and overseers found guilty of operating unsafe mines and maltreating Indians were brought to book, if then rather lightly punished.

The series of cases just summarized includes two instances of maltreatment in refineries, but none of injuries there. The absence of such cases is perhaps not just a matter of chance. Ingenio work was often cold and wet—an entry in one ingenio's account book records the hiring of Indians to break the ice impeding the water-wheel on winter mornings[27]—but it was inherently freer of accidents than mining itself. Capoche, to be sure, gives an instance of a refinery wall's falling on and killing four Indians; but that was clearly a freak accident.

On the other hand, the ingenio presented more insidious dangers of long-term and often fatal *disease,* caused by the dust raised during the crushing of ore. That the work of the morteros who tended the stamp mills was immediately unpleasant and hazardous was recognized at the time;[28] but that the dust particles could both cause direct damage to the lungs and predispose the suffering to other respiratory diseases seems not to have been appreciated. The progression from silicosis (damage to the lungs from silica particles) to other, fatal infections has been demonstrated through examination of remains of colonial mine workers in Peru. These remains—from an encomienda near Arequipa embracing part of southern Peru and northern Chile, that had its own mines—have been preserved in mummified form thanks to the extremely

---

27. BAN Minas tomo 9 (Minas catalog No. 720): account book of the ingenio of Doña Francisca Campuzano, f. 46, entry for July 26–31, 1632.

28. Capoche, *Relación*, p. 159, ". . . asistir al mortero, que es lo de más trabajo por el polvo que reciben en los ojos y boca, basta para hacerles mucho daño."

low humidity of the region. An examination of twelve mummies reveals that the lungs contain particles of silver, iron, and copper, as well as silica; and of the twelve, no fewer than ten seem to have died of pneumonia, while three show signs of tuberculosis. Silicosis can lead to both these diseases. Lung disease was probably the reason for the enlargement of the heart also found in some of these mummified workers.[29]

Other stages of the refining process presented further hazards. The danger of lead poisoning from vapors given off during the preparation of lead flux for smelting silver, or in the recovery of lead after smelting, was recognized in Toledo's mining ordinances of 1574.[30] To recover lead, refiners should use an enclosed building with chimneys some 7 meters tall (4 estados). More severe a poison than lead, however, was mercury—a far more common substance in Potosí, once amalgamation came in, than lead had been previously. Here again, the danger was recognized in Toledo's regulations, or at least recognized in part. The furnaces used to drive off mercury as vapor from the finished amalgam should be set apart from the refinery itself, and equipped with chimneys some 5 meters in height (3 estados), "so that the Indians shall not receive the smoke in any fashion."[31] Some early problems evidently occurred over this. Attacking in the late 1570s an allegation that mercury processing was killing Indians, Toledo acknowledged that initially some Indians had been affected (*"se azogaron"*) in Potosí, but that, on enquiry, he had discovered only seven or eight

---

29.   Marvin J. Allison, "Paleopathology in Peru," *Natural History*, 88:2 (1979), pp. 74–82. This article also shows from examination of other mummies that tuberculosis existed in Peru in pre-European times. There can be little doubt, however, that its incidence among miners was increased by silicosis. The disease for that reason remains one of the most serious scourges of modern miners in Potosí and elsewhere in Bolivia. Allison does not distinguish between miners, strictly speaking, and refiners, in his discussion. For reasons given above, it is likely that refiners were the main victims of silicosis in colonial times. Also, it is impossible to say what proportion of either class of worker suffered from lung diseases. Allison identifies his "miners" precisely by the presence of mineral particles in the lungs; others not showing these signs may also have been miners or refiners.

30.   Ordenanza 8 of the title "De los desmontes, trabajo y paga de los indios," in Levillier, *Gobernantes*, tomo 8, p. 234.

31.   Ibid.

cases; and most of those had occurred when Indians took stolen ores to their houses to refine them: the implication of some sort of natural retribution being quite clear! Nowadays, Toledo wrote, "if any Indian dies [in Potosí], he dies as if in his own lands."[32]

This sort of dismissal of the problem seems to have become normal once amalgamation was familiar and firmly established. Colonial observers do not comment on it, nor are there further safety regulations on the handling of mercury. It is inconceivable, however, that poisoning by mercury vapor did not continue in some measure, since silver and mercury amalgam could be separated only by heat; and it was also standard practice to heat tailings from the washing process so as to recover mercury from them by volatilization. Furthermore, the treading by Indians of the initial mixture of ore, mercury, salt, and so on, to promote amalgamation, brought mercury into direct contact with the skin, and hence by absorption into the body. But this particular danger is not raised at all in contemporary writings. Possibly the effects of mercury poisoning—loss of teeth, shaking, and paralysis—did not appear quickly or dramatically enough to call attention.

With the evidence available, it is impossible to arrive at satisfactorily definite conclusions about working conditions in Potosí, and particularly about the degree of danger and the chance of death faced by Indians working in silver production. Of working conditions it can only be said that they were bad, but that in other Spanish American colonial mines (Huancavelica, for example) they were plainly worse. Mitayos were obviously worse off than mingas. Regulations on working conditions were minimal; but precisely because of their scarcity, the degree to which they were enforced, and offenders punished, is mildly surprising. The colonial government did try to safeguard Indians against risks; and very probably those safeguards had some effect in reducing injuries and deaths. Regarded in one sense, any deaths of workers in silver production, especially among the drafted labor force of mitayos, can be seen as reprehensible; but mortality does not seem to have been as high

---

32. "... y si algún indio muere, muere como en sus tierras." Para. 14 of an undated letter, probably Lima 1578–79, "Lo que por Don Francisco de Toledo . . . se responde a los capítulos que los inquisidores de este Reino le dieron . . . ," in AGI Lima 30, tomo 4, f. 213.

in Potosí as has sometimes been thought, and certainly was not on what might be called a "Black Legend" scale.

Rather more can be said of abuses of Indian workers by Spanish employers. (By "abuse" here is meant treatment that was forbidden by law, or thought by the colonial authorities to be contrary to good custom.) Some of these have already been mentioned—the physical and verbal attacks on workers by dissatisfied supervisors and employers. But native laborers, mitayos especially, constantly suffered from a wider range of abuses than those. Probably the commonest was overwork.

On the hours to be worked by Indians, both mitayos and mingas, Toledo laid down detailed regulations in 1574. Labor should start an hour and a half after sunrise and cease at sunset, with an hour reserved for rest and eating at midday. On account of the winter cold, Indians engaged in washing ores should work only from 10 a.m. to 4 p.m. in May, June, July, and August.[33]

These rules must have been dead letter from the day they were issued. It is clear from various sources that work in ingenios went on around the clock, at least during the wet season, when advantage had to be taken of every hour of adequate water flow.[34] Shift work on some pattern clearly developed early, though its organization is uncertain. Slight evidence from the 1630s suggests that at least in some refining tasks (roasting magistral and pulverizing iron) day and night shifts of twelve hours were used;[35] and there is obviously a good possibility that other refinery workers were organized in the same way.

Certainly, in mining, day and night shifts seem to have developed early. Capoche in passing mentions, while recounting the

33.   Ordenanzas 2 and 3 in the title "De los desmontes, trabajo y paga de los indios," of Toledo's mining ordinances of La Plata, February 7, 1574: Levillier, *Gobernantes*, tomo 8, p. 231.

34.   See, for example, AGI Indiferente General 857, "Copia de los ingenios del asiento de Potosí, visitados por Francisco Miguel de Orruño, veedor del cerro," nd, ca. 1576, passim.

35.   See, e.g., ff. 51 and 53 of the ingenio account book for 1632–33 in BAN Minas tomo 9 (Minas catalog No. 720).

36.   *Relación*, p. 158: "Y fue el caso que en la veta rica, traía un español en compañía de otro cincuenta y seis indios; con los veinte y ocho trabajaba de día, y con los otros tantos, de noche."

collapse of the mine whose owner ignored the veedor's safety orders, that the fifty-six Indians working there were divided into equal day and night shifts.[36] Clearly, then, within ten years of the issuance of Toledo's regulations on working hours, the ban on night work implicit in them went unheeded.

Twelve-hour shifts in mining would perhaps have been tolerable to the Indians, though immensely hard work, if they could have been sure of having the other twelve hours to rest. Many of them very probably could not rest, however, because the custom quickly arose among mine owners and supervisors of demanding a certain *amount*, rather than *period*, of labor from the men. This was in direct contravention of another of Toledo's ordinances of 1574— that forbidding miners and refiners to demand piecework of any Indian employed by them.[37] Nevertheless, piecework soon came onto the scene. It may not have been demanded of barreteros, who, being characteristically mingas, were on the whole in a better position to resist such demands than mitayos. But it was most certainly demanded from apires, who were nearly all mitayos. They were expected to carry up to the surface a certain amount of ore in a week's work. The amount demanded varied with the depth of the mine and other conditions, but undoubtedly was set on the high side; and if an apire fell short, he could expect quick and severe punishment. In 1594, for example, an apire by the name of Alonso Yana complained that the minero supervising him had whipped him for bringing up one heap *(montón)* too few during the week. This happened after sunset on a Friday, officially the end of the working week. Alonso decided to cut ore himself, and evidently undermined a support, since a collapse ensued, as a result of which his arm was broken. Or again, in 1596, a mine *mayordomo* accused two apires of not having formed all the heaps required of them ("los montones que les había dado de tarea"); punished them with fifty lashes apiece; and, so they complained, counted as only one or two days' work what they had taken the whole week to accom-

---

37.   Ordenanza 7 of the title "De los desmontes, trabajo y paga de los indios": "Y porque algunas personas acostumbran dar tareas a los dichos indios, tomando esto por medio para acrecentarles el trabajo: ordeno y mando que ninguna persona limite a los dichos indios alquilados lo que en un día han de trabajar, sino que hagan lo que pudieren. . . ."

plish ("lo que habían trabajado en una semana, se lo contaba por uno o dos días").[38]

The setting of quotas for ore extraction continued, and very probably expanded, as time passed. This was only a natural consequence of the declining yield of ores that generally afflicted Potosí. A clear statement of economic pressure's leading to an increased work load on at least the apires comes in 1611 from Carlos Corso de Leca, a highly experienced miner and refiner in Potosí, and at the time alcalde mayor de minas. As such, he had responsibility for Indian welfare in mines, a duty that he seems to have taken seriously enough. He found that mineros were quite consciously trying to balance the silver content of the ore that was being mined against the costs of producing silver from it. Many of the extraction costs were all but fixed: those, for example, of ladders, tools, and wages of supervisors; and the refining costs were outside the minero's control, since his province was strictly extraction. So the obvious means of economy available to the minero was to press the apires into extracting more ore for their wage. Corso found that apires who worked as nearly continuously as they could for five days and nights were at best credited with five day shifts' worth of ore extracted, and sometimes with as little as two day shifts' worth.[39]

Further detail comes from the 1630s on the matter of quotas. In one mine on the Veta de los Ciegos of the cerro, the apires were obliged not only to extract newly cut ore, but also to gather up fragments that had been previously mined but left underground *(brozas)*. Of these they had, in return for twelve hours' wages, to extract some 260 pounds per day; and of the newly mined mate-

38. Cases heard by the alcalde mayor de minas, Potosí, December 9, 1594, and December 20, 1596: ff. 48v. and 54 respectively in BAN Minas tomo 125, item 13 (Minas catalog No. 859).

39. AGI Charcas 51, "Información nueva de servicios de Carlos Corso de Leca," La Plata, November? 1611, unfoliated (JHR). Corso's account of the mineros' attempt to balance production against costs, and the resulting overworking of apires, is fully confirmed by Felipe de Godoy, a former treasurer of the caja of Potosí, in 1608. See BL Sloane mss 3,055, "Felipe de Godoy a la magestad de Felipe 3° en respuesta de una carta . . . ," La Plata, February 14, 1608.

rial they had to bring up enough, in a day, to yield 260 pounds of clean, sorted ore *(metal limpio)*, ready to be sent to the refinery.[40]

No evidence has come to light about work quotas in refineries; and it is possible that none was imposed there, since refining was done largely with minga workers.

Mining mitayos suffered first as quotas were imposed; but the evidence just presented suggests they may have suffered more from the progressive increase of quotas as the average quality of ore gradually declined. Although the statutory mita wages continued to be paid, the worker in effect seems to have received ever less for each unit of effort he made. Exacerbating this abuse was the mine owners' demand that mitayos should provide their own basic equipment: candles and something in which to carry ore. Regulations ordered that owners should buy these, and initially some, at least, did so. Once again, however, economic pressures caused by declining ore yields placed ever greater burdens on the mitayos. A report of 1613 asserted that Indians had to spend over 100,000 pesos a year on candles, though mine owners did provide some. The account books of two mines in 1632–33, however, contain no entries at all for candles (though they do include such things as crowbars and steel, as well as wages, which suggests they are complete).[41] The high cost of providing candles for the mitayos is suggested by the writer in 1613, who estimated that on average each spent 4 reales a week to make up the shortfall of what the owners failed to supply. This was obviously a very sizable slice from a mitayo's weekly wage of 20 reales. The writer is clearly arguing on the workers' behalf, and so may exaggerate somewhat their spending on candles; but still the cost seems likely to have

40. BAN Minas tomo 15, item 1 (Minas catalog No. 953), f. 548, para. 2. The amount demanded of both brozas and metal limpio is expressed as 1.5 cargas; and the carga in question is one of 7 arrobas, with 25 pounds to each arroba. In another section (f. 871) of the same ms, it is stated that Indians working through the Sojo adit were expected to extract 525 pounds (3 cargas of 7 arrobas) of ore in 24 hours; though here it seems that they were being paid for two twelve-hour shifts.

41. AGI Charcas 19, Don Hierónimo Maldonado de Buendía to crown, La Plata, March 1, 1613, f.1. BAN Minas tomo 9 (Minas catalog No. 720), accounts of the Los Ciegos mine, and of another in the veta Centeno.

been considerable, especially when owners stopped providing candles altogether. The mitayos' expenses for ore receptacles—usually, it seems, woolen blankets—are not known; but they must also have been considerable, since the cloth cannot have long survived being dragged and bumped, full of sharp rock, along tunnels.

The expansion of piecework, though it was forbidden in law and laid a great burden on the mita work force, seems rarely to have been noticed by officialdom, and was even less often condemned. There was another abuse of mitayos, however, which though possibly less grave for the workers, attracted constant attention and attempts at correction from the authorities. This was the selling or leasing of mita workers by the employer to whom they were assigned, to some other miner or refiner. From these practices the mitayo certainly suffered economically and often physically; but the main reason for the concern of government (and of a surprising number of citizens, it must be said to their credit) was that this sort of alienation seemed an attack on the fundamental freedom that the state had declared was inherent to American natives under Spanish rule.

It is obvious enough that the mita itself, as draft labor, was an infringement of that freedom. But the state could adduce, if rather uneasily, reasons of public good in justification of the draft. It was not willing, though, to let private citizens extend the infringement, especially when in doing so they were obviously taking advantage of what the state saw as its own generosity to those same citizens. The mita was, in fact, a sort of compact for the mutual advantage of both state and silver producer: as a result of it the state received wealth, produced by the efforts of miners and refiners with the aid of mitayos; and in return for those efforts the producers might keep any profit they made after paying their taxes and costs. There were thus obvious reasons for the state to take exception to miners and refiners who failed to use the mitayos granted to them for producing silver, and instead sold the labor of these workers to someone else. That was a perversion of the tacit agreement.

It is easy enough to see why sale of mita labor began. Once amalgamation had come in, and the resulting expansion of mining was in progress, demand for labor drove the cost of free hands above that of mitayos. This was quite in accord with the intentions of Toledo and others—mita labor was to be artificially cheap so that silver production should be maximized. But there were always some miners and refiners who, through idleness, lack of capital, or lack of good ores, preferred selling the work of their mitayos to using it themselves.

Toledo himself provides some of the earliest evidence of sale of mita labor. Writing in the late 1570s, he admitted that under his mita organization some producers in Potosí had transferred the use of their mitayos to others for gain, although, he hurried on to say, the Indians had not suffered, since they were paid the regulation wage. Fake companies had been set up to conceal such transfers—a fraud that continued to be used down the succeeding decades: the recipients of mitayos would form a partnership with, for example, a mine owner lacking labor; articles would be drawn up before a notary stating that the first man contributed workers as his investment in the partnership, while the second contributed the mines; typically both would agree to put in their personal labor, and share the profits. But in reality the contributor of the mitayos frequently did nothing at all, merely taking a cash payment from the miner. Clearly such arrangements stretched the concept of a company rather thin; and they were considered fraudulent, not only by Toledo but by many other administrators who followed him. Toledo indeed reported that he had banned such companies, and in general had forbidden sale of Indians in any form. Moreover, the mitayos assigned to a refinery or mine were not to be included in any sale of the property, but to be considered unassigned (*vacos*) in such cases.[42]

Toledo's prohibitions could do little, however, against the forces of the labor market, and sales continued, as Capoche's fierce condemnation of the practice patently shows.[43] His objections are typical of those raised by other and later commentators. One is founded in law, the other in morality. The first holds that sale of Indians deprives them of their liberty and sovereignty (*libertad y señorío*). They are passed around like cash or some commodity—"the poor Indian is a coin with which is attained everything that is necessary,

---

42. AGI Lima 30, No. 4, Lima?, 1578–79?: "Lo que por Don Francisco de Toledo . . . se responde a los capítulos que los inquisidores de este Reino le dieron. . . ," f. 204, para. 34.
43. *Relación*, pp. 167–69.

just as if he were gold or silver, but much better."[44] Slaves from Guinea are better off, because they are sold only once. Indeed, says Capoche, sale of Indians subjects them to slavery (esclavonía). Second, the selling of mitayos deprives them of due reward for their labor. They are paid the going mita rate of 2.75 reales a day; but the seller charges 8 reales a day per Indian, so gaining over 5 reales while doing absolutely nothing.[45] This outcome was clearly built firmly into the mita system. The only means of blocking it would have been to raise the price of mita labor to equal that of mingas in the free labor market; and no miner, certainly not Capoche, would have advocated that. Nor, indeed, would many administrators, however conscious of their responsibilities to Indians, have pressed for such a change, since the value of cheap labor in stimulating silver output was well realized. Nevertheless, Capoche, like many after him, was conscious that the Indians were being cheated of due reward for their efforts. They were equally cheated, of course, when they were used by the miner to whom they had officially been assigned. But an active silver producer was regarded by other active miners and administrators as deserving of the Indians' cheap labor, whereas the seller of mitayos was parasitic. "Commonly those who sell them are dissolute and vagabond people, who serve only to drive up prices in the town and to go around betting, sometimes staking even the Indians allotted to them."[46]

As the quality of ores fell, and Potosí's output leveled off and then began to drop, more and more producers who, in Capoche's day, would have concurred with him in considering sellers of Indians as parasites must have found themselves driven to that same expedient. A report from the 1590s holds that over 1,300 mitayos were being sold weekly in Potosí "like pack llamas."[47] One common selling procedure was the fake leasing of refineries. An oidor of La Plata in 1606 described the practice to the king. Owners would lease their ingenio along with its allotment of mitayos to someone who had no intention of using it to produce silver, but who wished

44. *Relación,* p. 168, ". . . el pobre del indio es una moneda con la cual se halla todo lo que es necesario, como con oro y plata, y muy mejor."
45. *Relación,* p. 168.
46. *Relación,* p. 169.
47. "Como carneros de carga . . .": AGI Indiferente General 1,239, Luis Osorio de Quiñones to "muy poderoso señor," Madrid, nd, but clearly 1590s.

merely to have access to the men—either to use them elsewhere, or to sell their labor at 150 to 200 pesos a man per year.[48] Such leases had been forbidden by various viceroys; but a large loophole had been opened by Viceroy Velasco's permitting them in the case of refinery owners who owed money to the crown. The purpose of this decision was that part of the rent should go to pay the debt; but undesirable consequences followed, as the Audiencia of La Plata pointed out in 1608.[49] Ingenio owners were purposely putting themselves into debt to the crown in order to be able to lease their refineries, and, under cover of the leases, sell the labor of their Indians. It was simple to become a debtor to the crown: mercury could easily be bought on credit from the treasury. The mercury debt had therefore increased to a level of 2,340,000 pesos (1,500,000 pesos ensayados). What had been intended as a means of reducing indebtedness to the crown had, in fact, increased it. An ingenio owner selling the labor of his mitayos might expect, the audiencia said, to charge some 235 pesos (150 ensayados) a man per year. So, if he had a hundred workers, he would surely gather in over 20,000 pesos annually, which might well be more than he would make by employing the workers himself. (In reality, allotments of a hundred mitayos to a single ingenio were rare; half that number would be closer to the average.)

In spite of this clear demonstration of the principle that governmental action may well produce the opposite of its intended effect, leasing of the ingenios of those who owed to the crown continued. Indeed, by 1620, and probably before then, the treasury itself was putting the ingenios of mercury debtors out to lease, and including the mitayos in the contracts. A number of curacas and mita captains wrote a bitter complaint to the king about that, saying that they and their people suffered ill-treatment from the renters: ". . . this is the name they give us, saying 'Work, dogs, for you are costing me good silver which I have put in the royal treasury on your master's behalf'. . . ."[50]

---

48. AGI Charcas 18, Licenciado Ruiz Bejarano to crown, La Plata, March 1, 1606, "No. 95" (on verso).

49. BAN Minas tomo 123, item 3 (Minas catalog No. 522), Audiencia to crown, La Plata, March 13, 1608.

50. ". . . Este es el nombre que nos dan, diciendo 'trabaja perros, que buena plata mi costais que he metido en la real caja por vuestro amo' . . .": AGI Charcas 5, "los caciques indios" to crown, Potosí, March 25, 1620, f. 1v..

In addition to this direct official encouragement of sales of Indian labor, there was also a good deal of administrative inefficiency and even connivance on the matter, which tended to expand sales. Several reports show that curacas sold the Indians they were supposedly gathering and shepherding to Potosí for mita service. Those sold were known as *indios de ruego*.[51]

Selling was further encouraged by inefficient allotment of the mita itself. Despite policy to the contrary, inertia and favoritism sometimes led to mitayos' being assigned to mines and ingenios that were run down or in some cases no longer functioning at all. The owners then naturally seized the opportunity to profit as best they could from the labor granted to them. A well-documented case of favoritism is the assignment by the second Viceroy Marqués de Cañete (1588–95) of 151 Indians to his brother-in-law, Don Beltrán de Castro, the owner of a single ingenio in Potosí. Viceroy Velasco, the next viceroy, discovered this while taking Cañete's *residencia*, and reduced the allocation to thirty. Castro, meanwhile, had been selling the labor of his mitayos.[52]

And so it continued. In 1635 and again in 1638, the president of the Audiencia of La Plata, Don Juan de Lizarazu, attempted to justify the inclusion of mitayos in leases by the argument that the Indians themselves were not, and indeed could not, be sold, since they were free. Only the *use* of their labor was transferred.[53] Another supple-minded governor, Toledo himself, had in fact already produced this argument many years before, in refutation of accusations that he had created a system in which free men were sold.[54] But the down-to-earth reaction of simpler men like Capoche was

---

51. For example, AGI Indiferente General 1,239, Luis Osorio de Quiñones to "muy poderoso señor," Madrid, nd, but clearly 1590s.

52. AGI Lima 34 tomo 4, Viceroy Velasco to crown, Callao, April 28, 1601. For negligent distribution of mitayos to people without functioning mines or ingenios, see AGI Charcas 32 ms 36, cabildo of Potosí to crown, Potosí, March 3, 1596; and AGI Charcas 51 [Carlos Corso de Leca] "En cumplimiento de lo que Vuestra Excelencia me manda haga relación tocante al repartimiento de los indios de la mita. . . ," Potosí, March 1, 1617, para. 4 (JHR).

53. AGI Lima 45, Lizarazu to crown, Potosí, February 28, 1635, No. 6, para. 16; and AGI Charcas 266, item 12, Lizarazu to Viceroy Chinchón, Potosí, June 12, 1639.

54. Source as in n. 42 above.

closer to the truth. Sale of a mitayo's labor was, in the circumstances of Potosí, tantamount to at least temporary sale of the man himself. That in itself was illegal, if the concept of the Indians' freedom had any meaning. And the effortless profit made by the employers who rented out their men was immoral.

A connected abuse of mitayos that received the moral condemnation of some administrators was that of indios de faltriquera. This term has already been mentioned in connection with minga labor, as signifying the acceptance of cash by an employer in place of mitayos assigned to him. A mitayo might himself decide to pay the employer a cash substitute for his labor; or, probably more commonly, the curaca or captain in charge of supplying mitayos from some town or district would hand over cash to replace the worker he did not supply in person—either because the population in question no longer could yield the requisite numbers, or because the Indians themselves had given cash to their curaca with which he could buy them out of the mita.

The phrase "indios de faltriquera" seems to belong to the seventeenth century, and possibly the practice was not common before then. Signs of it do occur, however, in the 1590s. For example, Viceroy Velasco's mining ordinances of 1599 forbid it.[55] The extent of the practice in the 1600s is difficult to gauge, but may have been large. Don Juan de Lizarazu calculated in 1635 that no fewer than half the mitayos due to Potosí were being "delivered in cash."[56] Another official, Licenciado Blas Robles de Salcedo, an oidor of La Plata, asserted four years later that only a third of the mita actually appeared in person, implying that the rest bought themselves out, or were bought out.[57]

Lizarazu, Robles de Salcedo and other officials objected to the practice of indios de faltriquera on moral and practical grounds.

55. AGI Charcas 134, clause 9 of the ordinances accompanying the "Repartimiento general del Señor Don Luis de Velasco . . . de los indios que repartió para las minas e ingenios," Lima, August 31, 1599. Rather than a cash substitute, Indians or curacas were to provide another worker.

56. AGI Lima 45, Lizarazu to crown, No. 6, Potosí, February 28, 1635, para. 14, ". . . sobre el uso de los indios del cerro."

57. AGI Charcas 21, "Respuesta del Licenciado Robles de Salcedo . . . ," Potosí, October 28, 1639, various foliations.

The moral criticism was the same as that directed at sales of Indian labor: that the employers received something for nothing, at the Indians' expense. Miners and refiners claimed that with the cash received in lieu of missing mitayos, they hired mingas. But, of course, they could hire only at the minga rate, and so demanded payments for the missing mitayos on that scale: from 7 to 9 pesos a week (after 1600). A mitayo therefore had to pay heavily to avoid a week's labor for which he would have received 2.5 pesos. This discrepancy the likes of Lizarazu considered unfair, although their objections were milder if the silver producer used the cash he received to hire a minga for a week, as some clearly did. The severe moral censure of administrators was, rather, aimed at those producers who merely pocketed the money. And the officials' practical criticism also resulted from this failure to hire—for its outcome was that the total labor force producing silver was reduced, and so less silver was forthcoming.

From the point of view of economics, this second, practical criticism was nonsense. Presumably some of the employers who, as it were, "put their Indians in their pockets" rather than hiring mingas, did so because even with that free minga labor, they could not produce silver profitably because the ores available to them were of insufficient quality. Doubtless some employers were merely idle; but others took "indios de faltriquera" because producing silver no longer paid. Administrators, however keen that Potosí should continue to fill the king's coffers, could not reasonably expect miners to produce at a loss.

It is, indeed, arguable that both the practice of indios de faltriquera and that of sale of Indians previously discussed were, in strictly economic terms, advantageous to the Potosí industry. Both can be seen as devices that had developed to cope with rapid shifts in demand for labor in a market in which supply had been made inflexible by the mita system. Mita allotments were remade roughly every ten years between 1582 and 1633. At that rate of adjustment they could not distribute labor to miners and refiners in exactly the quantities needed by each, simply because mining was such a volatile business. An owner whose mine was producing poorly one month might strike a good pocket of ore the next, and suddenly need more workers for extraction and refining; and then a month later, find himself back in difficulties. Clearly the mita system, with its fixed allotments, hindered production in such cases.

Sales of mitayo labor were therefore economically useful, in allowing those who truly needed workers at any moment to obtain them. The practice of indios de faltriquera had the same effect, since the mitayos who bought exemption from draft work could, and did, hire themselves out as mingas. Indeed, it is extremely likely that it was only through working as mingas, at high pay, that many Indians were able to buy themselves out of mita labor.

Consideration of the cash flows taking place in both the faltriquera and sale systems raises another interesting and perhaps advantageous possibility that they may have presented to silver producers. Suppose, as has just been suggested, that the mitayo used money he had earned as a minga to escape a spell of mita service: money then passed from the producer who engaged him as a minga, through his hands, and into those of the mita employer. Suppose, again, that the first employer was hiring mingas because he had a prosperous mine and refinery (and so found advantage in using even expensive labor), while the second employer preferred "Indians in the pocket" because his mining operations were stagnant and unprofitable. Then the faltriquera system appears as a mechanism for passing funds from the prosperous part of the industry to those in difficulties. This might well seem undesirable. In most industrial situations, it would be considered foolish for the successful to support the failures. But, again, the volatility or unpredictability of mining must be taken into account. This year's successful enterprise might be next year's failure. In such a situation it might be useful to have a mechanism by which the producer passing through a lean spell had some source of income—an income which, in fact, came originally from his more successful (though in all likelihood only temporarily more successful) colleagues. The faltriquera practice may thus have functioned as a sort of insurance system. The sale of mitayo labor would have had the same effect, though there the cash passed directly from the buyer to the seller of labor, without Indian intermediary.[58]

58. If, as some evidence suggests, Indians who bought themselves out of mita work did not use money earned as mingas to do so, but wages from some other job they had previously taken in or around Potosí, then it could be argued that the community at large was contributing to the support of miners and refiners who found themselves in difficulties.

All this is not to suggest that among sellers of mitayos and recipients of indios de faltriquera no parasites roamed, who merely cashed in on their privileged position as silver producers. Clearly such men were to be found. But these dealings in Indians may well have had economic connotations that escaped the colonial administrators who so roundly condemned them.

The Indian whose labor was sold by his employer could not but suffer from the arrangement. According to reports, he received the same amount as he would have earned as a mitayo working for his assigned employer, but often with far harsher treatment. The Indian who paid to escape his mita turn, on the other hand, may have had some gain in doing so. In avoiding mita service, he also avoided the heaviest mining job of carrying ore below ground. Instead, he could hire himself out as a minga, and if he possessed any skill, work as a barretero, thereby increasing his opportunities of gathering good ore for himself; or he might choose some refining task, where hours of work were reportedly short, and the labor lighter than below ground. It is easy to imagine, in fact, that once a man gained some skill, he could permanently escape mita service through the faltriquera system. He might work permanently as a minga, using part of his wages as such to avoid the one week in three (or two, after 1600) that he should have served as a mitayo. If the cost to a mitayo of buying himself out of a week's mita work were the same as the minga wage (7 to 9 pesos in the early seventeenth century), and the mita wage for a week of mine work were 2.5 pesos; then a minga who worked for two weeks would earn 14 to 18 pesos, and if buying himself out of a week of mita labor, would pay out 7 to 9 of these, keeping 7 to 9 pesos. If he worked for one week as a minga and one as a mitayo, he would earn a total of 9.5 to 11.5 pesos. Balancing, and perhaps outweighing, the cash advantage of doing his mita stint, however, would be the easier work and the incidental profits of minga labor. (Any worker who, after 1600, by good fortune found himself doing mita work only one week in three could, of course, opt for permanent minga work in just the same way as the man faced with being a mitayo half the time, and enjoy similar advantages.)

If the practice of indios de faltriquera was not as hard on native workers as some contemporary commentary suggested, it is also worth noting that few signs appear in Potosí of another abuse of Indians often thought characteristic of colonial Spanish America:

retention of labor by debt. Indeed, the only evidence of this practice in Potosí itself emerging from sources consulted for this book refers not to mining or refining, but to bread baking. In 1602 the corregidor of Potosí found that the corregidor of the province of Lipes, acting apparently in cahoots with the Potosí bakers, was sending Indians from his jurisdiction to the town, where, according to the corregidor of Potosí, "with evil intent they give them silver so as to put them in debt for the rest of their lives."[59] He had ordered that the Indians be allowed to leave the bakeries on Sundays to go to Mass, and on other days to exercise their *miserables constituciones*. For some unexplained reason, the Lipes Indians were found particularly adept at baking, so that even the corregidor of Potosí was unwilling to order their release from what he himself termed their slavery; it would be better, however, if the bakers bought black slaves.

What is interesting about this case is that the corregidor of Potosí cited no legislation banning retention of labor by debt, or limiting how many months' wages could be advanced. Regulations of advances certainly existed in New Spain by the early seventeenth century. The corregidor's failure to quote any such rule may, of course, merely have been the result of his ignorance. But it might also suggest that no such regulations existed. Certainly, research has brought none to light for Potosí in its first century. And possibly the reason for lack of such regulations was that retention by debt was uncommon in the town. In the outlying mines of the district, debt may well have been used to keep a hold on workers, though only one piece of evidence has been found for this, referring to an ingenio and mine in the province of Chichas in the early 1630s. A priest who had been *cura* of various small mining centers of southern Charcas, one Dr. Lorenzo de Mendoza, returned to Spain and there lodged a suit against several mine owners, accusing them of ill-treatment of Indian workers. Whether any personal animus lay behind his charges cannot be known; but they were certainly vehemently presented. Among other abuses, Mendoza described a classic type of debt peonage. He alleged that Indian

---

59. ". . . con malicia les van dando plata para tenerlos empeñados toda la vida." BAN Cartas 786, Don Pedro Córdoba de Mejía to Audiencia of La Plata, Potosí, October 4, 1602, para. 1.

workers were forced to buy food and all other supplies from their employers at double the common price; that they were not allowed to pay for them in cash, but only in labor, and were thus reduced to "permanent captivity" *(perpetuo cautiverio)*; that these debts were transferred along with the Indians when the ingenios were sold; that, indeed, the amount of the debts was exaggerated in such cases; and that the work performance of the Indians was undervalued, so that repayment of the debts was made even less possible. (It should be said that all the workers in question were mingas. No mita labor was provided for the Chichas mines.)[60]

An oidor from La Plata, Don Martín de Arriola, was sent to investigate these charges, and others of wanton cruelty, lodged by Dr. Mendoza. The surviving manuscript gives an account of his activities at only one ingenio, owned by Captain Pedro de Espinosa y Ludueña. Arriola examined sixteen Indian mine and refinery workers, who in general denied the accusations brought by Mendoza. They asserted that they were paid partly in cash and partly in goods, which they themselves requested, since otherwise supplies were hard to find in the isolation of the region; they did not complain about the prices of goods; some stated they owed money to the owner, and others said they owed nothing. The owner allowed them and their womenfolk to leave the ingenio to visit their pueblos, and they returned of their own accord. In general they denied being ill-treated.

It is impossible to know, of course, how far the Indians were coerced into making these favorable replies. Evidently the investigating oidor, Arriola, thought they had been, since he found the owner, Espinosa, guilty on several counts: that he had charged excessive prices for goods, which he should have sold at cost; that on buying an ingenio, he had received with it Indians who owed debts to the previous owner, and obliged them to work the debts off to him with labor, which was illegal (presumably what was illegal was the transfer of the workers with the ingenio); that he had, illegally, forced Indians to stand as guarantors that other Indians

---

60. For the case, see BAN Minas tomo 131, item 2 (Minas catalog No. 690a), "1634. Visita general que el Licenciado Don Martín de Arriola . . . tomó del ingenio nombrado Nuestra Señora de Guadalupe, provincia de los Chichas. . . ," f. 207ff.

would not escape, whereas Indians, because of their legal status as minors, could not serve as guarantors; and that he was guilty of depriving the workers of their freedom through threats and ill-treatment.

Without Arriola's adverse findings, this case would be inconclusive evidence for debt peonage: the Indians' statements counterbalance the original charges. But Arriola, despite the Indians' testimony, and probably using other evidence also (there is one mention of his examining local Spaniards), does in his verdict describe a situation that bears some of the stamp of debt peonage. That such a situation should exist in the district mines but not in Potosí itself is hardly surprising. Their isolation made clothing and other materials hard to come by, and facilitated monopolization of supplies by the owners of mines and refineries. Potosí, by contrast, was a great market place. In Potosí, furthermore, there were legal authorities as well as Indian leaders to whom aggrieved natives could go, and sometimes find redress. Dr. Mendoza, the originator of the charges against Espinosa and others, acknowledged this, and more, when he said that only in the provinces of Chichas and Lipes did Indians lack Spanish legal defenders *(protectores)*; and that there they also lacked their own curacas, since they all came, singly or in small numbers, from other areas. Finally, in the small mining towns or isolated ingenios of the district, individual Indians were recognizable and traceable. In the teeming population of Potosí, they were far less so; and if they could not easily be traced it was far harder to pursue them for debts, and haul them back to work off their time.

Against the ill-treatment and abuse of mitayos so far described was set a concern for Indian welfare that was realized in several ways. Whether this concern was more the result of the authorities' self-interested desire to preserve a valuable labor force than of an altruistic concern with the natives' well-being is hardly worth debating on present evidence from Potosí. Doubtless both motives were present, in different proportions at different times in different people.

One manifestation of official concern for Indian welfare has already been shown: safety regulations for mines and ingenios, in limited numbers. Regulations for the good treatment of workers in other respects were given by Toledo and by successive administrators at various levels after him. The type and range of these orders existing by the late sixteenth century is well shown by an account given in Capoche's *Relación* of the duties of the officially appointed Spanish protector of Indians in Potosí.[61] By this account, the regulations were as follows. The protector should see that Indians were paid at statutory rates, in cash, and in person *(en su mano)*. Curacas and mita captains were not to be given their men's wages to distribute (the implication clearly being that they would keep them). The protector should enforce the limitations set on working hours. He should order Indians removed from dangerous mines and from those that were rented, since these were the least well maintained and hence the most perilous. The protector should ensure that Indians were used for mining tasks alone and not diverted into some other activity. He should prevent their being assigned to the mita during the rest period, and see that they were declared unassigned if the ingenio to which they were previously allotted were sold (this to forestall sale of the Indians themselves). He should make certain that Indians employed in freighting coca and other goods were paid for the time they had served and not for the distance they had covered (another attack on piecework). Not least should he protect mitayos from abuse by their own leaders—by which Capoche meant such things as the underhandedness with wages that he criticizes in the same passage, or the curacas' habit of selling mitayos' labor to influential Spaniards, which he condemns elsewhere. Finally, the protector must represent any Indian who suffered these or other grievances, taking cases before the appropriate justice.

Clearly, far from all the welfare rules underlying Capoche's definition of the protector's responsibilities were enforced. Sale of Indian labor did persist, as did illegally long workdays, to give only two examples. But the existence of the protector does seem to have limited infraction of the rules. And indeed the creation of the office of protector, along with other offices designed to safeguard Indians' interests, is a second major manifestation (after the issuance of safety rules) of the administration's desire to protect mitayos in Potosí. The office of protector was created by Toledo at some date before May 1575, according to a report by an oidor of La Plata in that month. At the same time the viceroy appointed inspectors of

---

61. p. 188.

mines, and special judges to hear cases involving Indians.[62] From then on, the protectorship continued to exist for the rest of the period considered here, though Capoche refers to the recent arrival of a royal cédula ordering abolition of the post. This he thought undesirable. And so did the Audiencia of La Plata, with the result that the crown revoked its order for abolition in 1588.[63]

The protector, among other duties already related, represented Indians before the law, or arranged for their representation. Most cases came before judges specially appointed to hear suits concerning Indians. According to Ramírez de Quiñones's statement of 1575 (note 62 above), Toledo was the first to install such judges; though Capoche strongly implies that it was the succeeding viceroy, Enríquez, who initiated the office in Potosí.[64] Specifically mining cases involving Indians were probably heard in general by the alcalde mayor de minas, who, according to Capoche, rather confusingly "also deals with Indian matters with the title of juez de naturales,"[65] though this alcalde might also carry cases before the same juez.

The *alcaldía mayor de minas* is another early office. It, or something very like it, existed in Toledo's viceregency and was possibly instituted by him. In 1578, for example, one Juan de Bengoechea described himself as *alcalde de minas y veedor de los ingenios de Potosí*.[66] The alcalde mayor de minas acted as a first instance criminal and civil judge in mining cases, and also had responsibility for enforcing the regulations governing mines and refining. A special

---

62. "... jueces particulares y defensores para su tratamiento y veedores para que no sean defraudados en sus jornales . . .": Pedro Ramírez de Quiñones to crown, La Plata, May 6, 1575, in Levillier, *Charcas,* tomo 1, p. 323. Ramírez does not use the term *protector,* but *defensor* seems to have been a synonym. In April 1575 Toledo had installed his first *defensor general de los indios* in Lima, a central official to see to Indian welfare for Peru as a whole. See the preamble to the "Ordenanzas del Virrey Don Francisco de Toledo relativas al defensor general de los naturales," Arequipa, September 10, 1575, in Levillier, *Gobernantes,* tomo 8, pp. 281–98.

63. Crown to Audiencia of La Plata, San Lorenzo, May 11, 1588: BAN real cédula 208 (Minas catalog No. 271).

64. *Relación,* p. 146.

65. "... que también conoce de los negocios de indios con título de juez de naturales. . . ," *Relación,* p. 146.

66. AGI Charcas 31 ms 31, Potosí, March 2, 1578.

duty, which makes it necessary to include this post in an account of offices dealing with welfare, was investigation of accidents, and prosecution of any negligence causing them. This duty was laid down in Viceroy Velasco's mining ordinances of 1599.[67]

The last in this list of offices, whose purpose was at least in part to safeguard the interests and lives of Indian mining and refining workers, was that of the veedores, or inspectors, of mines in the cerro. These men were the executive arm of the alcalde mayor de minas's power to enforce safety rules. The desirability of appointing a veedor was remarked on in the 1561 mining ordinances for Porco and Potosí,[68] but again it is not until Toledo's time that the office can clearly be seen to have existed.[69] By the end of the century there were two veedores, and by 1611, three.[70] Their duties, according to a title of appointment to the office in 1597, were to see that all mita Indians assigned to a particular mine actually went to work in it, keeping the statutory hours of labor; that their lunch-break was observed; they they heard Mass on appointed days; that they were paid in coin at the appointed rates; that they were in general well treated; and that mines were kept in repair, especially their supports and ladders.[71]

If this array of officials seems evidence of a laudable concern by the authorities for the Indians' welfare, it must be pointed out that the Indians paid for the protection. None of the salaries came from treasury funds. Toledo, as he fixed mitayos' wage rates in the 1570s, also declared that 1 grano (about 5 maravedís) should be deposited daily, per mitayo, into a special fund (the *caja de granos*) to pay the wages of welfare officials. It is not at all clear whether Toledo intended the grano to be deducted from the worker's wage, or whether the employer was supposed to pay it in addition to the

67. AGI Charcas 134, ordenanza 14 accompanying Viceroy Velasco's "Repartimiento general" of Lima, August 31, 1599.

68. Title 2, clause 21. See Matienzo, *Gobierno*, p. 141.

69. Ramírez de Quiñones refers to it in his letter to the crown of May 6, 1575. See n. 62 above.

70. AGI Charcas 35 ms 1, "Relación del oficio de contador de la caja de los granos en Potosí," anon., no exact date, but 1596; and AGI Lima 39, "Cuenta de los granos. . . ," March 10, 1611, accompanying letter of Don Diego de Portugal to crown, Potosí, March 12, 1611.

71. BAN CPLA tomo 8, f. 138v. (Minas catalog No. 434), title by Viceroy Velasco to Juan de Arce de Collantes, Lima, November 21, 1597.

wage. This point was indeed much debated among colonial administrators in the 1620s. Whatever the initial practice, it is not surprising that over time the Indians found themselves paying the grano from their regular wage. A group of mita leaders in 1620 protested to the king about this, exclaiming that they were forced to pay their own executioners—perhaps a reference to the efforts that the protectors made to collect the granos, even imprisoning curacas to extract the money.[72] By the 1620s, half a real (17 maravedís) was being collected weekly per Indian in granos, a somewhat lower figure than the 25 maravedís that would have accrued at the original rate of 5 maravedís daily over a five-day week; and the total gathered yearly was some 12,000 pesos. Against this sum were set the salaries of the officials already described, and some others. The alcalde mayor de minas received 2,345 pesos a year (1,500 ensayados); the protector, 1,876 (1,200 ensayados); each of the three veedores, 1,563 (1,000 ensayados); the corregidor of Potosí a 938 peso (600 ensayados) supplement to his normal salary, as recompense for his visiting the cerro twice a week and his general supervision of delivery of the mita (duties that different corregidores took with varying degrees of seriousness); each of the six provincial Indian mita captains, 313 pesos (200 ensayados); various *alguaciles*, or constables, who attended at the entrance to adits and who helped collect the granos, a total of 156 pesos (100 ensayados); the chaplain of the jail, to say Mass for Indians there, 78 pesos (50 ensayados); and finally the accountant of granos, 1,250 pesos (800 ensayados) for his efforts. At one time the sacristan of the principal church had been paid 234 pesos (150 ensayados) annually for ringing the bell at dawn to signal the beginning of the working day; but this was no longer done, since the mitayos on the cerro stayed there from Tuesday to Saturday, and the refinery workers were mingas whose working hours were flexible. The total of salaries actually due from the granos income was 13,207 pesos (8,450 ensayados), or some 1,200 pesos more than what was being collected. So salaries were underpaid.[73]

A good deal of opposition to the payment of granos had arisen

72. AGI Charcas 52, "los caciques indios" to crown, Potosí, March 25, 1620, f. 2v.
73. The salaries, and history of granos, given here are taken from AGI Lima 39, tomo 5, Esquilache to crown, "Gobierno" No. 5, Lima, April 29, 1620.

by the early seventeenth century, not only from Indians but also from administrators. President Portugal of La Plata was particularly critical of the levy;[74] and eventually in 1618 the Council of the Indies concluded that it was unjust and must stop.[75] The question then immediately arose—how were the offices hitherto funded from the granos to be paid for? The Council merely recommended using the "means and items that may seem most suitable"—perhaps, it surmised, the income from some vacant encomienda could be applied to these expenses. As far as possible silver producers were not to be burdened with the extra cost. These airy directives left the Peruvian authorities in a quandary. No conveniently unassigned encomienda income was available. It was hardly sensible of the Council to think there would be. The result was that nothing was done for over a decade. The mitayos continued to pay granos until 1632, when Viceroy Chinchón, a man sincerely concerned about the grievances of the native people in his charge, acting in collaboration with Don Juan de Carvajal y Sande, his visitor to the Audiencia of La Plata, decided that until other sources appeared, no choice remained but to transfer the salary costs to the silver producers and the treasury. The alcalde mayor de minas should be paid from the treasury. The office of *contador de granos* should go, since there would be no more granos to count. The supplement to the corregidor's salary should be canceled. A fifth of the other salaries (principally those of the protector and the three veedores) was to come from general treasury funds, and the balance from a levy of 10 reales on each bar of silver of 120 marks brought in by refiners for assay and taxing (the levy to vary proportionally with the weight of the bar).[76]

It is hard to tell if the mitayos received value for money over the five and a half decades they had to pay granos. On the one hand

74. See, e.g., para. 6 of his letter to the crown from Potosí, March 12, 1611, in AGI Lima 39; and para. 2 of his letter to the crown from Potosí, April 2, 1613, in AGI Lima 39.

75. AGI Charcas 19, crown to Esquilache, real cédula, Madrid, December 10, 1618.

76. AGI Charcas 20, a small untitled expediente on salaries of veedores and the alcalde mayor de minas, containing the decisions of an *acuerdo general de hacienda* convened by Chinchón, Lima, December 17, 1631, and an auto by Carvajal y Sande, Potosí, May 24, 1632.

are the mita leaders crying out at having to support their "executioners" (note 72 above); on the other are records of at least some instances in which the officials did their jobs. What proportion of total instances these represent is, of course, the crucial and unanswerable question. An interesting account from 1656 relates how the alcalde mayor de minas was summoned before nine on a Saturday morning to a mine in which a number of Indians had been trapped by a fall, and responded exactly as bidden by Velasco's ordinance 14 of 1599—making an immediate enquiry into what had happened, finding who was to blame, and prosecuting. Indeed, that same day, May 14, 1656, the mine owner, no less than one of the aldermen (*veinticuatros*) of Potosí, was found responsible and was ordered confined to the cerro and his ingenio.[77] In this same incident the three veedores can be seen in action, organizing rescue squads of Indians and overseers called in by the alcalde mayor from surrounding mines. The case makes forbidding reading. For fear of further collapses, the corpse of an Indian found buried up to the chest, deep in the mine, was, after much debate, left there; and an attempt to extricate another corpse in a somewhat less perilous position was carried to success, if that is the word, only by cutting off one of the legs.

This same manuscript contains brief accounts of earlier cases in which the alcalde mayor de minas had a part. They show him prosecuting mine owners and supervisors for a variety of offenses against Indians; and they demonstrate that the protector (or *defensor*) did represent Indians before the alcalde mayor.[78]

One of the most energetic of alcaldes mayores de minas was Carlos Corso de Leca, an innovative refiner of the late sixteenth century, and probably the leading member of the mining community in the early seventeenth. In 1607 the crown appointed him alcalde mayor. In 1611 he claimed, in recounting his services, that he had much reduced bad treatment of mitayos, all but eliminating whipping; he had cut down the overtime that mitayos were forced to work on Sundays and fiestas to fulfil their quotas of ore; he had

---

77.   BAN Minas tomo 125, item 13 (Minas catalog No. 859), "1652–1656. Competencia de jurisdicción suscitada entre Don Francisco Sarmiento de Mendoza y el Capitán Pedro de Montalvo. . . ," f. 7–7v.

78.   BAN Minas catalog No. 859, ff. 46–62. (See previous note for title).

visited all workings, ordering repairs and widening of narrow galleries; and he had ensured that the mitayos were paid more regularly. All this should perhaps be taken with a little scepticism, since it is of Corso's own saying. His most original tactic for protecting Indians' interests is described, however, by both himself and a witness. He took to sending six Indians, disguised as mitayos, onto the cerro, with each week's new group of workers, as spies to observe treatment of the draftees. This led to prosecutions. On the other hand, said Corso, once the mitayos realized that they had an ally in him, they began to slack in their work, "as they are badly inclined and each day their slyness grows. . . ." So he had also had to punish the idle.[79]

Other examples of actions by these various welfare officials could be cited, to no conclusive effect. It is more profitable to turn now to the final instance of Spanish concern for the Indians' living and working conditions to be described here—the hospital.

The Real Hospital de la Veracruz was probably the only significant physical institution for the well-being of Indians in Potosí. It was founded in the mid-1550s.[80] From the start it seems to have been a secular institution. Toledo, in a report of 1573 on religious matters in Potosí, makes no mention of participation in the hospital's affairs, past or present, by any of the three orders (Franciscans, Dominicans, and Mercedarians) then resident;[81] though some early friars, at least, did treat Indians in their parochial charge, but apparently not in the hospital.[82]

The medical side of the hospital's history is not revealed in the

---

79. "Demás de esto ahora de presente, como los indios son de mala inclinación y cada día crece en ellos la malicia, van aflojando en el trabajo." AGI Charcas 49, Carlos Corso de Leca to crown, No. 249, Potosí, March 22, 1612, para. 1 (JHR). See also AGI Charcas 51, "Información nueva de servicios de Carlos Corso de Leca," La Plata, November? 1611 (JHR).

80. Arzáns, *Historia*, tomo 1, p. 150, gives 1555. A memorial of the cabildo of Potosí, alluded to in a provisión of Viceroy Velasco, El Cercado, May 6, 1599 (BAN Rück mss No. 2, provisiones of Velasco, f. 49) prefers 1556.

81. AGI Lima 29, tomo 1, Toledo to king, Potosí, March 20, 1573, "Eclesiástica," f. 102v.

82. For example, treasury accounts of 1561 record payment of royal funds to Dominicans in Potosí for the purchase of remedies for Chucuito Indians in their charge who were suffering from smallpox. AGI Contaduría 1801, *data* for 1561, *pliego* 26.

records consulted for this book. Gross numbers of patients alone are available, and those for only two years: 150 in 1593, and over 100 ten years later.[83] Inevitably, mining injuries—fractured or crushed limbs, torn or strained tissues—would have been common; and bonesetting, amputation, and bloodlettings must have occupied the surgeon for much of his time.[84] Sugar was a standard "drug" in the treatment of infectious ills such as smallpox. (Rural people around Potosí still today consume it mainly as a medicine.) The records do say a little more about the structure, funding, and organization of the institution.

The *Planta general* of Potosí of the late sixteenth century shows the hospital situated in the town center, across the street to the east of the principal church, and facing onto the Plaza de la Fruta. The initial structure was improved in 1573 by Toledo, with the addition of further rooms and a large cemetery for Indians who died during treatment.[85]

The town council ran the hospital, probably from the start until about 1620. In 1589 it described itself as the patron, when appointing an administrator, one Father Antonio de Escobar. His task was to say Mass, confess the sick, and help them to "die well."[86] Medical staff were also named by the council—in 1603 the hospital had a physician, surgeon, barber, nurse, and presumably a pharmacist in charge of the pharmacy *(botica)*.[87] Responsibility for the hospital's operation was removed from the cabildo with the formation, shortly before 1620, of a brotherhood, or *hermandad*, to attend to it. This was ordered by the king in 1617, but in fact an hermandad had arisen spontaneously before the royal order arrived, on the pattern of those serving the Santa Ana and San Andrés hospi-

83. Cabildo of Potosí to crown, February 25, 1593, cited by Gunnar Mendoza in Arzáns, *Historia,* tomo 1, p. 220, n. 2; also, "Descripción de . . . Potosí . . . 1603," p. 378.

84. Treasury accounts of 1561 show the crown disbursing 4 pesos for a lancet, and 3.5 pesos for a syringe, whether to the hospital or to a religious order is unclear. AGI Contaduría 1801, data for 1561, pliego 28.

85. Arzáns, *Historia,* tomo 1, p. 150.

86. BAN Minas catalog No. 294b: Potosí, Libros de acuerdos, tomo 5, f. 405v., acuerdo of November 15, 1589.

87. "Descripción de . . . Potosí . . . 1603," p. 378.

tals in Lima.[88] The hermanos, twenty-four in number, described themselves as "rich private persons," impelled by charity and desire to serve king and God, and thus eminently suited to assume control of the hospital. Apart from doing that, they visited the patients and contributed money. They made an initial gift of some 6,300 pesos, which was spent on structural repairs.[89]

The brotherhood put much emphasis on its restoration of the building. Whether its initial generosity continued remains to be seen. In the past, funds had sometimes been a source of difficulty. In the first two decades of the hospital's life, charity seems to have been the main support, with perhaps a minimal contribution from the treasury. Viceroy Cañete is reported in 1561 to have ordered a grant of some 470 pesos (300 ensayados) to be paid yearly from royal income.[90] But, as usual, it was Toledo who created more permanent arrangements, ordering that each mitayo should contribute about 7 reales (a half-peso ensayado) from his wages. By Capoche's time this levy was bringing in some 10,300 pesos annually for the hospital,[91] or about what would be expected while the mita was still arriving in numbers close to those set by Toledo. In 1603 the income stood at 30,000 pesos annually, which is remarkable, considering that delivery of the mita had declined by then.[92] The source of this wealth (beyond the mitayos' contributions) is unknown, though it is true that the hospital received an assignment of some sixty Indians a year from the mita, whose labor it sold, possibly so gaining between 9,000 and 12,000 pesos a year.[93]

88. AGI Charcas 55, eleven hermanos to crown, Potosí, April 25, 1620.

89. AGI Charcas 55, cabildo y hermandad del hospital real de la Veracruz to king, Potosí, nd (clearly 1620s). In justification of the royal title of the hospital, which was certainly in customary use by then, the brotherhood argued that silver produced by the Indians became royal patrimony (a dubious point, apart from the quinto), and hence Indians injured in mining and treated in the hospital could be said to have suffered in the king's service.

90. AGI Contaduría 1801, data for 1561, pliego 34. The date of Cañete's order is not given.

91. *Relación*, p. 146.

92. "Descripción de . . . Potosí . . . 1603," p. 378.

93. Forty-eight mitayos had originally been assigned by Toledo in 1575 in a personal grant to the physician whom he appointed to the hospital, Dr. Vázquez. See PBN ms B511, ff. 435–470v., "Repartimiento general que el Excelentísimo

At the same time as the Council of the Indies ordered an end to granos, the king in 1618 canceled the mitayos' payments to the hospital. In fact, however, mitayos continued to make their payments for some years—until at least 1627; but they had been relieved of this expense by 1632.[94] After then, the hospital apparently depended on bequests, which in 1629 brought in over 34,000 pesos; and it also enjoyed, by the crown's gift, the income from a play yard *(corral de comedias)* in Potosí, however much that may have been.[95]

The ending of the mitayos' contributions to the hospital by the early 1630s removed one justified source of complaint on their part: that Spaniards were treated there without charge—and hence, to some degree, at the Indians' expense. Although the Hospital Real de la Veracruz had apparently been founded to care for Indians, and was certainly regarded as an Indian hospital by the viceroys from Toledo onward, people of all sorts entered it because it was for several decades the only hospital in the town. In 1610, however, another institution was created, the Hospital de San Juan de Dios, which may have catered to Spaniards and others who were not Indians.[96]

On balance, it seems safe to say that the hospital performed some useful services for the community of Indian workers in mining and refining—but that at the same time it fell considerably short of what

---

Señor Don Francisco de Toledo . . . hizo de los indios que han de venir a la labor y beneficio de las minas de la Villa Imperial de Potosí," Arequipa, October 10, 1575. They were to work Vázquez's ingenio. Later, Toledo increased the number to sixty. The Viceroy Conde de Villar (1584–88), however, assigned these mitayos to the hospital and provided a cash salary for his appointee as physician, Dr. Castillo. The salary in 1596 was reported at some 2,800 pesos (1,800 ensayados). See, for these developments, BAN Rück mss No. 2, provisiones of Velasco, 1596–1605, f. 37, provisión, Lima, December 1, 1596; and AGI Charcas 32 ms 42, "Lo que informó el Marqués de Cañete sobre el negocio del hospital de Potosí," Valladolid, September 18, 1603.

94. AGI Charcas 20, auto of Don Juan de Carvajal y Sande, Potosí, May 24, 1632, in an untitled expediente (see n. 76).

95. AGI Lima 41, tomo 3, Viceroy Guadalcázar to crown, Lima, March 8, 1627, "Gobierno No. 4;" and AGI Charcas 55, Don Pedro de Andrade y Sotomayor to crown, Potosí, January 18, 1629, f.2.

96. The foundation of the San Juan hospital is given by Gunnar Mendoza in Arzáns, *Historia*, tomo 2, p. 142, n. 2.

should, or might, have been done. This same unsatisfactory, and inevitably impressionistic, verdict applies to the whole machinery for protecting Indians' lives and interests in Potosí. Rules for welfare and safety were few and far from comprehensive; but in view of the inadequacy, it is somehow surprising to find them being applied at all—and applied they were, at least at times. It can be said with certainty that without the protective legislation that existed, and without the hierarchy of officials that from time to time enforced it, the Indians who labored in the production of silver at Potosí would have been worse off than they were. A further statement that can confidently be made is that working conditions were far from equal for all classes of workers, just as wages were far from equal. The specialization of labor that developed in response to the scale and complexity of silver production by amalgamation implied, as would be expected, that those with greater skills (broadly speaking, mingas employed in cutting ore and in refining) fared far better in conditions and treatment than did the mitayos who were set to carrying ore and other unskilled tasks. At the same time, however, the very size of Potosí may have given some safety in numbers to all Indians working in its silver industry. The possibility of anonymity in the mass seems to a degree to have protected workers against being retained by debt—a practice much more possible in the district mines, as a consequence of their isolation and small populations.

6

Conclusion

The labor systems of Potosí in a wider American context

In discussing how silver producers in New Spain and Peru dealt with any shortages of labor they might anticipate, Immanuel Wallerstein proposes that "In Mexico they resorted to wage labor, and in Potosí they simply drew the forced labor from farther distances."[1] In their instructive and useful survey of Indian labor in the Spanish American empire, Juan and Judith Villamarín contend that "In the Central Andes free workers went to the urban centers and their surroundings. They also worked in small mines. Their proportions in the large mines for most of the colonial period, however, were not significant; in Huancavelica and Potosí mita labor continued to be of primary importance."[2] Other examples of persistence of the belief in the "primary importance" of mita workers at Potosí are not hard to find. The vitality of the notion is certainly of some ideological and historiographical interest—reflecting, perhaps, as much preconceptions of the Black Legend variety as the unexplored state of Andean colonial history. Certain sallies had been made into that history, however, that should have put later writers on guard. For instance in 1946, George Kubler, with his usual keenness of eye, noted a report that by 1601 40,000 resident mingas were at work in Potosí.[3] And in 1960 Donald L. Wiedner repeated the figure, arguing for a "substantial class of permanent

---

1. *The modern world-system II. Mercantilism and the consolidation of the European world-economy, 1600–1750* (New York 1980), p. 149.
2. *Indian labor in mainland colonial Spanish America* (Newark, Delaware, 1975), pp. 19–20.
3. "The Quechua in the colonial world," (pp. 331–410 of the *Handbook of South American Indians* Volume 2—*The Andean Civilizations*, ed. Julian H. Steward, Washington, 1946), p. 372.

free Indian labor" in seventeenth-century Potosí.[4] Finally, David
Brading and Harry Cross, in an admirable conspectus of colonial
silver mining in Peru and New Spain, have noted the presence of
permanent workers in Potosí, though presenting these as above
all workers from the mita who worked voluntarily for wages in
their periods de huelga.[5]

It has been the contention of this book that, from the beginning
of mining activities at Potosí, an economically significant number
of voluntary Indian workers was to be found there, engaged in
the production of silver. *Voluntary* means here that these workers
were not obliged to labor in Potosí by any compulsory arrangement imposed by the Spanish colonial government. Involuntary
workers were, of course, also to be found in Potosí from the earliest days. A double labor structure therefore characterized the silver-producing industry of Potosí from the outset, the difference
between its two parts being the degree of coercion attached to them.

The duality of the labor structure can be traced to preconquest
origins. The freer group of workers had its origins in the yanaconas
of Incaic times. Many early workers at Potosí (and Porco) seem,
indeed, to have been yanaconas in preconquest years—men who
then transferred their allegiance and services to the conquerors.
Some, at least, of these freer workers became the indios varas of
the pre-Toledan decades in Potosí—small-scale native mining entrepreneurs, who in essence rented sections of mines from Spanish owners, and organized work teams of other Indians to extract
ores. The more coerced section of the early work force was de-
scended from the preconquest mit'a (the draft-labor institution of
the Inca state). Control of the immediately postconquest mita (to
use the Spanish spelling) did not belong, however, to the Spanish
state, but to encomenderos. These sent gangs (mitas) of natives in
their charge to Potosí to produce silver, sometimes from places as
far away as present northern Peru.

With the increase of complexity, and above all, capital intensity,
in silver production resulting from the introduction of refining by

---

4. "Forced labor in colonial Peru," *The Americas*, 16:4 (April 1960), p. 369.

5. D. A. Brading and Harry E. Cross, "Colonial silver mining: Mexico and
Peru." *HAHR*, 52:4 (November 1972), pp. 558–59. Brading and Cross do, however,
judge that, in matters of Indian mining labor, "To pass from Mexico to Peru is to
enter a vale of tears." The contrast does not, in fact, seem quite so severe, as the
following section of this conclusion will explain.

amalgamation in the early 1570s, the possibility of Indians' continuing their early entrepreneurial activities in mining seems to have
declined greatly. Once amalgamation became dominant, in the
1570s, figures such as the indios varas seem to have had no place
in the silver industry of Potosí. The current of voluntary labor was
nevertheless still strongly present. It now consisted of laborers
termed "mingas." These were men who worked in mining, but
more commonly in refining, for a wage—and a wage that was substantially greater than that paid to forced laborers. The term *minga*
does not occur before the mid 1580s; but it seems inherently likely
that such wage laborers were present, though perhaps in small
numbers, before then.

In the 1570s, Viceroy Don Francisco de Toledo brought about a
reversion to state control of the more coerced side of the Potosí
labor force. In the course of that decade he gave formal shape to
the mita of Potosí. The term *mita*, in the context of Potosí, now
ceased to mean the periodic despatch of a work gang by an encomendero. It signified, instead, the gathering of some 13,400 adult
males each year from many communities of the Peruvian and Bolivian highlands, and their forced residence, for one year, in Potosí,
for mining and refining work. The gathering, delivery, and return
of the mita were directed by the state, and were enacted by local
native officials and by Spanish corregidores, acting under the authority of the corregidor of Potosí. Although Toledo gave formal
shape and legal expression to the mita, strong signs of the transi-
tion from individual to state organization of the draft can be seen
in the decade before he arrived in Peru. Colonial officials had
pointed to the necessity for such a change, and some practical
arrangements in that direction had clearly been made by the time
Toledo began to put his own scheme into effect.

By 1600 slightly over half the Indian laborers working in silver
production in Potosí at any particular moment were mingas, and
slightly under half were draftees, or mitayos. These proportions
remained about the same for the rest of the period examined in
this work. And indeed they can be found in Potosí more than a
century later.[6]

The fact that a large contingent of wage workers was present in

6. Enrique Tandeter, "Trabajo forzado y trabajo libre en el Potosí colonial
tardío." *Estudios Cedes* 3:6 (Buenos Aires 1980), p. 7.

Potosí by the end of the sixteenth century goes a long way toward resolving an apparent conundrum in the labor history of colonial Spanish America. Up to now (with the exceptions mentioned at the beginning of this chapter), it has generally seemed that Potosí, and, by extension, other Andean mining centers, relied largely, or wholly, on forced labor. Certainly, the general assumption has been that conditions of labor were particularly onerous and nasty in Potosí. In contrast, it has been clear for some time that, by the end of the sixteenth century, silver was being mined in New Spain largely by wage workers, and that these workers enjoyed considerable freedom of movement. The presence of a large number of mingas in Potosí by 1600 lessens this contrast. The contrast is shown, indeed, to be essentially false, although some differences and irregularities may benefit from commentary.

In the final years of the sixteenth century, the mining labor force of New Spain stood as follows:[7]

Treasury district:	Black slaves (esclavos)		Indian wage workers (naborías)		Drafted Indian workers (repartimiento)		Total
	total	%	total	%	total	%	
Mexico City	892	14.6	3,582	58.8	1,619	26.6	6,093
Zacatecas	200	9.3	1,956	90.7	0	0	2,156
Guadalajara	110	16.4	559	83.6	0	0	669
Guadiana	61	27.1	164	72.9	0	0	225
	1,263	13.8	6,261	68.5	1,619	17.7	9,143

One immediately striking conclusion in these figures is that the total number of workers engaged in silver production in New Spain at the end of the sixteenth century (9,143), was slightly smaller than that so employed in Potosí alone in the early years of the seventeenth century (about 9,900—see chapter 4 above). The pre-

7.   The figures in this table are drawn from an untitled table in BL Additional Mss 13,976, item 61 (ff. 346-47). They refer to the final years of the 1590s (probably 1597). For a closer description of the source, and analysis of the figures, see P. J. Bakewell, "Notes on the Mexican silver mining industry in the 1590s," *Humanitas*, 19 (Universidad de Nuevo León, Monterrey 1978), pp. 383–409.

dominance of Potosí in Spanish American silver production is emphasized in this similarity. Also immediately noteworthy is the appreciable proportion of black slave labor in Mexican mining—whereas in Potosí blacks hardly participated in producing silver. (See Appendix 1 for explanations of the scarcity of black labor in mining and refining in Potosí.)

In New Spain, just over two-thirds of the silver-producing labor force (68.5 percent) were naborías: Indians working for wages. As the table shows, however, these wage laborers were not evenly distributed among the regions of the colony. They were concentrated in the mines of the west, northwest, and center-north (respectively, the treasury districts of Guadalajara, Guadiana, and Zacatecas). All draft (repartimiento) workers, though, were concentrated in the center and south of the viceroyalty, in the district of the treasury office of Mexico City.

It is clear that while the balance of forced and salaried labor in Potosí more closely resembles the balance in New Spain than it differs from it, a particular parallel exists between the composition of the work force in Potosí and that in the treasury district of Mexico City (exception always being made of the presence of blacks). Potosí employed slightly under half forced labor (mita), and the Mexico City district, 58.8 percent forced (repartimiento) workers. It is perhaps illustrative to consider why this should have been so.

The absence of repartimiento workers in mining, outside southern and central Mexico, can be explained in several ways. The native population of the north and northwest, apart from being smaller in number than that of the center and south when the Spanish arrived, was also more primitive and less adaptable to the demands of draft work in mining. The people of the northern plateau, whom the Spanish, following the Mexica usage, called Chichimeca, were nomadic, bellicose, and without experience of the discipline of organized labor. They were, therefore, of little use to Spanish miners in the north, even as slaves. They could not be gathered into drafts. Indeed, far from that, they offered severe armed resistance to Spanish settlement of the north, in the Chichimeca war, for much of the second half of the sixteenth century.

But in the center and south of New Spain—the district of the treasury office in Mexico City—the native population was long accustomed to draft work (under, for instance, the *coatequitl* of the

Mexica-Aztec), and hence easily subjected to Spanish repartimiento. The mines of the center and south, having been on the whole discovered earlier than those of the north and west, as it were "captured" this supply of draft labor. The north and the west, having no possibility of finding draft workers locally, or of gaining access to drafts from farther south, necessarily came quickly to rely on wage workers. These quickly gathered in the northern mining centers from many places of origin in central and western New Spain.[8]

It is conceivable that if New Spain had had a viceroy of Toledo's will and organizational abilities after the middle of the sixteenth century, some transfer of the repartimiento workers from the center to the newly discovered, and rich, mines of the north might have been organized. But, although Mexican viceroys such as Don Martín Enríquez (1568–80) and the Marqués de Villamanrique (1585–89) were men of great ability, no figure of Toledo's stature came onto the Mexican scene. And severe obstacles to changing the mine labor system existed in New Spain that even Toledo might have had difficulty in resolving: the greater maturity and fixedness of social and economic structures there, in comparison with those of Peru, by the middle of the century; and, perhaps most difficult, the persistence of the Chichimeca war in the north until the 1590s, which would obviously have offered practical and political barriers to the organization of a draft for the northern mines. If it had not been for these special circumstances, the northern and northwestern regions of New Spain would perhaps have resembled the center and south of the viceroyalty in having some percentage of draftees in their mine labor forces by the end of the sixteenth century; and the labor structure of Potosí would have resembled that of the whole of New Spain, rather than just its southern section.[9]

Despite the regional unevenness of mining labor systems in New

8.   For a discussion of mining labor systems in sixteenth-century New Spain, see Enrique Florescano, "La formación de los trabajadores en la época colonial, 1521–1750," pp. 69–79, in Enrique Florescano et al., *La clase obrera en la historia de México*, tomo 1, *De la colonia al imperio* (2nd. ed., Mexico City 1981).

9.   James Lockhart, in a personal communication to the author of December 1983, makes the strong point that the resemblance in composition of the mining labor forces of Potosí on the one hand, and central and southern New Spain on

Spain, however, the essential point remains that Potosí, with a work force consisting of roughly half mingas by 1600, was much closer in its labor arrangements to the silver districts of New Spain than has previously been apparent. The reasons for this similarity do not seem complicated. The same pressures operated in the labor markets in both Charcas and New Spain: a growing demand for mining and refining workers (coupled with a rising estimation of skilled labor), at a time of falling native population. The results were the same: an increase in the number of salaried workers. This was a process, of course, that took place not only in the mining section of the Spanish American economy. In various places and occupations where demand for native labor (especially for skilled workers) began to press on the supply provided by coercive systems, wage labor appeared surprisingly early in colonial history. The principal Spanish cities were typically such places. Gibson's discovery of contractual wage labor in textile *obrajes* during the sixteenth century in Mexico City is well known.[10] But also in regions lacking large towns, wage labor appeared early in certain circumstances. MacLeod, for example, finds it in Central America in the first decade of the seventeenth century—a time when population loss to the plague resulted in labor shortage and, apparently, a rise in wages as employers competed for men.[11] Closer to Potosí, in the southern Peruvian highland town of Huamanga, Stern notes a proliferation of labor contracts between individual Indians and Spaniards from the 1590s onward.[12] To do justice to Stern's interesting and perceptive work, it should be said that he attributes the appearance of wage labor in Huamanga to more complex causes than mere imbalance of supply and demand in the labor market resulting from demographic changes. The Indians' growing suc-

---

the other, derives from the fact that in both cases the mines lay within the normal preconquest ambit of sedentary peoples; whereas the northern and northwestern mines of New Spain were outside that ambit.

    10.   Charles Gibson, *The Aztecs under Spanish rule. A history of the Indians of the Valley of Mexico, 1519-1810* (Stanford 1964), p. 245.

    11.   Murdo J. MacLeod, *Spanish Central America. A socioeconomic history, 1520-1720* (Berkeley 1973), pp. 216-17.

    12.   Steve J. Stern, *Peru's Indian peoples and the challenge of Spanish conquest. Huamanga to 1640* (Madison 1982), pp. 144-45.

cess in evading mita service by various means, including skill in litigation, drove employers to hire native workers under contract.[13]

Potosí, therefore, was far from unusual in employing substantial numbers of wage laborers by the beginning of the seventeenth century. Given the numbers of laborers that silver production required after the introduction of amalgamation, and the utility to employers of specialized skills among those laborers, it would indeed be surprising if substantial wage labor had *not* appeared in Potosí in the late sixteenth century. To show, however, that there existed a large and economically influential number of mingas in Potosí by 1600, is not necessarily to have said all that can or should be said about the degree of coercion to which labor in general in Potosí was subjected in that first century of silver production.

On the one hand it is clear that the presence of large numbers of mingas modifies the established view of Potosí's labor arrangements. While a persuasive case could be made for the view that mingas were faced with substantial economic pressures that led them to stay in Potosí to earn money—tribute requirements, the demands of their curacas, the need to support themselves and their families—it is still undeniable that those who remained in the town to work as mingas in mining and refining were not forced to be there in at all the same way as were the mitayos. The legal obligation to work—the force of the state compelling presence in the mine or ingenio—did not weigh on the minga as it did on the mitayo. Nor did the Indian who decided to live in Potosí have to work in mining or refining of silver ores. Many other tasks brought a wage on which thousands of native people resident in the town seem to have survived: craftwork, freighting, charcoal making, to name but three. Some observers of the situation might argue that "free wage labor" is too benevolent a term to apply to mingas; but to deny that there existed a difference between the degree of coercion experienced by them, and that felt by the mitayos, would be to neglect substantial differences in the conditions of life of the two groups in Potosí. Ultimately it is hard to avoid the conclusion that mingas were there because they chose to be.

On the other hand, as earlier parts of this book have shown, the simultaneous presence of mingas and mitayos in the work force

13.   Ibid., ch. 5.

of Potosí was not a simple matter. They were not separate groups. On the contrary, close economic links connected them. The cost of the higher wages of the mingas did not fall on the mining and refining employers alone. Rather, through the substitute minga arrangement, much of it devolved onto the draft laborers, and thence widely onto native communities supplying mitayos to Potosí—communities that lay in some cases far from the city.

Contemplation of the economic relationship between mitayo and minga brings to mind a puzzling general question that can be asked of many regions of Spanish America in the middle period of colonial history. Why, in the face of growing imbalance between the supply of Indian labor (resulting from the loss of native population in the sixteenth century) and the demand for workers (resulting from immigration of colonists and broad development of local economies)—why, in this situation, did not greater coercion generally arise, instead of the generally freer system of Indian wage labor? (Why, for example, in Potosí did retention of wage workers by debt not appear?) Various answers to this question can readily be imagined. Undoubtedly, Spanish legislation controlling the further spread of coerced labor had its effect. (It certainly contributed to ensuring that the silver ores of Oruro were worked entirely by wage labor.) And perhaps it is an indication of the rooting of a broadly capitalistic economic system in Spanish America in the sixteenth century that market forces in the supply of, and demand for, labor were able to exert themselves in some regions, and bring about the emergence of wage labor. But the case of Potosí suggests yet another process—one that runs parallel to developments found around Huamanga by Stern.

By the early seventeenth century, Stern finds, a distinct group of hispanized Indian leaders existed in that region—a group including, but not entirely composed of, the traditional leadership of native communities. These people imitated the settlers in seeking to accumulate wealth in various forms—cash, buildings, and land. The methods they used to gather wealth were also imitated from the Spanish world, and can be broadly described as the individualization—the making private—of property. Their procedures were far different from, and even antithetical to, their traditional sources of wealth—that is, goods and rights received through the ancient reciprocities of the Andean economic system. For instance, curacas sometimes now used a device of Spanish law (the *compo-*

sición de tierras) to convert into their private possessions community lands to which they held long-standing rights of usufruct. Stern finds in these processes a deep change in the nature of relationships among Indians within communities. In sum, those relationships were growing more Hispanic: grounded in an increasing measure in differences in ownership of material possessions rather than in the traditional exchanges of goods, services, and rights that characterized preconquest Indian society.[14] "A widening gulf of suspicion, tension, and conflict accompanied the differentiation of Indian society into rich and poor. . . . Success assimilated the most powerful and dynamic fraction of Indian society to an exploitative class of aristocrat-entrepreneurs; the more modest success stories often represented a drain from ayllu society of needed people, skills, and resources, and weakened its internal solidarity."[15]

It seems reasonable to draw a parallel between the native group in Huamanga to which Stern refers here, and the minga component of the labor force in Potosí. It is arguable that, in Potosí at least, the answer to the question that was posed two paragraphs ago—why did not still more coercion of native labor appear as the balance between supply and demand of workers was lost?—is that a large number of laborers avoided coercion (or minimized it for themselves) by hispanizing. That is, they adopted a characteristically Spanish relationship with their employers, that of the hired man. It is tempting, furthermore, to propose that the mingas "assimilated . . . to an exploitative class of aristocratic-entrepreneurs," to use Stern's phrase, in taking up hired work in silver production. The substitute mingas certainly became a conduit through which the wealth of the communities supplying mitayos to Potosí flowed into the silver industry of the town. Whether that is something that they did knowingly cannot be said. What seems clear enough is that the mingas, in taking up salaried employment with colonists, created a social and economic distance between themselves and the mass of transient mitayos, in a way similar to that described for the native leaders of Huamanga by Stern. This process of separation is visible, of course, in the earliest relationships between

14. For development of this argument, see Stern, *Peru's Indian peoples*, ch. 7.
15. Ibid., p. 181.

Spaniards and yanaconas in the central Andes. And it was suggested early in this work that the yanaconas were the start of a dual labor system in Potosí—the ultimate occupants of the less coerced side of that system being the mingas.

The best judgment that can be made, therefore, on the basic question posed early in this book—the degree of coercion attaching to native mine labor in Potosí in the first century—is that, when the labor structure is viewed as a whole, the forced quality of mita work seems mitigated to a substantial degree by the growth of the minga system; but that that system concealed in itself a further coercion in the form of the battening—though probably unintentional—of the hispanized mingas on those of their fellow people who chose to stay in traditional communities.

Appendix 1

Slavery

If the preceding pages have made no reference to the labor of slaves (that is, chattel slaves), the reason is that the primary sources in which this book is grounded give hardly a hint of such labor in the production of silver in Potosí.

Indian slavery seems scarcely to have been known in Potosí. An early suggestion by Juan de Matienzo was that the Chiriguanaes—the people of the foothills and lowlands beyond La Plata—might be enslaved, since they were so warlike.[1] This suggestion was given the crown's approval in 1596,[2] but it seems never to have resulted in the presence of any Chiriguana slaves in Potosí, in mining or any other occupation.

Occasional references to the presence in or around Potosí of enslaved Indians from other regions do occur. Toledo issued an auto in 1573, for example, stating that colonists of Tucumán and Santa Cruz de la Sierra brought back or sent Indian servants to the highlands, and then rented them out for agricultural and other work (though not, apparently, for mining). Some were sold to *chacareros*, and never returned home. Toledo considered this an infringement of regulations prohibiting personal service of Indians, if not outright slavery.[3] Despite his attempts to put matters right, Indians of Tucumán were still suffering the same treatment in 1586.[4] But, it should be repeated, no evidence has appeared to sug-

---

1. Matienzo to crown, La Plata, October 20, 1561—in Levillier, *Charcas*, tomo 1, p. 55.
2. BAN Cartas No. 601, crown to Audiencia of La Plata, San Lorenzo, September 17, 1596.
3. AGI Charcas 16 ms 57, auto by Toledo, La Plata, November 2, 1573.
4. AGI Charcas 42 ms 1, Governor Juan Ramírez de Velasco to crown, Santiago del Estero, December 10, 1586.

gest that such slaves, or quasi-slaves, took any part in the production of silver.

Finally, a sale in Potosí of Indian slaves from Chile in 1635 should be recorded.[5] Whether the four people sold—aged 18, 19, 20, and 34, and all apparently male—were Araucanians, whose enslavement was permitted in the seventeenth century,[6] is not stated; nor is the purpose for which they were bought mentioned. Research to date has revealed no other examples of Chilean Indians' being sold in Potosí in the first century, though other cases cannot be ruled out.

As for the labor of black slaves in Potosí, the sources consulted for this book offer nothing with which to contradict, or substantially add to, the conclusions drawn by Inge Wolff.[7] These are, in brief: that the great altitude of Potosí limited the blacks' capacity for hard physical labor; that, according to contemporary reports, subjecting blacks to such labor in the mines of Potosí led to their rapid deaths; and that, in view of these problems, miners did not find it worthwhile to invest in black slave labor the several hundred pesos that each slave cost. According to Wolff, some 5,000 blacks lived in Potosí by the start of the seventeenth century. Many were domestic slaves of merchants, officials, and silver producers. Numerous others were craftsmen, while several dozen black slaves were employed in the mint. Some of the 5,000 were undoubtedly freedmen, especially since freedmen were found in chacra agriculture around Potosí.

A little detail may be added to these findings. Much discussion, originating with the home government, took place in the first decade of the seventeenth century about the desirability of replacing forced Indian labor with that of black slaves. Replying to the crown on this subject, Don Rafael Ortiz de Sotomayor, corrregidor of Potosí, wrote in 1610 that although Potosí was too cold for blacks to work in mines there, perhaps they would be useful in refineries—

5.   PCM EN 89, ff. 2087v.–90, Potosí, September 26, 1635, "venta de indios esclavos."

6.   Arnold J. Bauer, *Chilean rural society from the Spanish conquest to 1930* (Cambridge, England, 1975), p.7.

7.   "Negersklaverei und Negerhandel in Hochperu, 1545–1640," *Jahrbuch für Geschichte von Staat, Wirtschaft und Gesellschaft Lateinamerikas*, Band 1 (1964), pp. 157–86 (and especially 160–69).

notwithstanding that their having "to work surrounded by earth and water gives ground for fear."[8] In fact, another report of the same year says that blacks had already been tried in refining, particularly in work with the cajones in which amalgamation took place, but had been found wanting (for reasons unstated) and removed. Another problem with the labor of black slaves in silver production was that Indians feared them—more than they feared Spaniards.[9] Perhaps the Indians were not the only ones who were afraid. A current of trepidation runs through several of these official objections to increasing the numbers of blacks in Potosí: they are "gente tan libre y de mala inclinación."[10]

8.   AGI Charcas 49, Ortiz de Sotomayor to crown, Potosí, February 16, 1610— with real cedula to corregidor of Potosí, Lerma, July 26, 1608 (JHR).

9.   AGI Charcas 35, ms 109, reales oficiales of Potosí to crown, Potosí, February 18, 1610, para 1.

10.   AGI Charcas 19, Don Diego de Portugal (President of the Audiencia of La Plata) to crown, Potosí, February 15, 1614.

Appendix 2

Selected Prices in Potosí, 1587–1649
(pesos corrientes of 272 maravedís)

Item

year	coca *(cesto)*	llamas	Peruvian wine *(botija)*
1587	11.43 [4]	10.52 [13]	12.73 [3]
1589	10.86 [32]	8.65 [21]	15.10 [11]
1594	none	8.10 [15]	12.37 [3]
1599	none	none	12.00 [1]
1604	9.64 [5]	6.05 [19]	none
1609	7.00 [1]	8.84 [7]	16.78 [11]
1614	8.12 [4]	6.95 [8]	none
1620–21 (Jan.–July)	6.84 [3]	5.71 [10]	12.36 [17]
1625	7.16 [9]	7.49 [14]	14.07 [13]
1630	6.21 [18]	5.08 [11]	11.91 [5]
1635–36 (Jan.–May)	4.77 [7]	4.59 [20]	13.00 [1]
1640	none	4.85 [3]	none
1645	none	4.51 [4]	none
1649	5.51 [4]	4.06 [5]	15.00 [1]

Note: Figures in brackets following each price indicate the number of sales from which the price is calculated. "None" signifies that no sales of the item were recorded in sources consulted for this table for the year in question.

Source: Contracts of sale recorded in notarial books of Potosí for the years listed. All are from PCM, Escrituras Notariales.

Glossary

apire
: A laborer, usually a mitayo, employed to carry ore, or other material, in a mine. From Quechua: apay (to carry).

ayllu
: Quechua: the basic corporate group in central Andean native society, holding title to land, organizing cooperative labor teams, and having various other collective functions. The Quechua word means, fundamentally, lineage or kin relationship.

azoguero
: In Charcas, the owner of a silver refinery, or ingenio. Most azogueros also owned mines.

barretero
: A mine worker whose principal task was to cut ore, using hammer, wedge, and crowbar (barreta).

cabeza de ingenio
: A stamp mill in a silver refinery. In a water-powered refinery, the water wheel might power one or two cabezas, depending on whether the drive shaft extended on one side, or both sides, of the wheel.

cabildo
: A town council, consisting of aldermen (termed *veinticuatros* in Potosí), magistrates *(alcaldes ordinarios)*, and a variety of other officers.

cacilla
: A rich silver ore, suitable for smelting by guayra (q.v.) in the early decades of Potosí's existence.

cajón
: A tank for refining silver by amalgamation. A cajón was a division of a *buitrón*, which was a large, rectangular stone container built over vaulting. A buitrón might be divided with planks into twelve or more cajones. In Potosí a cajón held 50 quintales (or c. 5,000 pounds) of milled ore. In the sixteenth century, the refining process in cajones was often accelerated by the application of heat from a fire set in the vault below the buitrón.

chacra
: A small farm, privately owned. From Quechua: *chajra*—farming, or sowing, land.

charqui
: Jerked beef.

chicha
: A fermented drink, prepared from maize. Its preparation

	includes mastication of the grain by humans—usually elderly ladies. The action of salivary enzymes doubtless accelerates the conversion of starch to sugar. An acquired taste.
chuño	Undoubtedly the earliest form of freeze-dried potato. Andean native peoples developed a process of preserving the potato (itself native uniquely to the Andes) by alternately soaking it in running water and exposing it to day and night air. The result, a grey substance of putty-like texture, is another acquired taste (see chicha).
curaca	An important district leader in the Incaic decimal structure of government. Curacas retained authority, or indeed sometimes increased it, after the Spanish conquest. They were often termed *caciques* by the Spanish, after Mexican and Caribbean practice.
de huelga	A term applied to the part of the mita gruesa (q.v.) not engaged, at any given moment, in draft labor connected with silver production.
encomienda	The fundamental organizational device of the early Spanish empire in America. The crown, or some agent of it, assigned the tribute (in kind or labor) of one or more native communities to a settler. In return the settler (encomendero) was to provide the assigned native people (encomendados) with physical protection, evangelization, and instruction in Spanish customs and practices. The aim was to promote a dispersed Spanish settlement, economic activity, conversion, and acculturation of the conquered population, and defense.
entero	The delivery of the mita gruesa or mita ordinaria (q.v.). I.e., the number of laborers actually provided by the draft for silver production in Potosí—annually, or for each of the mitas ordinarias into which the gruesa was divided once the men were in Potosí. Figures cited in contemporary sources for the entero may, however, be misleading, because they often include workers *enterados en plata*—i.e., men in place of whom curacas or other workers made cash payments to employers.
estado	A linear measurement of two varas (q.v.): 1.67 meters, or about 66 inches.
gremio	(De azogueros). See mining guild.
guayra	A small furnace of native Andean design, for refining metallic ores. From Quechua: huayra (air, wind)—since

	draft for the furnace was provided not by bellows, but by exposure to wind.
hatunruna	Quechua: *Jatunruna*—the common man in preconquest times.
indio de faltriquera	A "pocket Indian" - that is, the payment received by an employer in substitute for a draft worker.
indio vara	In pre-Toledan Potosí, a native mine worker who, in essence, rented a certain portion (number of varas) of a mine from its Spanish owner. Indios varas seem to have been quasi-independent, small scale mining and refining entrepreneurs, active for a quarter of a century or so after the discovery of ores in the cerro rico of Potosí.
ingenio	The standard term for a refining mill in Charcas, corresponding to the *hacienda de minas* of New Spain.
leguaje	Payment to mitayos for the time spent traveling to and from Potosí.
llampo/ llampería	Silver ore of poor quality, surrounding cacilla (q.v.) in the vein.
maray	See quimbalete.
minero	The supervisor or majordomo (but never the owner) of a mine.
minga	A hired, waged, worker. The word, and the related terms mingar and mingado (one hired), derive from Quechua: mink'ay (to contract reciprocal labor).
mining guild	The formal, collective body of the mine and refinery owners of Potosí. The guild, or gremio, was legally constituted in 1611. (See Arzáns, *Historia,* tomo 1, p. 167, n. 4.)
mita gruesa	The total number of forced workers brought to Potosí annually by the draft system created by Viceroy Toledo. From Quechua: mit'a (a turn at some task) and Spanish: grueso (large, gross).
mita ordinaria	The portion (nominally a third) of the mita gruesa (q.v.) that at any moment was drafted for mining or refining labor in Potosí.
mitayo	One who works in a mita (q.v.). From Quechua: mit'ayuj.
pallar	To pick over discarded ore in search of neglected pieces of metal-bearing material. A worker doing this is a palliri. Both derive from Quechua: pallay (to gather, collect).
pella	In the amalgamation process of silver refining, the amal-

	gam of silver and mercury remaining after the refining "soup" of ore, mercury, salt, water, and sometimes other "ingredients" had been washed.
peso	The term given to various monetary units of account and exchange in the Spanish empire. In this book, prices and wages have been converted to pesos de plata corriente of 272 maravedís. This was the standard unit for day-to-day transactions—a silver coin weighing one ounce, and subdivided into 8 reales of 34 maravedís. It corresponds to the *peso de oro común* of New Spain, and to the *peso de a ocho [reales]* (known in English as a "piece of eight"). The standard unit of account in the Potosí treasury was the peso ensayado, valued variously at 425 and 450 maravedís.
piña	A piece of refined silver remaining after mercury had been volatilized from the pella (q.v.).
pongo	An Indian supervisor in some group task. The term derives from Quechua: punku (door), via the notion of doorkeeper, guard.
quimbalete	A primitive device, of native Andean design, for triturating ore. It consists of a small boulder, of half-moon shape in profile, to the upper, flat, edge of which is lashed a beam. The projecting ends of the beam are alternately pushed down by a worker on each side. The boulder (maray) rocks to and fro, crushing ore placed beneath it.
quintal	A unit of weight, equivalent to some 46 kilos, or 101.5 pounds avoirdupois.
quipu	A native Andean device, consisting of colored and knotted strings, and serving to record numerical data, and generally as a mnemonic instrument.
ranchería	A native dwelling quarter in Potosí. The principal ranchería lay between the town center and the foot of the cerro.
repartimiento	In the context of Potosí and the mita, the periodic assignment, by a viceroy or some other prominent official, of draft workers to employers for mine and refinery work. In the period discussed in this book, repartimientos in Potosí were revised at intervals of roughly ten years. In New Spain, repartimiento was the general term for the state-directed draft labor system, the counterpart of the mita system of the central Andes.
socavón	Adit. From Spanish: *socavar* (to dig under, undermine).
vara	A linear measurement of 0.838 meters, or some 33 inches.
veedor	An officially appointed, and salaried, inspector of mines.

veinticuatros   See cabildo.

yanacona   In preconquest times, a person not belonging to any ayllu
                 (q.v.), but attached to some dominant figure in native
                 society, and working at any of a wide range of tasks. The
                 status was hereditary. After the conquest, many surviv-
                 ing yanaconas transferred their allegiance and services
                 to Spaniards. By the middle of the sixteenth century, the
                 term's connotation was of close, personal attachment to
                 a Spaniard, and freedom from obligations of tribute and
                 draft labor.

Primary Sources

Manuscripts in the following archives were consulted during the preparation of this book: the Archivo General de Indias (AGI), the Archivo de la Universidad, Seville (SAU), the Biblioteca Nacional of Spain (SBN), the Biblioteca Nacional of Peru (PBN), the archive of the Casa Nacional de la Moneda in Potosí (PCM), the Archivo Nacional de Bolivia, Sucre (BAN), the Archivo General de la Nación of Argentina (AAGN), and the manuscript division of the British Library (BL) (formerly the British Museum). The following is a listing of the volumes or bundles of papers from which information has been taken for this work. The titles of individual documents have been given in footnotes.

Archivo General de Indias (AGI): Charcas 16, 17, 18, 19, 20, 21, 31, 32, 35, 34, 36, 40, 42, 46, 47, 49, 52, 51, 54, 55, 56, 80, 134, 266, 415; Contaduría 1,801; Escribanía (de Cámara) 865A; Indiferente General 857, 1,239; Justicia 667; Lima 28A, 28B, 29, 30, 34, 35, 38, 39, 40, 41, 44, 45, 54, 270, 313; Patronato 238.

Archivo de la Universidad, Seville (SAU): vol. 330/122.

Biblioteca Nacional (Spain): ms 3,040.

Biblioteca Nacional of Peru (PBN): ms B511.

Casa Nacional de la Moneda, Potosí (PCM): Cajas Reales (CR) 7, 30, 72, 201, 229; Escrituras Notariales (EN) 8, 44, 89.

Archivo Nacional de Bolivia (BAN): Audiencia de Charcas, libros de acuerdos 3; Cabildo de Potosí—Libros de Acuerdos (CPLA) 5, 8; Escrituras Públicas (EP) Aguila 1559, Soto 1549, 1551, Reinoso 1559, Rojas 1550; Minas 3, 9, 15, 123, 125, 131, 143; Reales Cédulas 3; Rück collection 2, 3, 6.

Archivo General de la Nación of Argentina (AAGN): sala 13, cuerpo 23, ms 10-2.

British Library (BL): Additional mss 13,974; Sloane mss 3,055.

Select bibliography

(Works cited in notes, or substantially consulted in the preparation of the text).

Adams, Catherine F. *Nutritive value of american foods in common units.* Agricultural handbook No. 456, Agricultural Research Service, United States Department of Agriculture. Washington, D.C., 1975.

Agricola, Georgius. *De Re Metallica.* Translated from the first Latin edition of 1556 by Herbert Clark Hoover and Lou Henry Hoover. New York 1950.

Ahlfeld, Federico E. *Geografía física de Bolivia.* Cochabamba 1969.

Alonso Barba, Alvaro. *Arte de los metales, en que se enseña el verdadero beneficio de los de oro y plata por azogue.* [Madrid 1630] Potosí 1967.

Arce Quiroga, Eduardo. *Historia de Bolivia. Fases del proceso hispano-americano: orígenes de la sociedad boliviana en el siglo XVI.* Cochabamba 1969.

Arzáns de Orsúa y Vela, Bartolomé. *Historia de la Villa Imperial de Potosí.* Edited by Lewis Hanke and Gunnar Mendoza L. 3 tomos, Providence, Rhode Island, 1965.

Bakewell, P[eter] J. *Antonio López de Quiroga (industrial minero del Potosí colonial).* Universidad Boliviana "Tomás Frías." Potosí 1973.

———. "Notes on the Mexican silver mining industry in the 1590s." *Humanitas* 19 (Universidad de Nuevo León, Monterrey, 1978), pp. 383-409.

———. "Registered silver production in the Potosí district, 1550-1735." *Jahrbuch für Geschichte von Staat, Wirtschaft und Gesellschaft Lateinamerikas* 12 (1975), pp. 67-103.

———. *Silver mining and society in colonial mexico: Zacatecas, 1546-1700.* Cambridge, England, 1971.

———. "Technological change in Potosí: The silver boom of the 1570s." *Jahrbuch für Geschichte von Staat, Wirtschaft und Gesellschaft Lateinamerikas* 14 (1977), pp. 60-77.

Ballesteros Gaibrois, Manuel. *Descubrimiento y fundación del Potosí.* Zaragoza 1950.

————. "Notas sobre el trabajo minero en los Andes con especial refer- encia a Potosí (s. XVI y ss.)." *CIM 1*, pp. 529-57.

Bargalló, Modesto. *La amalgamación de los minerales de plata en Hispano- américa colonial.* Mexico City 1969.

————. *La minería y la metalurgía en la América española durante la época colo- nial.* Mexico City 1955.

Barnadas, Josep M. *Charcas. Orígenes históricos de una sociedad colonial.* La Paz 1973.

————. "Una polémica colonial: Potosí, 1579-1584." *Jahrbuch für Geschichte von Staat, Wirtschaft und Gesellschaft Lateinamerikas* 10 (1973), pp. 16-70.

Basadre, Jorge. "El régimen de la mita." *Letras* (Universidad Mayor de San Marcos, Lima, 1937), pp. 325-64.

Bauer, Arnold J. *Chilean rural society from the Spanish conquest to 1930.* Cambridge, England, 1975.

Benino, Nicolás del. "Relación muy particular del Cerro y minas de Potosí y de su calidad y labores, por. . . , dirigida a Don Francisco de Toledo, virrey del Perú, en 1573." *Relaciones geográficas de Indias—Perú*, tomo 1. Biblioteca de Autores Españoles, tomo CLXXXIII, pp. 362-71. Madrid 1965.

Brading, D. A., and Harry E. Cross. "Colonial silver mining: Mexico and Peru." *HAHR* 52:4 (November 1972), pp. 545-79.

Cañete y Domínguez, Pedro Vicente. *Guía histórica, geográfica, física, po- lítica, civil y legal del Gobierno e Intendencia de la Provincia de Potosí* [1791]. Potosí 1952.

Capoche, Luis. *Relación general de la Villa Imperial de Potosí.* Edited by Lewis Hanke. Biblioteca de Autores Españoles, tomo CXXII. Madrid 1959.

Cieza de León, Pedro de. *La crónica del Perú, nuevamente escrita por. . . , vecino de Sevilla.* Biblioteca de Autores Españoles, tomo XXVI, *His- toriadores primitivos de Indias, II.* Madrid 1947.

Cobb, Gwendolyn B. "*Potosí and Huancavelica: Economic bases of Peru, 1545- 1640.*" Ph.D. dissertation, University of California. Berkeley 1947.

————. "Potosí, a South American mining frontier." In *Greater America: Essays in honor of Herbert Eugene Bolton.* Berkeley 1945.

Cole, Jeffrey A. "The Potosí mita under Hapsburg administration: The seventeenth century." Ph.D. dissertation, University of Massachu- setts. Amherst 1981.

Collier, George A., Renato I. Rosaldo, and John D. Wirth (eds.). *The Inca and Aztec states, 1400-1800: Anthropology and history.* New York 1982.

Cook, Noble David. *Demographic collapse: Indian Peru, 1520-1620.* Cam- bridge, England, 1981.

Crespo Rodas, Alberto. "El reclutamiento y los viajes en la 'mita' del Cerro de Potosí." *CIM 1*, pp. 467-82.

————. "La 'mita' de Potosí." *Revista Histórica* 22 (Lima, 1955-56), pp. 169-82.

"Descripción de la Villa y minas de Potosí. Año de 1603." In *Relaciones geográficas de Indias—Perú*, tomo 1, edited by Marcos Jiménez de la Espada. Biblioteca de Autores Españoles, tomo CLXXXIII, pp. 372-85. Madrid 1965.

Dobyns, Henry F. "An outline of Andean epidemic history to 1720." *Bulletin of the History of Medicine* 37:6 (November-December 1963), pp. 493-515.

Escalona Agüero, Gaspar de. *Gazofilacio real del Perú. Tratado financiero del coloniaje*. Biblioteca Boliviana. La Paz 1941.

Fox, K. V. "Pedro Muñiz, Dean of Lima, and the Indian labor question (1603)." *HAHR* 42:1 (February 1962), pp. 63-88.

Garcilaso de la Vega [the Inca]. *Royal commentaries of the Incas and general history of Peru*. Translated by Harold V. Livermore. Austin 1970.

Gibson, Charles. *The Aztecs under Spanish rule: A history of the Indians of the Valley of Mexico, 1519-1810*. Stanford 1964.

Helmer, Marie. "La 'encomienda' à Potosí, d'après un document inédit." *Proceedings of the Thirtieth International Congress of Americanists* (London 1952), pp. 235-38.

————. "Notas sobre la encomienda peruana en el siglo XVI." *Revista* 10, pp. 124–43. Facultad de Derecho y Ciencias Sociales, Instituto de Historia del Derecho Argentino y Americano, Universidad Nacional. Buenos Aires 1965.

————. "Notes sur les esclaves indiens au Pérou (xvie siècle)." *Bulletin de la Faculté des Lettres de Strasbourg* 5:7 (April 1965), pp. 683–90. Travaux de l'Institut d'Etudes Latino-Américaines de l'Université de Strasbourg [TILAS].

Jiménez de la Espada, Marcos. *Relaciones geográficas de Indias—Perú*. 3 tomos. Biblioteca de Autores Españoles, tomos CLXXXIII-CLXXXV. Madrid 1965.

Julien, Catherine J. "Inca administration in the Titicaca basin, as reflected at the provincial capital of Hatunqolla." Ph.D. dissertation, University of California. Berkeley 1978.

————. "Inca decimal administration in the Lake Titicaca region." In Collier et al., *The Inca and Aztec States*. . . .

Keith, Robert G. *Conquest and agrarian change: The emergence of the hacienda system on the Peruvian coast*. Cambridge, Mass., 1976.

Kubler, George. "The Quechua in the colonial world." *Handbook of South American Indians*, vol. 2—*The Andean civilizations*. Washington, D.C., 1946.

Lara, Jesús. *Diccionario qhëshwa—castellano, castellano—qhëshwa*. Cochabamba 1971.

Levillier, Roberto. *Gobernantes del Perú.* 14 tomos. Madrid 1921-26.
———. *La Audiencia de Charcas.* 3 tomos. Madrid 1918-22.
Lockhart, James. *Spanish Peru, 1532-1560: A colonial society.* Madison 1968.
Lohmann Villena, Guillermo. *El corregidor de indios en el Perú bajo los Austrias.* Madrid 1957.
———. "Enrique Garcés, descubridor del mercurio en el Perú, poeta y arbitrista." *Studia* 27–28 (Lisbon 1969), pp. 7-62.
———. *Las minas de Huancavelica en los siglos XVI y XVII.* Seville 1949.
MacLeod, Murdo J. *Spanish Central America: A socioeconomic history, 1520-1720.* Berkeley 1973.
Málaga Medina, Alejandro. "Las reducciones en el Perú." *Historia y Cultura* 8 (Lima 1974), pp. 141-72.
Matienzo, Juan de. *Gobierno del Perú (1567).* Edited by Guillermo Lohmann Villena. Travaux de l'Institut Français d'Etudes Andines, tomo XI. Lima 1967.
Matos Mar, José. *Yanaconaje y reforma agraria en el Perú. El caso del valle de Chancay.* Lima 1976.
Menéndez-Pidal, Gonzalo. *Imagen del mundo hacia 1570, según noticias del Consejo de Indias y de los tratadistas españoles.* Madrid 1944.
Mesa, José de, and Teresa Gisbert de Mesa. *Bolivia: monumentos históricos y arqueológicos.* Instituto Panamericano de Geografía e Historia, Comisión de Historia, 122. Mexico City 1970.
Murra, John V. "Aymara lords and their European agents at Potosí." *Nova Americana* 1 (Turin 1978), pp. 231–43.
Formaciones económicas y políticas del mundo andino. Instituto de Estudios Peruanos. Lima 1975.
"Pareceres de los Padres de la Compañía de Jesús de Potosí." In *Pareceres jurídicos en asuntos de Indias,* edited by Rubén Vargas Ugarte. Lima 1951.
Petersen, Georg G. *Minería y metalurgía en el antiguo Perú.* Arqueológicas 12, Museo Nacional de Antropología y Arqueología. Lima 1970.
Polo de Ondegardo, Juan (attributed). "Relación de las cosas del Perú." In *Crónicas del Perú,* tomo 1, edited by Juan Pérez de Tudela. Biblioteca de Autores Españoles, tomo CLXIV. Madrid 1963.
Probert, Alan. "Bartolomé de Medina: The patio process and the sixteenth century silver crisis." *Journal of the West* 8:1 (January 1969), pp. 90-124.
Recopilación de leyes de los reynos de las Indias, mandadas imprimir, y publicar, por la Magestad Católica del Rey Don Carlos II, nuestro señor. . . . 4 tomos. Madrid 1681. (Facsimile edition, Ediciones Cultura Hispánica. Madrid 1973.)
Rivas, Salomón, and Raúl Carrasco. *Geología y yacimientos minerales de la región de Potosí.* 2 tomos. Servicio geológico de Bolivia "Geobol," Ministerio de Minas, Boletín 11. La Paz 1968.

Rowe, John H. "Inca culture at the time of the Spanish conquest." *Handbook of South American Indians*, vol. 2—*The Andean civilizations*. Washington, D.C., 1946.

————. "Inca policies and institutions relating to the cultural unification of the Empire." In Collier et al., *The Inca and Aztec states*. . . .

————. "The Incas under Spanish colonial institutions." *HAHR* 37:2 (May 1957), pp. 155-99.

Rudolph, William E. "The lakes of Potosí." *The Geographical Review* 36 (1936), pp. 529-54.

Sánchez Albornoz, Nicolás. *Indios y tributos en el Alto Perú*. Instituto de Estudios Peruanos. Lima 1980.

————. *La población de América Latina. Desde los tiempos pre-colombinos al año 2000*. Madrid 1973.

Sempat Assadourian, Carlos, et al. *Minería y espacio económico en los Andes, siglos xvi-xx*. Instituto de Estudios Peruanos. Lima 1980.

————. "Potosí y el crecimiento económico de Córdoba en los siglos XVI y XVII." In *Homenaje al Doctor Ceferino Garzón Maceda, Universidad Nacional de Córdoba*. Córdoba, Argentina, 1973.

Spalding, Karen. "Exploitation as an economic system: The state and the extraction of surplus in colonial Peru." In Collier et al., *The Inca and Aztec states*. . . .

————. "Social climbers: Changing patterns of mobility among the Indians of colonial Peru." *HAHR* 50:4 (November 1970), pp. 645-64.

Stein, Stanley and Barbara. *The colonial heritage of Latin America*. New York 1970.

Stern, Steve J. *Peru's Indian peoples and the challenge of Spanish conquest: Huamanga to 1640*. Madison 1982.

Tandeter, Enrique. "Trabajo forzado y trabajo libre en el Potosí colonial tardío." *Estudios CEDES* 3:6 (Buenos Aires 1980).

Vargas Ugarte, Rubén (ed.). *Pareceres jurídicos en asuntos de Indias*. Lima 1951.

Villamarín, Juan A., and Judith E. *Indian labor in mainland colonial Spanish America*. Newark, Delaware, 1975.

Villar Córdoba, Sócrates. *La institución del yanacona en el Incanato*. Lima 1966.

"Visita hecha a la provincia de Chucuito por Garci Diez de San Miguel en el año 1567." Transcription by Waldemar Espinosa Soriano. Lima 1964.

Wachtel, Nathan. *La vision des vaincus. Les indiens du Pérou devant la conquête espagnole, 1530-1570*. Paris 1971.

————. *Sociedad e ideología. Ensayos de historia y antropología andinas*. Instituto de Estudios Peruanos. Lima 1973.

Wallerstein, Immanuel. *The Modern world-system II: Mercantilism and the*

consolidation of the European world-economy, 1600-1750. New York 1980.
Wiedner, Donald L. "Forced labor in colonial Peru." *The Americas* 16:4 (April 1960), pp. 357-83.
Wolff, Inge. "Negersklaverei und Negerhandel in Hochperu, 1545-1640." *Jahrbuch für Geschichte von Staat, Wirtschaft und Gesellschaft Lateinamerikas* 1 (1964), pp. 157-86.
Zavala, Silvio. *El servicio personal de los indios en el Perú*. Tomo 1: *Extractos del siglo XVI*. Tomo 2: *Extractos del siglo XVII*. Mexico City 1978-79.
Zimmerman, Arthur F. *Francisco de Toledo, fifth viceroy of Peru, 1569-81*. Caldwell, Idaho, 1938.

Index